Letters to Loretta from the Radio Shack

A True World War II Teenage Love Story

By Laura Lynn Ashworth

LL Ashworth
1/4/15

Letters to Loretta from the Radio Shack
A True World War II Teenage Love Story

ISBN: 978-0-9909500-0-4

Acknowledgements

A special thank you to the following individuals who so generously gave their time, thoughts and talents to me to ensure the successful completion and distribution of this book:

Eric Flint

New York Times Best-Selling Author, The 1632 Series

Mark Huston

Contributing writer, The 1632 Series

Paula Goodlett

Editor, The 1632 Series

Rick Boatright

Technical formatting, The 1632 Series

Tim Fanning, Handelan-Pedersen

Cover design

Part 1—1943

Chapter 1, January 1943

January 5, 1943

US Naval Training Station
Farragut, Idaho
1330 So. Washington Ave.
Chicago, IL

Dear Loretta,

Gee, but aren't you thoughtful. By the way, every time I write a letter to you, you seem to be writing a letter back home. Isn't that a co-incidence or isn't it? I received two letters to date, so "keep em flying."

It was just a month ago that I left and I'll be damned if I know whether it seems like a year or a week. As far as concerning you, it seems like a year. I presume you're still as sharp as a whip, you old prankster. Say, in your next letter send me a couple of pictures of yourself, one of them recently taken and you may charge it to Uncle Sam and his fleet.

So I see your stepping out now, you're really cooking with the right kind of material. Don't forget I've got a date with you when I get back home, which I hope won't be any longer than a year.

Had a lot of fun at the rifle range this week as no doubt Joe will tell you. I still get three square meals a day, and are they square. A slice of bread with plenty of nothing.

This weather we have up here now surely reminds me of Chicago. It's dingier than a campaign speech and it just knocks the hell out of these Californians out here. They're just used to beautiful women and mild weather, while we in Chicago are used to gales and violent women.

Do you know what? In "Frisco" the taverns close at midnight. Now isn't that a whacky thing to do?

Haven't seen many movies lately except for a few Navy films showing recent battles to get us boiled. But if we don't get our liberty Wednesday, I'll boil over like a frozen motor. They're going to keep an eye on our company while we're on liberty (now what the hell do you call liberty like that?) and if we're good we'll get one every two weeks. Very, very thoughtful, don't you think? I'll leave you know how I make out, so until then.

Lots of love, Slab

January 31, 1943

Dear Loretta,

Say, you aren't kidding that you're going to be sixteen? I can really look towards you with interest when you hit that old age. I bet your hair is turning grey already. Say, when does this glorious day arrive?

I think that's pretty wicked of you being afraid to go home with a sailor for fear of being kissed. Maybe you think he would want to play a spelling game or something. As far as figures are concerned (not the ones in bookkeeping either) you were never a slouch, in my opinion.

Are you telling jokes when you mention my love life? What can a jockey do way up here in Indian Territory? When you go to town, the old ladies drag their daughters in and hide them in the basement till we leave. The only thing left are the hags (the Paradise style) and I'll be damned if I'm going to suffer a broken nose from a brawl over them.

I just came back from dinner and you could hit me with a club and call me deadbeat if you'd guess what we had. Some nice chili and spaghetti, two chunks of apple pie and ice cream. What a difference between this meal and cold beans.

I forgot how to spell spaghetti so I told a guy next to me that I'm going to ask the old man for a dictionary in my next letter. This jerk asked me "what in the hell is the old man going to use then?" As I continue this letter, this guy is lying on his back groaning like he lost all his teeth. He's a nice boy, but he writes out loud and also snores the same way.

Well, Honey, the sun is setting and as it throws a beautiful red glow over the heavily snow capped mountains covered with pine trees; it brings back a memory of your lovely face. (Okay buddy you can put the gun down now.)

You should hear one guy from California read a letter from his sister. You would laugh your wig off. It's a little too risky to send to you; 'cause ten years in Statesville is a long time.

By the way when do I get your (my) pictures? Do I have to come home and wring your neck or send a shotgun by telegram?

Say, I noticed the way you spell "Whacks." You didn't think I would get the wrong impression did you?

There is some Waldo from Frisco who's bothering the hell out of me. Any mistakes in this letter is purely coincidental and no connections whatsoever between living and dead. He thinks two "frees" written on his envelopes are equal to an air mail envelope. He sends letters to his old man in code. (Shut your eyes and listen to this one, 'cause it'll kill you.) His dad runs a garbage barge off Frisco so he wrote to the Navy Rating Board and wants to be commissioned as an Ensign. He's still waiting for his papers (his citizen papers).

There's one dumb hick that laughs his head off when he receives a letter from home 'cause he can't make head or tails of it. He never puts an address on his envelope 'cause he doesn't give a damn whose hands the letters fall in.

Well, Babe, write again and send that physique of yourself, but in a hurry.

Lots of Love, Sal

Chapter 2, February 1943

February 7, 1943

Dear Hearthrob:

Well, Duchess, so you're having troubles, too. Why don't you write to the President and get some of these guys deferred. There's no getting away from it, Joe is a nice-looking and nice fellow, but where in the hell is he going to now? Say, does that guy come around the corner anymore? I haven't heard from him in three weeks. Guess what, Scully wanted to send me a bottle of whiskey. That's very thoughtful, but I want to win my stripes on my sleeves not all over my body.

Where is that picture I asked of you? Did you run out of film or were you in an accident. You might get a picture of me any day now, so hold on to your pants. Hey dodo, in the Navy you get a leave, not a furlough. That taking into point if you get any at all.

Thursday, I was at Spokane and it's the first modern city I have seen in almost two months. Was it flooded with gorgeous "de icers." These babes out here drink like a sewer and always have a cigarette in their mouth. They've got some spiffy dancers, too. They like to boog it with a solid four. I don't remember much, though, until I woke up the next morning. You don't have enough time, these fourteen hour liberties. Five hours of it is spent on traveling. What I want is about thirty-six hours, so I can enjoy the women and the town.

But every damn time after we crawl back to our barracks after liberty, they slap us immediately on some detail as soon as we get up at five. Friday, I worked in the rifle range running around holding the target. Saturday, I helped put up chairs for the movies and shoveled snow for miles. That night, I went to the show for the first time in five weeks. I saw one of our modernest pictures out here, *Sweater Girl.* Some mellow babes were in it. Tonight must have been the captain's birthday or his wife must have had a baby, 'cause the picture will be *George Washington Slept Here.* I'm a guard in the show from 1700-2000, but I'll be able to see it. It still is popular, isn't it, or did it come to Ogden (Theater)?

I'll try to rustle you a Valentine card, but it's like trying to rustle buffalo out here. In case I don't, you know what I think. I hope the feeling is mutual.

Lots of Love, Sal

P.S.

Hey, I'm not Greek and I don't understand shorthand.

February 17, 1943

Dear Loretta:

Have nothing much to say except that I'll be home sometime next week. I'm getting thrown in Arm Guard (Floating Coffins). Boy, am I lucky.

Well here's a picture of myself. If you don't like it, you can feed it to the sharks or something.

I'm really disgusted that I didn't have a chance to go to school. I had excellent marks, but when I put down Arm Guard as fourth choice I might have as well put a gun to their heads begging for it,   I'm really stuck with it and that's no kidding.

Well, I'll be seeing you, Sal

February 25, 1943

Dear Loretta,

I'm in O.G.U. (Outgoing Unit) now and what a joint. Trying to describe it is like trying to find a needle in a haystack. The chow is delicious and all you want. If it wasn't for them working the hell out of us we'd get fatter than a pig in a pigpen. It's really nice in O.G.U. though, you only work about eight hours a day, six days a week. Of course we're supposed to get an overnight liberty every four days but every damn time it comes up to my liberty it seems to get cancelled. I'll be getting one, one of these years I hope.

Speaking of the work, you'd die laughing if you're not dead already. Can you imagine carrying flour sacks all day long (Crane Co. was never like this.) One hundred pound sacks, too, fifteen on the left and ten on the right. I walk a few steps and then they start pulling me back up through the deck. Sometimes I hit the basement. You get out of the flour warehouse and you look like Snow White and the Seven Jacks. From there we went to unload a boxcar of grapefruit juice. I never drank so much in all my life. I just visualized that it resembled beer and drank and drank. They carried me home in a wheel-barrel. Yesterday was a pay-off. We were shoveling coal from box-cars all day. They didn't have any gondola to ship the coal in but boxcars. Whoever thought of that brainstorm should die a slow miserable death. I never swallowed so many tons of coal in all my life. I lit a cigarette and I looked like a blast furnace with full speed ahead. Got back to the barracks and took a shower. The drain is still clogged. I work 2000 to 0400 tonight. That's how I managed to find time to write today. Well enough of this "Paradise" and we'll get back to you.

Of course you're feeling fine and it's good to hear that you're getting around. Of course I meant the Valentine. Say, by the way, it's a hell of a time to send a goodnight kiss when I'm only 2,000 miles away and not a human being in sight. What's a matta, baby, don't you trust me? Keep on sputtering, I like your talk.

Lots of Love, Sal

Chapter 3, March 1943

March 12, 1943

CCC—B.20
NTS (Radio) University of Idaho
Moscow, Idaho

Dear Loretta,

Received your letter or letters.

I should say and I see you're becoming quite educated. Where did you pick up that title of a letter. When I read it, it knocked me right through the damn wall and back again. Remind me to feed you to these sharks when we meet again. I have a hint, though, that I'll get shipwrecked off of some island and lead the life of Riley the rest of my life. He was a drunken, happy go-lucky dog, wasn't he?

Well, you probably noticed on the envelope that I moved from the land of the Indians to the land of the co-eds. It's only a hick town out in the wilderness, but these "barbecues" out here are really sweet. Get liberty every Wednesday night for three moldy hours but have every other Saturday and Sunday off.

When I don't get the whole weekend off, I get either Saturday or Sunday off. That's what I call a rosy life. Some nice looking girls go up to these U.S.O. dances. There's only a few that can really wheel it out, but as long as they have what it takes that's all that counts.

This university is really a nice looking place and I don't know what in the hell I'm doing out here. I guess I'll find out sooner or later. We have school eight hours a day and our evenings are rather crowded. If we're not washing clothes, we are compulsed to see a movie. Beefing, beefing that's the action word in the Navy that really makes you enjoy it. You don't give a damn if you're here today or shot tomorrow as long as they keep throwing grub at you.

Speaking of grub, it really is delicious and I don't mean maybe. I'll probably come out of here fatter than a hog with all the butter you want and you can just about take a bath in all the milk they sling you. No siree, home was never like this.

Going to school is really a riot. We have two periods of typing, two of procedure and four of code. That damn code takes quite a while before it's pounded in one's head, especially when it's as thick as mine. I've just finished my first week of school and I came out all right. Every Friday we have tests in spelling and procedure and I got 3.8 on both. The highest mark you can get is 4.0 so that isn't bad.

Well, Duchess, I'm on guard duty right now and I better end this data before I get caught and thrown in the "hoosegow."

Lots of Love, Sal

Chapter 4, April 1943

April 6, 1943

Dear Lor,

Yeah, I think I know what you did. I thought you eloped or maybe was caught by a tornado, I just received your letter yesterday so don't harp about answering 'cause you no doubt understand the conditions.

Say, you mean to tell me that you haven't reached sixteen yet? Boy, I hope the cops don't find out or they'll probably throw me in the brig. Don't you think? So you're graduating in June, good girl. If your old man sends you to law school that will be a good move "Exlax," 'cause sometime you might get me out of a tight jam.

So you're joining the Coast Guard Reserve and all the time I thought you were going to be a "Whack." Well it's a lot of fun riding Waves so what's the difference. I bet that ensign has plenty to do with your joining.

Say, how about a snapshot of yourself, you chubby rascal, or am I an orphan? Don't forget I'll be waiting for one (years have gone by) so don't forget.

Well, things are pretty nice around here, the weather is really beautiful. It doesn't rain more than six days a week, so that isn't bad. Have just about every weekend off in which I usually end up blinder than 0/20. On Wednesdays, we have a three hour liberty at night in which I usually go dancing at one of these girl fraternities. They're not very good dancers, but I've never kicked one out of bed, that's for sure. Every now and then I run into a babe that doesn't know what the "score" is. Sometimes they don't even know what "game" we're playing, and that is the type that's hard to shoot a line to. You know that type, I presume, or don't you? I met some babe that lives in Evanston that's attending the University out here. I asked her who shot her brains out when she got the idea of coming out here to God's country, but she said she just wanted to get away from herself. Believe me, when she came out here she was not kidding herself.

Well, there's very little left to say except that I'm doing pretty good in school (so far) and that at last I have a room. Share it with five others, but it's a nice room with a radio, easy chairs, wash bowl, mirror, dresser and a mattress thicker than my head.

Gobs of Love, Sal

P.S.

I thought you were eating a pair of shoes not a piece of fruit (pear).

April 29, 1943

Dear Loretta:

How are you, babe? So you're working at "Monkies" (Montgomery Ward) now, good girl. So you're a regular "gold-brick," too that was my specialty when I was in "civvies." It's a great world, isn't it? So you're going with a Marine now, well them "Bellhops" are all right. I suppose in your next "war maneuvers" you'll be "striking" for a Canadian or Australian. Variety is the spice of life, so don't change your tactics and you'll get a big kick out of it.

I'm doing okay out here, especially pertaining to the "barbecues." I never did go for "Exlax," two or three weeks is plenty of time to spend with a babe. After that they start getting monotonous or they ask the "wackiest" questions. Some of these babes are really "built" though, and I have no objections. I like them when they fill their clothes in "nice." Boy, I wish the babes out here could swing their chases like some of the "hep-cats" in "Shy" can. Just 'cause they have two feet, they think the only appropriate thing to do is the two-step. Boy, do they get my water boiling in a hurry.

13

So Dolores has struck oil, well what you know. What's she heading for now, a yacht or a penthouse? She's all right and I like to "shoot-the-breeze" with her. Tell her I said hello. How's your darling little "educated" sis? She's really got a "bean" on her shoulders. How's the old man, still going to church?

Boy, these Idaho potatoes are a fattening food. I've been eating so many potatoes since I've been here that I'm beginning to look like a spud. If I ever get back home and a spud or a bean just as so much looks me in the eye, I'll break its God-damned back.

Well, there's not much to say right now, so "Keep em smiling" and don't go "beefing."

Puddles of Love, Sal

P.S.

Send that picture on the "double"

Chapter 5, May 1943

May 24, 1943

Dear Loretta:

I received your letter today, but why bawl me out so? After all one and a half pages is pretty damn long considering the time I have to myself. You know I always liked to "bounce the blubber" with you and on that night I had to rush over and stand for "Fox Watch." If you think that's any fun, you're completely lost. That damn stuff comes over like a trip hammer and boy does it make your ears feel like you were swimming sixty feet under water.

Hey "luscious," how's "Monkies" treating you? I bet it won't be long and they'll be eating right out of your hands. Go get them, Duchess, and before you know you'll be the queen of the joint.

By the way, where in the hell is a picture of yourself? Are you dropping me like a waterfall or are you just dropping me? I think I'll have a couple for you next time I write. Say, how are these Merchant Marines? Does he like it very much? Leave me know because that's where I'm going to try to get in so how about doing some "scouting" for me? Don't "bum steer" me or else when I get home (it sounds like something to eat) I'll put the gloves on with you and go about ninety rounds. Fifty-seven isn't a bad score for a beginner, especially for a "barbecue." Look at me, I very seldom bowl over 300. I "liked" the way you said "I think of you every time I go out with a sailor." What are you trying to do, make me pull my hair out?

So they're trying to throw all your father's "best" friends in the army. Well, that's the way it goes. Drinking from the bottle one day and smelling the cork the next. How's your jitter bugging getting along? I heard you can really swing your "frame around." By the way, what "holes" are left to go dancing in? Is Pilsen (Park) closed yet?

Did you see that picture *Reveille with Beverly* yet? If you didn't, don't miss it. It'll have your blood corpuscles swinging it out with beads of perspiration on your forehead. It's the hottest musical you ever saw. Freddie Slack swings out "Cow Cow Boogie." Duke Ellington "tickles the keys" playing "Take the A Train." Count Basie does his part by "ripping off" "One O'Clock Jump." Last, but by no means least, we have Bob Crosby beating out "Big Noise from Winnetka," and boy is that a nice mellow song. So don't miss it or you'll be kicking out somebody's teeth the rest of your "sweet" life.

Well, sweets, I'll be closing now and I'll be waiting impatiently for that picture. You'll have to excuse the writing this time 'cause I gave up quality for quantity so you won't be biting my head off.

All the Love in Idaho, Sal

Part 2—1944

Chapter 6, July 1944

July 11, 1944

1323 S. Fairfield
Chicago, IL
R.M. 3/c
NOB Navy 1504 Gr. 7
c/o Fleet Post Office
San Francisco, Calif.

Dear Sal,

I know you're surprised to hear from me, but Carmine mentioned that he got a letter from you and I asked him for your address. Say, would you mind telling me why you never wrote to me after that short leave you had? What's the matter, haven't you got time for an old friend anymore?

Well, today is Tuesday and I'm just about to go swimming at Douglas Park. It's social night. I hope I have some fun. I'm going with Tillie (remember her), Dolores, and Rita.

Tommy was in on leave. I was at the beach with him and, boy, is he a good swimmer (also a wolf). He showed me where the whole bunch of you went swimming. Way by the rocks by the Planetarium. Remember?

Say, when are you coming home on a leave? I'm anxious to see how you look. Did you grow any taller or get any smarter? Maybe in spelling or something? Do you recall that time in Douglas Park, the little spelling contest we had?

I hear that you went up for a rating and after passing the exam they closed the doors on your T.S. eh.

You know it's been about a year and a half since I last heard from you. I'm seventeen now in case you've forgotten. Gee. It seems like I will never reach eighteen. Say, I bet you're old enough to vote now. Well, don't forget Roosevelt.

Well, I'll have to leave you now. The girls are here now and practically dragging me out the door. I'll be with you in about two and a half hours.

Well, here I am back again and guess what happened? I got a black eye. For the first time. Did you ever have one? It seems I was dancing with this fellow at the pool when he threw me out to "jive." He turns around a silly way and pokes me in the eye with his elbow. Boy, everything happens to me! I was surprised that they had records there. By the way, do you still jitterbug? You were the first one to teach me the fundamentals at your house that spring. That was good wine you had. Does your father still make it?

My sister sends you a kiss (X) like the one you had in our basement. Remember?

I'm listening to the radio now. Gee, I don't know what to want anymore. Say, I hope you are not prejudiced or anything and answer this letter. So as the radio plays "Goodnight Wherever You Are" (that's my favorite song, what's yours?), I'll bid you the same.

Love, Loretta

July 19, 1944

1330 So. Washtenaw Ave.
Chicago 8, IL
RM S/C
N.O.B. Navy 1504 Gr. 7-A
c/o F.P.O.
San Francisco, Calif.

Hiya Lor,

Say, you could have knocked me over with a sliver from a tooth-pick when I received your letter. Not only did you surprise me, but I was also overjoyed to receive it.

I realize that it was pretty damn wicked and silly of myself not to write to you before, but I was afraid you were going to throw hatchets at me through the mail and I can't afford to have any more holes in my "noggin" than I have at present. I began to think of your happy family the other week so I wrote a letter to Dolores but I sent it to the Washtenaw address and no doubt the little Russian got it and thinks it's a letter from the Czar. I'll say again though, it's really nice writing to you again.

So black eyes are contagious with you, well, that's what you get for bumping them into other people's elbows. Boy, those jitterbugs must really be getting rough back there, but how.

You asked if I changed much, well, to tell you the truth that is a hell of a long story. In reality, not much except that I'm about five feet ninety inches and weigh about a hundred and three eighty, not very much of a change, eh?

Now how about yourself? In fact to accommodate you, I'm going to send a blank form for you to fill out and don't forget to send a couple of pictures. I'm warning you I won't take nothing short of an affirmative for an answer.

Say, do you think I forgot how to tell time? I'll admit the only thing I seem to notice out here is the months (I should have said "are" but I'm happy) flying by, but and I do mean period. At a rough estimate, I'd say it was closer to six hours as reported "missing in action" than a mere two and a half. What are you trying to do, hold out on me? Probably strolling through the park and at your old "she-wolf" tactics. My, my ain't that something?

Boy, you're sure getting "chintzy," just one kiss. Don't be so tight with those puckered up lips, Duchess, after all that's what they were made for. It's just like old times when something like that comes over. I remember I practically used to have to break a leg to make you give in, but usually my arm ended up in a sling.

You'll have to excuse this "mill" I'm using but it's practically impossible to compete with that handwriting of yours and believe me I'm not kidding. I'm on watch right now and am absorbing in a little of rather hot music. Maestro "Licorice-Stick" Shaw is really giving out with the notes and I mean he's really giving out. Old "Moon Glow," "Temptation," "Frenesi" and what not. I really feel like squirming with some cute little worm right now, but women are negative out here and what a crime that is (suffer boy, suffer). Speaking of songs I really get a kick out of Cass Daley bellowing out "Willy the Wolf of the West." Boy, that song is really a killer. That song you mentioned I recollect that I used to dance to it at Old Melody Mill. I don't think I have any favorite melody to think of, but that's what an island like this will do for you. Coming to think of it though, I think "When They Ask About You" and "Holiday of Strings" is pretty snazzy, or don't you think? Well, sweets, I guess I better close for now.

Love, Sal

July 25, 1944

Wow! All the trouble to go out with a sailor— What's the matter are they finally getting particular?

Dear Sal,

Just received your letter and was glad to hear from you again.

Say, what made you think I was going to "throw hatchets at you." What reason would I have? I still don't know.

So, you thought of my family and then write to Delores? What's the matter, did you forget how to spell Loretta? Boy— that was something.

I go through all the trouble of writing to you and "breaking the ice," then two days later my sister gets the letter. Some boyfriend you are.

Judging from your letter, I see you're just as "sharp" as ever, but don't forget I don't belong to the Navy Intelligence, so take it easy on the "lingo."

How's your dancing getting along? I'm beginning to get the hang of it finally.

Say, Slabby, do you know that as long as we've been writing to each other, you never write me a love letter. Silly isn't it? But I was wondering what kind of a "line" you'd pass on a girl. Or maybe you haven't got a steady. Have you?

Even though, write me one the next time. Even if you have to copy it from a *True Story*.

Oh, yes, about the address. Well I don't live with the "old bird" (her father) anymore. Yep! I finally up and left him. I live across the alley by my aunt's house. Of course, there's no hard feelings between us. I still argue with him.

My, how affectionate you were at the end of the letter— you called me sweets.

When are you coming home, Slabby? You know I miss you a lot, even though I never mention it to you. Boy, was I mad at you when you were in on leave. Before you came in, you wrote and told me that when you get leave you'll come over to the house and take me out. But no, you had to come over at the last minute, (12:o'clock) and drunk on top of it and then expect me to go for a walk with you. Humph!

Maybe I should have been glad that you came at all. But I wasn't, I was mad!!! By the way, is that why you never wrote again?

What's a "mill"?

So "When They Ask About You," is your favorite song— well, I guess it's okay—but it is "kinda" old. Did you ever hear that song "Time Waits For No One"? Now, that's a song that has a pretty melody and words.

I see Scully once in a while. He's getting a little fatter and Healey is getting a lot fatter. Do you write to any of them? Sonny is engaged again. This time he says he means it, but then you know Sonny.

Well, I'll have to be closing now, seeing as how I'm coming to the end of the page. So, darling, wherever you are I send all my love (which isn't much) and I wish you pleasant dreams of me.

Love & Kisses etc.

Loretta

P.S. My, ain't I getting braver?

Chapter 7, August 1944

August 6, 1944

Dearest Lore:

Well, this might seem a bit strange (of course it really depends on how you look at it) but I just wrote you a letter three or four days ago (I'll be damned if I can remember which). It just so happens that our faithful reliable and what not mail plane ran into a slight accident and had to discard the mail it was carrying from our little "pebble" into the deep blue sea. As I was about to say before, I don't know for sure whether my letter addressed to one sweet chick was on it or not but just to be on the safe side I'm dropping you another line. After all, I can't afford to break our "love affair" once we have it rolling again after a twelve month recess, now can I?

I went over to the other island this afternoon to listen to our Navy Band out here and man, are they really mellow. They were (the band of course) all from big time bands before the war broke out and they know their business. They have a few sweet arrangements of "G.M." (Glen Miller) and boy, when they play them how do I long for Chicago and old times. Getting on the jumpy side, they have "G.M's" "American Patrol," Count Basie's "One O'clock Jump" and Bobby Sherwood's "Elk's Parade." When I hear the above three records (pardon me, I mean arrangements) my blood starts tingling and my toes start doing handstands 'cause they are really "alreet" and three times as mellow. I have seemed to forgot, slightly, the knack of rug-cutting but with a sweet chick like yourself to put me back in the groove again it wouldn't take me over three seconds. I hope I'm not taking a lot for granted but I'm sure counting on you to help me steer myself right (steer—I don't mean cattle, either), seeing that you're getting to know the art of "toe-tangling" backwards, so don't leave me down.

By the way, I never was the fussy type so why don't you fill out that form and make two of us happy? After all, I want some means of security and I guarantee you I will not use it for blackmail purposes ha, ha, heh. How about a few variety pictures of yourself starting from a bathing suit to a heavy date gadget. I'll try my best to obtain a few for you as soon as I get back to halfway civilization, mainly, Honolulu. I'll be back there in maybe two weeks so, sister, can't you spare a few pictures?

I'll say again that I was sorry about the way things went on my long three day leave, but when I get back to "Shy" (Chicago) again I'll make up for it but tenfold. That's a promise, by the way, so you can count on having a good time. A few moonlight swims (we'll see who can "drown" who) dancing in a few nice ballrooms and last but not least, we'll have to take in a few night clubs on the rumba side. Have you got a car, by the way (now what in the Hell made me bring that up)?

Say, did you forget that this year is still "leaping" or were you telling jokes. Just the same I always did (and I always will) like you a heck of a lot, whether you know it or not. If not in the above case of "like" then I'm afraid it'sits love. I hope you don't think I was trying to work my way through college when I was spending much time "Whistling at Your Doorstep and a Knocking at Your Door" or do you? Well, you had better not. You're a nice-looking girl (almost a woman—boy, that word seems vulgar) and I think we could get along together very nicely. I sure wish I had you in my arms at this very moment 'cause I'm fit as a fiddle and ready for pitching woo but on a big scale. I'm afraid that will have to wait for a while (you can wait, now can't you?) 'cause I haven't the faintest idea when I'll get home again, but keep on smiling in the meantime, which isn't very hard for a happy-go-lucky female like yourself. But you can bet your last pair of nylons on one thing, and that is I can't wait until I see you again.

There's nothing on this island but lovely moonlight and nothing else. It really is a shame to leave it to go to waste like this, but that's old Mother Nature for you. I had better close for now but my love for you is quite perpetual so write again but soon.

Love & the Sweetest Dreams, Sal

August 11, 1944

1323 So. Fairfield
Chicago, 8, Illinois
R.M. 3/c
N.O.B. Navy, 1504 Gr. 7-A
c/o F.P.O.
San Francisco, Calif.

Dear Sal,

Just received your letter and was very happy to hear from you again.

Well, here it is Fri. and I've just gotten home from work, and boy, was it miserable working. The mercury must have hit 120° or more. So, the girls and I have decided to go swimming tonight at the beach. Maybe I'll get a "moon burn." Say, I bet you've got a nice tan. Do you ever go swimming in the ocean or have they got sharks in those waters?

So I see you're keeping up with modern music. I haven't heard any of G.M.'s records in a long time. Boy! You talk like a real hep-cat, sure would like to see you in action. (Ahem!)

Oh, Slabby, about that application you sent. I didn't think you wanted it back so I was fooling around with it and I don't want you to get the wrong impression, but you know how it goes. (I hope.)

Dolores and I are taking pictures Sunday so I'll send some to you in the next letter I write. That reminds me, did you ever know that I had my hair bleached blond for about six months this last winter? I'm sending you a snapshot of me as a blond and on the other side as I looked a couple of weeks ago. But, you have to promise to send it back because I like to keep it for a souvenir. Promise????

Say, did you know that Dolores has a new steady boyfriend? Yeah! She's at it again. But this time it's quite for keeps. He was wounded, but in France about three weeks ago. Both of his legs are in a cast and he has a "slight" chest wound. Dolores expects to marry him on his next furlough. I'm going to stand up at the wedding. (Some wedding.)

Say did you really mean every thing you wrote in your former letter or were you first "spoofing" me? By the way, are you old enough to go to nightclubs now or am I kidding? Say, Slabby, I came to think of it, did you know that you were the first fellow I ever kissed? And, remember the "helluva" time you had trying. Spelling games and such. And you know, you asked me something else, but at that time I didn't know what you were talking about. But I know now and it makes me laugh now as to how dumb I was then. Oh yes! I'm changing little by little. Now don't think I'm throwing hints but my sister and I made a little wager of five "bucks" that I would have a "steady" by my eighteenth birthday and I say I will. She thinks I'll never get one because I'm so "cold" towards the fellows. But I think I know what I want, so why "play up" to ever T.D. & H (Tom, Dick and Harry).

I'll have to close this letter now but I'll be expecting to hear from you P.D.Q. (Pretty Damn Quick)

Love and that one kiss from me,

Loretta

APPLICATION FOR A DATE WITH A SAILOR

Name: Loretta (Cuddle up a little closer) **Age:** 71 1/2
Address: Juvenile Court Roosevelt & Ogden
City: Chicago **County:** Cook **State:** Ill.
Color: White – sometimes **Thighs:** Nosey, eh! **Height:** 10 ft.
Weight: 99 lbs **Bust:** 42 ¾ ins. **Complexion:** so-so **Hips:** 32
　　　Waist: 32
Color of Eyes: Black **Figure (check one): Good** X "braggin"
Do you go to dances: Yep **If so, how much:** About that many
　　　times
Not enough: Why **Do you neck:** But, definitely **When:**
　　　Whenever I get the chance
Anytime? Yeah **Like it:** and how **Why:** "ummm"
Are you married: not legally **If so does your husband travel:**
　　　You're not kidding
Type of residence: X **Can you cook:** and how
What: water **Is it good:** I don't know I never tasted it
Do you get up early: Are you kidding **Why:**
Will you try anything once: Sure **More than once:** that all
　　　depends **HM'MMMM**
What: Going to Church **Now it's getting interesting...** fooled
　　　you
What do you estimate your capacity for the following to be:
Wine: all you got in the cellar **Bourbon:** ? **Scotch:** ? **Rum:** ?
　　　Gin: ?
Milk: ? (milk is crossed out)
What is the approximate car-fare from your home to the
nearest park: Walking distance **Swimming pool:** walking
　　　distance
Movie: walking distance **Depot:** walking distance **Shindig:**
　　　walking distance
If you live at home indicate on diagram the exact position of:
　　　Parents bed room
Light switch living room Back door Sofa Nearest window
　　　(open): Yes
Quickest way out: window

29

Please(Note answer (F.) Truthfully, it might save my life some day)

Points of interest: The other window

Most logical place your brother would hide:

Don't have to worry about him. He's in the army.

Please note: The reverse side of this is
excellent for drawing diagrams:

A close up. Place a small photo of yourself,
one in a bathing suit is plenty satisfactory...

Sorry.

(The sketch below was drawn in Pencil on the back of the form.)

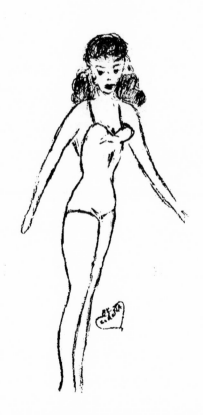

Chapter 8, September 1944

September 6, 1944

Next time I'll send you a picture. I'll show you how I look in a dress.

Dear "Pijouk" (Drunk)

Well, well, so you finally managed to "squeeze" out a ten day leave from the Navy. My, how did you ever do it? Say, I didn't think you'd have any trouble getting to dance with a girl for a whole month with all those hidden charms of yours.

That's awfully peculiar if you didn't hear about me being a blond. Boy! You should have seen how I shocked everyone in the neighborhood—especially the Russians—remember them? My father didn't notice my hair 'til two days later. Of course, that's just like him, you know.

Well, to keep you up-to-date about my jobs, I think the last time I wrote to you I was working at Superior Electrical Industries, then International Spring and now I work back at Continental Coffee Co. I use to work there once before. They sent me a letter to come back and work for them—I don't know why though! Laverne and her sister Elaine and my sister Dolores also work there. Yep! We have some pretty swell times at and after work.

Guess what? I got another black eye! Boy, this is getting monotonous. Why did I have to wait 'til I'm seventeen to get 'em? I never had any before.

Well, my brother is coming in on another furlough next week. I think he averages a furlough every three months. Here he's been in the army for seventeen months and he's never been "across" yet. Now, that's why you call connections.

Oops. My little cousin (bless her heart) just spilled the ink over my stationery and boy what a mess.

Dolores just honored the household with her presence. "Lucky we." She says hello to you. Should I tell her you say hello too? Okay! Hello Dolores. —She thinks I'm crazy.

Excuse me—telephone.

2 minute intermission.

Speaking of Dolores and that little "wager" we made—I have until March 22—and just think I'll be eighteen. Boy, I hope that day never comes. I'll be happy just to be seventeen all my life. I don't want to get any older, but I guess "Time Waits For No One."

I was going "steady" once, but my goodness! I got tired of seeing him every day almost. And didn't I have a time getting rid of him—He was a German fellow and you know how domineering they are and I hate someone to tell me what to do and what not to do. Boy! If that's what it means you have to go through, Hell! I'll never get married—never. Although, I will say this for him. He was a good dancer—he had looks and money. And he knew how to act—he wasn't any silly jerk either. But why am I telling you this? I like to hear how you spent your time since the last I saw of you. Meaning your social life with the girls. Did you ever find any special one yet?

Well, I'm signing off for now.

With all my love, (and that's plenty)

Loretta

RM 3/c

Radio Navy #41

o/o F.P.O.

San Francisco, Calif

Dearest Lor:

Well, Sweets, it was awful nice to hear from you again. I'll try and make a half way attempt to answer your letter right now, but don't hold anything against me 'cause I'm still a bit groggy from the ten day leave I just got through with.

I just got back from nine months of Gooney-Bird duty and I am now back from where I started previously. I've been on Oahu four months before I got shipped to that little pebble in the Pacific. I never did like island duty, but the case is just about hopeless as far as getting a ship goes. Maybe one of these days I might accidentally board a rig-cutter, but you can take my word for it that it will be strictly on the accidental side.

So you've been a blond for six months and I haven't heard a word of it, how come? Am I an orphan or just lacking citizenship papers? That blond layout sure knocked me off my "poles," in fact I was just about ready for the "Blue-Kidney" when my gazers looked at the picture. As to my opinion, I think you look sweeter as a luscious brunette. Mind you, it's only one man's opinion but I think your brunette hair was a natural combination with your eyes. Anyhow, it was nice to see a picture of you and as you request it back for future references, you'll find it enclosed within this letter. But don't forget to send me some to keep and to remind me of you or else I'll break your neck.

Getting back to my ten day leave, or "Bromo Seltzer Excursion" as one might call it, it was a pretty fair leave but I wished I could have spent it at home instead. I had to be satisfied with Honolulu and that was that. I really got lit up four of the nights, in fact the first Saturday night I was on leave we happened to visit a bird zoo in between drinks and I passed out like a light. Of course, the varnish I was drinking had something to do with it, but the bird I was gazing at, with a ten foot nose and still growing, re-clinched the matter. I woke up the next morning in my room wondering what the Hell happened until my buddies let me in on the info. I swore off drinks until three days later. I guess that's just the way things go.

I went to three dances while I was on leave and although they were nothing compared to Pilsen Park, they still served the purpose. It was the first time in about fourteen months and I guess you know that it was pretty tough breaking in the toe-nails. I finally got maneuvering after a bit but I'm afraid I'll have to have you polish me up a bit when we go on our first date when I get back. Now what am I afraid of? Don't answer that.

The biggest trouble in dancing out here is that there are too many GIs out here to each Wahine. It's strictly "breakin" and by the time you reach the babe there's twelve other guys throwing arms around her. It's similar to a Notre Dame, Northwestern football game but just a bit rougher.

Getting back to you now (it goes off and on like this throughout the whole letter), I certainly got a big kick out of that questionnaire. It was very humorous and you know I wouldn't take you serious over a joking matter like that but there were a few things I'd like to take into consideration. I wouldn't want to bring them up at this time though, so I'll just leave it ride for the present.

Seeing that you have a "fin" bet against your sis, I'd like to do everything utterly possible in seeing you come through with flying colors. Don't go thinking it's the money I'm after, either. By the way, how many more months have you got before the deadline? After all we just can't leave this wager slip by, now can we?

I haven't met up with Wiggler yet, but I hope to before too much time slips by. I tried to get on touch with him while on my leave, but no soap. I'll keep trying, though.

Well, Honey, it's about time I started hitting that beer line so I'll be seeing you.

Love as always, Sal

P.S.

Don't forget the pictures and take note that my address has changed.

September 18, 1944

Dear Sal,

Well, here it this Monday and am I happy. I first received my income tax refund and a check from the last place I worked at. That brings me close to $100.00. Boy, what a way to start a letter off. Talking about money. Instead, I should have told you that I was thinking of you and the fellows from the corner. And that's why I decided to write to you without waiting for an answer from you.

I had a pretty good weekend for a change. My sister's "old flame" (not that goldmine she used to go out with) is stationed at Navy Pier and will be there for about six weeks. Yes, he's a sailor, so he brought along a few of his mates and little did I know she was going to meet him at all—I was just an innocent bystander. When there they were, all four of them waiting outside of our factory to take us out. Lucky for us—we girls were all dressed up or we would've been in some predicament, now wouldn't we?

Well, to start the evening off, we went out to eat (we were hungry—after all, we did work eight long hours and on a Saturday too!) And after we ate (oh! Slabby what I'm about to tell—I hope you won't think too too bad of me. I don't know why I do it—but it's like a burning fever that when you start it once you can never seem to get enough of it!) But I've taken to drink— Yes, I know I shouldn't, but I have to pass the time some way since you're gone.

I had two beers through the whole evening (but you know something else— They call me "2 beers Loretta")—No, all kidding aside—I really had a swell time. After we ate, we went to a show because it was "kinda" early—after the show we went to the grand opening of a Tavern on 22nd street. And for that occasion they had a Hawaiian Band and a Hula Dancer (I bet you see a lot of those out where you are) —Boy! I never saw anybody do the Hula like she did— Never, whew! You should've had seen the fellows, they had to practically strap 'em to their chairs. I was lucky that the fellow I was with didn't like to argue—(meaning—that I didn't want to "mush" so he didn't persist.) But I kissed him goodnight. Yep! My sister and Laverne almost "fell over." You know it's not like me to kiss someone after only meeting him for the first time— (Look at Scully, remember how he tried) Of course not mentioning you, remember? Or how could you forget, but you had a lot of fun trying—so did I. Too bad you weren't stationed at Navy Pier. I'd have more fun with you, i.e. if you didn't change any, did you?

Yeah! How about sending me a picture of yourself? After all, I want to see if you got any "cuter." By the way, how tall are you now?

Well, I'll have to be closing now—so pleasant dreams to you—and make sure you dream one about me, and no nightmares allowed.

Love, Loretta

September 23, 1944

Saturday "Nite"

Dear Lor:

It was really nice to hear from you again, Sweets, but I was surprised to hear that you didn't receive my letter that I sent about a week and a half ago. Well, I guess it's about time the sharks got one of them but I don't see why in the Hell it had to be yours.

You'll have to excuse this broken handwriting tonight because I just got out of the pool about ten minutes ago and I have never come so close to resembling a polar bear as I have tonight. Sister! I am freezing but definitely. Boy, do I wish I had something like you to cuddle up close to keep me comfortable, my, my, would that be Heaven or a reasonable facsimile. But you can't have your cake and eat it too, but mind you I'll be looking toward the future with high hopes. That's about the only way I can see 20/20.

Say "Sis," I hope you don't go putting your nose so high up in the atmosphere that you could draw "flight pay" now that you're filthy with "majuma." Why don't you put a down payment on a nice little bungalow somewhere in Oak Park and then when I come home we could play house. I was just kidding you, Sweets, but on the second thought, it wouldn't be so bad. No sir, it wouldn't be bad at all. "You the mama and the papa is me," now where did I hear that before? Don't tell me, leave me guess.

Glad to hear that you had a nice time, but don't go overdoing it or else you and I are going to go through another wrestling bout but for high stakes. Whatever you do, don't go trusting a "Swabby" too far— Now what in the hell am I saying, it sounds like I'm trying to throw the wrench in on "yours truly." Oh well, you can't talk forever without putting your foot in the wrong place.

Boy, you bowled me over with the two beer gag (pant, pant and pant) and I'm still choking. Give me a break and leave me up for air will you, Honey?

Okay, be stubborn (boy, that word seems strange to me, Aw the heck with it, I'll leave it ride) and let rigor mortis set in, see if I yell. I hope I don't have to start calling you "Alcohol Lil" in the near future 'cause I'd look pretty hot going into a tavern with you and start ordering from the bartender; "Give me a case of Haig & Haig" and a half of barrel of beer." You have to admit that it wouldn't sound so "purty," but oh what a business old Bromo Seltzer would be doing the next day.

I don't know why I feel so good tonight, seeing that I have an eight hour Mid watch starting in about three hours from now. Maybe it was the swim or the letter I got from you, but frankly I think it was both. Don't go expecting me to dream about you tonight with a beautiful Mid staring me in the eyes, I'll be in there plugging tomorrow night but I don't see why you can't comply.

I don't know if I told you but I met Ed (Boo Boo) about a week and a half ago in Honolulu, and all there was to do was to drink and attend a dumb-dumb dance. Well, anyhow, we were happy in just seeing one another. I don't think I'll ever get use to this "off the street at ten o'clock," boy, it is really wicked.

I was supposed to meet Ed a couple of days ago "ashore," but he didn't show up so I went out with another buddy from Chicago. Of course, I don't think my being late forty-five minutes had anything to do with it, but one can never tell, can one?

Well, sweets, I haven't any worthwhile pictures as yet but I can't see why you can't send some of yourself. Go make haste with the celluloid. You know I'm still about 66 ½, so don't go yelping 'cause I got caught in a punch press. Well I'll close for now as "Licorice Stick" Shaw is giving out with "Begin the Beguine." Lots of love and kisses but be good.

Sal

September 28, 1944

Dear Sal,

Just received your letter and glad to hear from you again. My, it sure takes you a long time to answer. I think I'm one letter ahead of you. But why bother with such trivials. Say, why don't you write more often, or is that against your religion?

You know them "Mama and Papa" words you were telling me about, well, thems proposin' words where I come from—either that or you're a cad. —Cad!!!

My, how come you're so worried about what I do when I go out? Whatsa matter, don't you trust me? Well, it's good to know that someone worries about me. Yeah! But who's gonna worry about me when I go out with you?

Boy! Wait until you come home on leave and I see you for the first time—boy!! I'll give you the longest hand-shake you ever had—fooled you—yeah! I will fool you and kiss you. (Do you follow me?)

You know, since the war I only went out with two sailors, and that was on special occasions. So don't go telling me not to trust a "swabby" after all, I know what "the score is" —just call me Miss "know it all" from now on.

Remember the money I told you I had. Well my brother came in on furlough a couple of days ago. Now, I'm reminiscing of something gone and forgotten.

Dolores says hello.

Say—what was the meaning of that little warning at the end of your letter—quote "but be good,"—haven't I always been? And don't think I changed in that respect.

Well, I sent you some pictures in my former letter. You should have gotten 'em by now. And no criticisms either. After all, I'm not very photogenic. I'm still waiting for a picture of you. Will you send me a big one, "5x7" like the last time? I've got an empty frame I want to put it in. Your other one was lost in the turmoil of having the house cleaned, and I've looked "high and low" for it but haven't seen "head nor tail" of it since. (I've got a book of "sayings" that I'm copying those expressions from right next to me and also a dictionary.)

Well, Chicago is still the same except a little more quiet since you left, but we're getting used to the lull and quick. Say, have you got any idea of when you think you will be home? You'd better hurry up. I'll be eighteen in five months now and I'd like to see you while I'm still young.

I suppose you know Art is discharged. Yep, he walks with a limp. I remember when I used to play pinnacle with him, Scully and Monk. Laverne writes to the latter. She hasn't changed much since you last saw her. Only she put on a little weight around the "you know what."

Boy, I think she must be in love with Monk. She cries when she doesn't get a letter from him. I think she's jumping at conclusions for "his heart still belongs to Dolly." Boy, I sound like an old lady talking about my poor girlfriends like that. Well that's all for today.

Chapter 9, October 1944

October 1, 1944

Sunday Night

Dearest Lor:

How are those pretty little "Black Eyes" getting along these days? Before I go any further, I think I have a little boner to pick with you. What in the blankety blank blank _____ for putting "43" on that missing letter instead of "41"? It's a miracle it ever got here, but they happen now and then, you know, but mostly then. I got it just the other day and, boy, am I tickled that I did 'cause I couldn't afford to miss a letter like that.

Boy, those pictures were really Honeys and I'm not just flattering you either. That sure is a cute little bathing suit and a figure to match and I can say that again. What do you do when you go down to the lake, bring a club with you to beat off the opposite sex? If any get too fresh, just whistle and I'll come a swimming and a running and that, young lady, is a promise. I used to do quite a bit of swimming myself right off the "rocks" and those pictures sure made me yearn for Chicago, and that's not all that made my heart skip beats every now and then. The good old Navy Pier was in the background of one of the pictures also. Yes-sir, I can just picture myself swimming with you off the rocks and I can hardly wait until the "picture" develops. You had better practice on holding your breath for at least two months, I mean minutes. There you go again, you won't even let me concentrate for one single minute. Well, sweets, I guess you know how I feel about those pictures so I'll drop that pleasant subject for the moment.

I haven't been on liberty for eight whole days now, imagine that? Last time I went ashore we went down to the beach (you just can't keep me away from the water out here) and had a pretty good time, that is myself and the other guys. We brought two cases of beer and is it fun swimming when you get a little groggy. It was just a small beach, but the high breakers that were coming in really made it swell. We managed to take a few pictures, but I don't know as yet if they came out. I'll leave you know though. We had an old crate and went around the whole island after the swim. The mountains sure are pretty in certain places, but I'd rather be in the Chicago Theatre (with you at the side of me) watching the same scenes in a newsreel or some other reasonable facsimile, any old time.

I'm supposed to meet Ed in "Lulu" (Honolulu) this Wednesday and kill a few. He's still the same old Ed, as big as ever. I've also been talking to Wiggler over the phone. We're trying to get it arranged so the whole three of us can make liberty together. Boy, it sure would be pretty nice if three ex-corner boys could make the rounds again. I better start getting a new set of "blinkers" 'cause when we three meet in Lulu I'll get blinder than a bat.

They really have a nice swimming pool here and that's about all. The high dive is really a pip. I've the back flip and front and back jack-knife mastered already and maybe, in another year, I'll have them all under control—or else a broken neck.

No, Lor, I haven't fallen for any girl since I left Chi. I went to a couple of nice dances in Oakland while I was there for about a month, but nothing serious. I sure think that the girl this letter is addressed to is a bundle of charm and would be good company any old time. It's a little hard to explain through letters but I hope you know how I feel.

Well, sweets, I'll close for now, so think of me in the meantime as I always do of you.

Love plus, Slabs

P.S.

If you're going steady with anyone but me before I get back, I'll be throwing rocks at you the rest of our lives.

43

October 5, 1944

The USS Signet (AM-302) is an Admirable-class minesweeper built for the United States Navy. She is authorized May 2, 1942, keel laid April 8, 1943, launched August 16, 1943 and is placed in full commission in the United States Navy on June 20, 1944. On that afternoon, the officers and crew come aboard, stow their gear and settle down to shipboard life. The USS Signet spends the summer of 1944 completing her fitting out and undergoing minesweeping trials, shakedown, and antisubmarine warfare training. On August 25, she reports to the Commander, Western Sea Frontier, at San Francisco, California and on August 26, takes to sea with her first convoy of one ship heading for Pearl Harbor. Arriving on September 6, the USS Signet sails for Eniwetok in the Marshall Islands on September 10 with a different one-ship convey. On September 21, the USS Signet arrives at Eniwetok. She doesn't stay long and is soon off to Kwajalein, another island in the Marshall Islands. Arriving on September 23, the Signet arrives at Kwajalein, and then that evening heads back to Pearl Harbor, arriving on September 30 to load stores and provisions.

RM 3/c H.S.N.R.
Division 3
H.S.S. Signet—AM 302
o/o F.P.O.
San Francisco, Calif.

Dear Lor:

Well, my pretty little Polish girl (any similarity between "Amapola" and the above words is not purely co-incidental but accidentally on purpose), I suppose you're wondering what made me write so quickly after the last letter? Well, "Sweets," that is a long story, but since I'm no Mark Twain I'll have to make it short.

You can plainly see that I'm not stationed at Wahiawa anymore and that I finally got a ship. It came as a surprise to me, in fact, it almost made my "ticker" stop ticking. I put in a "chit" back at the base Monday afternoon, and before the ink was dry I was practically on my way to my new ship. The M.A.A. (Masters at Arms). came to my bunk Tuesday morning and told me to go down to the "Ad" Building and see the Executive Officer about a transfer (right after an eight hour Mid, too, imagine that). I thought the guy was "kibitzing" around so I went back to sleep, I got up about one and then went swimming till four when the M.A.A. came for the second time (incidentally I almost broke my neck trying to do the one and a half off the high dive.) This time when I went down to the "Ad" Building, did I get "read" off, but I got the ship and that's the main thing. I thought they were going to ship me out to Midway (Island) again.

Guess who came over to the base about two days before I left? None other than Wiggler. We just shot the breeze about the corner and the lucky young kids who seem to be making out okay in the wolfing department. I was supposed to meet Ed and him in Honolulu Wednesday, but I couldn't account of the transfer. He was looking pretty good and it was really nice to see him.

I managed to get liberty today and went out with some other buddy from Chicago. We went to a nice little place where they always have nice drinks and I'm still a bit woozy as I'm writing this letter, but I'll finish it if I have to break my big toe in trying.

I'm sorry that I couldn't get those pictures for you. They weren't ready when I left the base. But I sure am glad that I got those pictures of you because it'll bring me closer to you while I'm out at sea. I'll be leaving pretty soon and will probably be out for some time consequently. This will be my last letter for a while. But that doesn't mean that you can't write to me at least once a week 'cause I'm really crazy about you and hope you feel likewise. Don't forget, Honey, be good while I'm away and we'll really make up for lost time when I hit Chicago again, you can bet your last pair of nylons on that 'cause it's a cinch bet.

Love & Kisses, As Always, Sal

P.S.

Don't forget to keep writing.

October 10, 1944

The USS Signet, with Sal and 90 other crew members, ship off for Eniwetok escorting a 13-ship convoy. Sal is a radio man responsible for translating Morse code messages that come into the radio shack from US ships and Radio San Francisco.

October 11, 1944

Dear Sal,

Just received your letter and was very glad to hear from you again. (Same old thing, all the time.)

Well, judging from your letter, I guessed you liked the pictures. But don't be surprised if some day I ask for them back, then I'll send you a picture with all the camouflage print on it. You probably wouldn't recognize me then. Well, I'm still waiting for your pictures.

The radio is now playing, "After You've Gone." Boy! I wish you were here so I could dance with you. Say, remember the time I was dancing at your house with Laverne and Scully, and the two of you were teaching me how to "boogie it." "Youse" were telling me "Don't be so stiff." "Loosen up." Boy you should see me dance "it" now. Of course I go "in" for that slow boogie-woogie. I hate to move around fast. Now, instead of dancing with my feet I use the "hips." That's a lazy man's dance. Don't you think?

Well, I hope you meet Ed and Wiggler and have a shot and a beer for me. I suppose you've heard that no one has had any word from Monk for about six weeks now. Laverne says if he doesn't come back she's going to be an old maid. Should I believe her? Well, you better make sure you get back. Do you think I want to join her in her ambitions?

Continental Coffee Co. had a dinner party the 9th. They had some moving pictures of the whole company but I wasn't in any of them. I came too late. The dinner was fair but it broke up early. Anyway, three fellows from work and Laverne, Dolores and I went out. Oh yes, Laverne's sister Elaine had to tag along. We didn't get home 'til 3:30 a.m. Dolores, Laverne and Elaine all went to work. I stayed home and slept 'til 12:30, then took my little cousin to the show in the afternoon, came home, ate supper, then I went out again and didn't get home until 2 o'clock this morning. And by time I got to bed, it was about 3 a.m. And the funny thing about it is that I'm not tired now. I could start all over again. That's what I get for eating "Wheaties."

Say, I liked that last part of your letter. Do you think you'll still like me when you see me again? Maybe I've changed and you won't be able to "stand" me around. And then what would you do? What would I do? After all, it's been a long time since I last saw you. Maybe you're not that same sweet Slabby that left Chicago umpteen months ago. But I'm hoping for the best. The Army changed Monk and the Navy will probably change you. And that's if you wrote, well, I wouldn't even think about going out steady without first seeing you. Even though it will probably cost me five bucks. But what's five bucks between friends, and besides Dolores will most likely forget about the bet. Do you think you'll be able to get home for any of the holidays? I would like to be with you on New Year's Eve. Or am I too ahead of my time? Well, I'll be closing for now and until I hear from you.

Lots of Love and Kisses to My Favorite Sailor, Loretta

October 12, 1944

Dear Sal,

Just received another letter from you today. Boy! was I surprised. But then I said to myself (Before I opened the letter of course) this isn't like Slabby to write two letters right in a row. He must have changed his address or something. And sure enough, just as I suspected. Say, is this the first time you're being stationed on a ship? Then I'll hear from you even less than I did before. I answered your letter yesterday so you won't get it for awhile. Probably get this one first.

So, you finally met some of your old gang. Say what did Wiggler have to say about me? Or didn't you inquire? The last I heard about him was that he was supposed to have been going out steady with some "chick" out in Birmingham. Of course, you know how rumors are. There still hasn't been any word from Monk for six weeks now. He's got everybody worried—especially Laverne. Oh yes, what did Wiggler have to say about her— Don't worry, anything you tell me will be in the strictest confidence. Laverne and Wiggler had some sort of spat before she left and I'm just curious (not nosy).

Boy! All that the girls talk about now is getting married. And my sister and Laverne are on the head of the list. But that's not for me—nope. Just the thought of it scares me.

Did you ever think seriously of getting married? And don't think I'm throwing any hints. Not me. I'm having too much fun now, and I don't expect to spoil it yet anyway. But then you know, if I get married I won't have to go to work. Yeah, but then I'll have house work to do and I dread that. (See how I argue with myself.) So, I'll just let things go by and leave it all up to fate.

You really surprised me when you told me that you were "crazy about me." How come it took you so long to let me know how things are? I wish I could believe that you're really sincere about it. Don't forget that year's intermission and I think that if you really liked me, you wouldn't have waited until I wrote to you. But, I'll still write as often as I can, although I'm breaking my "letter for letter" rule. For you, anything goes. Well, almost anything.

Now that you are at sea, won't you have more of a chance of getting home? You know when you get in port or something. I'm still hoping. You know, I didn't see you for such a long time. I'm forgetting how you really are. I used to have a lot of fun kidding around with you. Oh yes, remember that time you were in the basement with my sister and I came down to fix the furnace. Boy! When my sister told me that, little did I know. I just asked her how you kiss, Mmmmm! She says. Boy, wait until I kiss you again. I'll really send you out of this world. I'm not kidding either. I want to find out how to "send" a person. I gather I must have missed a lot when you were home. Gee! How I talk now! I'm getting awfully free with my words lately. But I've already changed. I don't "run" every time a fellows looks at me. Well, I'll continue this letter as soon as I get the chance.

Always thinking of you, Loretta

October 22, 1944

The USS Signet arrives in Eniwetok. Ship and crew stay for two days and enjoy a couple of swimming parties. The crew distributes the potatoes and meat they were carrying, and then head south to Majuro.

Dearest Loretta:

Hiya, Sweets, just received three letters from you and I bet you can hear my heart jump for joy all the way back in Chicago and if you don't, try listening with the good ear for a change. Only kidding, of course, 'cause I'm pretty sure you can hear out of both ears without much trouble except for a hearing aid gadget and what's a small "gizmo" like that amongst friends. What am I saying?

Of course I assume that I can still kid around with you about small trivialities (the rest is all on the "legit") without letting myself become your "pet peeve." After all, we used to have quite some fun together just razzing on another, remember? A girl of your type is just my speed in your humorous and contented ways, and I can say that again without dropping a tooth (I've only got two to go and then you can call me "Gums" for short)!

If I could accidentally get back to Chi for the holidays, would you and I "make with" the red paint but and how. Of course, as I just stated, it would have to be an accident, but I'll get home sometime next year for sure, or I'll know the reason why (here's hoping I never know the reason why). You can bet your boots that we'll make up for lost time but pronto.

Say, Honey, before I go any further, I don't want you to misinterpret my delay in writing 'cause I can assure you it's no fault of my own. I can only write whenever we hit some port and then we don't stay very long but I'll always try in that short interval to get as many on its way to you as possible.

At last I'm getting to see some of this world as I always thought I would when I joined this outfit (long, long ago). I'd like to do all my traveling now 'cause once I get back into those good old "civvies" again you won't catch me going any further than the outskirts of Cicero, and that's a promise. Of course, there'll be some exceptions, mainly when it comes to taking a ten mile trip (boy, I'm desperate) to Brookfield and going for a moonlight dip in that beautiful old quarry.

I of all people had the radio watch this afternoon while most of the other "Jacks" went swimming in the drink. Boy, how I envied them. While I was in the (radio) "shack" sweating my poor brains out (what's left of them of course), those lucky dogs were "making with" the water, diving off the rails and what not. Well maybe I'll get the breaks in some other port, just as long as they aren't in the nose.

I saw a good picture tonight (first one in a week and a half, too) called *Mr. Winkle Goes To War* with Edward G. Robinson and that chubby little Irish kid (Donaldson or something, eh?) and it was really swell. Of course, it had to have a bit of that old Flag routine in it but the humorous and natural parts did much more than make up for it. They sure had some nice "jammy" music to go with it, plus some hot jitterbugs. Man alive, did it ever send my heart pumping like a

Whitney-Pratt engine. By the way, is good old Pilsen Park still open? I sure craved those grounds on Tuesday night, yea man.

Say, my pretty little Polish girl, what you mean "Do you follow me!"

Listen, sweets, I'd follow you almost anywhere except if you tried to swim across the ocean underwater. On top of water I'd be game but as for the former—tut, tut. I must have read your old letters about umpteen times while out at sea and gazed at your pictures until I almost wore the looks off of them, but that doesn't really show you how much I honestly care for you. But I will as soon as I get back, and then will I be in my glory. Take good care of yourself, Honey, and I'll always be thinking of you day in and day out. I'll close for now but I'll try and write to you tomorrow.

All my love, with a lot of kisses for frosting, Sal

October 24, 1944

Hello, Sweets:

Well, I told you two days ago that I'd write to you again just as soon as I had any available time, and I guess the time is right now if I'm ever going to get it out.

Did you ever hear Vaughn Monroe's "Pretty Little Busybody" (very mellow). Well, that song applies directly to you, but and how. I never saw you ask so many questions in all your life about what Wiggler had to say. What's the matter, have you got a guilty conscience? Just joking, of course, and the way it just goes to prove my fact. He didn't say much, but I believe it can hold until later. No sense of getting excited over such trivialities. But as the last line of the above mentioned song you can quote me ditto; "Pretty little busybody, I love you."

Don't go worrying about Monk, 'cause he gets a lazy spell in him every now and then and you couldn't make him write if you held a sledge hammer over his head.

That's the way I was during that so called brief intermission. I always meant to write but I had about as much zeal as a "Pool-room Commando." Say, you're not still holding that against me, are you? If you are, we'll really have a severe wrestling match when I get back, winner takes all, know what am I saying?

Well, I finally managed to go swimming today. The water wasn't what one may call clean, but it's the swimming that counts. Or should I say diving, 'cause that's all I did this afternoon. We dive from off of our ship right into the "drink." It's from anywhere to twenty feet and I always take the highest. There are much more higher places to dive from but there's no sense in breaking your back unless there's no other alternative. When I was about fourteen, I'd dive off of almost any height. "Cowb" and I dove off a forty foot ledge into McCook quarry in Brookfield. Not bragging nor complaining, so no wisecracks, please. That was about the best swimming hole I've ever been in and some day I'll take you there for a dip and you can see for yourself.

Have the babes gone gaga around the street, all wanting to take a dip in the sea of matrimony? You haven't any ideas about jumping into that category as yet, 'cause if you have, I'm going to start calling you scatter-brain.

After the war, it'll be perfectly alright, but as for now we need a few more physicharists (man did I "butcher" that word) or don't you think so? But you better be waiting or I'll be singing "Angry" the rest of my life.

Say, Honey, you'll have to excuse the second page 'cause the damn coffee boiled over, but I only have an hour to sleep before I get up again (it's 0500) so I'll try and dream nice but sweet dreams of us.

Love as Always, Sal

Dear Sal,

Well, here it is Tuesday—Pay Day—and just think I'm spending the evening at home. I'm taking care of my three little cousins. My aunt went to the show and my uncle is working late.

Dolores and Laverne are now working on their part jobs. Yes, they work eight hours at Continental, then go around the corner and work three and a half more hours. Today is their first day there. I wonder how they like it. They want me to start there too. But I don't know. I'm not so crazy about it. Maybe I will just before Xmas.

Oh! Oh! My aunt that lives upstairs just brought down my other two cousins. Seems that she's going to the show too. Oh boy! Five little cousins. Wish you were here to help me manage them. Three boys and two girls. I'm helping the little girl with her homework. She's just started first grade. I'm surprised I know all about the work. And I don't think I'm exaggerating.

My sister's boyfriend was shipped back in the States. He's at I.C. in the hospital. You should see Dolores. She's so happy. That's all you hear her talk about. Between Laverne and her, Laverne keeps telling her how she envies her. She says she wished Monk would get wounded so he'd be shipped home. Silly, eh? I wish you were being shipped home. Just think that if you came home, Monk got in and Dolores' boyfriend, we'd have some fun. Maybe you'd feel "out of place." After all, they're both infantry men. Boy, what's the difference just as long as you're home.

Last night I had such a funny dream. I still can't get over it. In fact, that's all I've been thinking about today. (Besides you, of course.) It seems that I dreamt I was married, the wedding was still going on and there I was in a white gown, real pretty like. And my husband, he looked just like that sailor I met. Here I was already married to him and I'm asking him why he married me. He told me (but I can't tell you that.)

And the part I can't quite understand is that the people are leaving and it was time for me to depart with my new husband and I got scared. I was shaking. I told him to excuse me for awhile and that I'd be right back, but instead I went to my room and changed my clothes and left out the back way. Wrote him a note telling him I wasn't meant for him and such. And the next thing I knew I was with a different fellow promising I'd marry him when my first husband found me. You should have seen his face. It looked as if any moment he was going to murder me. Usually I'd pass this nightmare off and blame it on something I ate, but it's the second time I dreamt that I just got married and got scared then ran away from my husband. Now Dr. Slabby, can you psychoanalys (I think) my dream? And don't laugh either. I'm serious.

I'll be closing and until I hear from you, which reminds me that I didn't receive any word from you for quite awhile, I remain,

Your "dream" girl, Loretta

October 25, 1944

Dearest Sal,

Well, here I am writing to you again, and still no letter from you. But I'm still hoping and waiting.

How's my little sailor getting along? Still being a good boy? Silly question, huh!

Guess what the latest rumor in the neighborhood is? That George was wounded in the knee cap. He wrote two letters to Laverne and signed 'em "Love George." She's soooo thrilled. And do you want to know a "lil" secret? Of course you know Rita. Well she is going to have a baby. Yep! A baby. The only trouble is that she forgot to get the marriage license. She's engaged, though! To Alex. You know, Tillie's brother. He was in on furlough about four months ago. Boy, I'd hate to be in her shoes.

I saw Hinks last night. He took us (Dolores, Elaine and I) out for a drink (of coke). We had pretty much fun. He's a good dancer. But I bet you could "outshine" him any day. Laverne started out with us yesterday but met up with Sonny. He took her to El Chicos. Personally I don't care for him, maybe it was because I never really got to know him, but I'm sure I'm not missing anything. Laverne always does that. When we girls get together occasionally, we tell each other "No one is to leave the crowd." But leave it to her (Ain't I the catty one?) Even though we got along without her. Hinks left us after a while. Tillie came later on and gave us back our foursome. Hinks is working today. Poor boy.

Well today is Sunday and I just finished washing my hair. And then I start thinking about youse. So I says to myself, I think I'll write youse a letter to let youse know I'm thinking of you—you great big hunk of a man, you.

Excuse me, I'll be back in five minutes. I have to go and put my hair up in curlers. I got me a date for tonight. You'll be there in spirit, and when I kiss him goodnight, I'll be wishing it were you instead. Now just close your eyes and picture me with my hair in curlers and be glad you're not here.

Well, I'm back again. Dolores says hello! Sends her regards, too.

Oh yes, I found your pictures. I had it folded in with my shorthand certificate diploma from high school and such.

Just think, work tomorrow, and can you imagine, I worked all last week—I wasn't out one day—the floor lady came over and congratulated me.

Well, I think I'll do my aunt a favor and do the dishes. Ooops! Just a minute, my aunt just passed by. You know dishes are a little out of my lines, but I'm making an exception today on account of I feel so good.

Laverne and Elaine just dropped in so I'll have to be closing now so write more often. After all, I need a little inspiration. So until I hear from you I remain as ever, yours truly and sincerely,

Loretta

Yeah! I send my love, too.

October 26, 1944

The USS Signet arrives at Majuro and the crew is pleasantly surprised to find a group of islands with palm trees and beer. All go ashore for a beer party and a baseball game with the Marines, which they win.

October 28, 1944

The Signet and her crew set off for Pearl Harbor.

Chapter 10, November 1944

November 3, 1944

Dear Sal,

Well, I've finally got down to answering your second letter. Boy, have I been busy! For the past week, ever since Dolores' future came in and is stationed at as Hine's Hospital, I've been going with her and Laverne to the hospital every evening, leaving us forty-five minutes to wash, dress and eat after we get home from work. It seems I've found me some soldier to "kibitz" with while waiting for Dolores. He's really nice. He comes from a small town in Wisconsin (and he's not as bad as it sounds). The one Laverne talks with comes from Minnesota. We were playing cards with them last night and boy! Those fellows from Minnesota and Wisconsin don't know nothing. The Wisconsin boy was wounded in the South Pacific, he has a fractured leg which is much better now, meaning he can walk around with a limp and they think he's coming down with Malaria. He gets a fever of 104 every so often. Seeing as how his folks are way out in Wisconsin, I go visit with him, and besides he asks me to. Well, that's one guy I can trust, especially when he gets the fever (ain't I terrible?)

I see that you go swimming pretty often. I won't be able to go for about eight more months. Lucky you. I can hardly wait for you to take me to the quarry, but I hope it's not like Lemont's quarry. They've got those water snakes out there and man! I'd hate to have one use me for a daily meal.

These are a couple of new songs that are really "easy on the ears" such as "I Don't Wanna Love You" and do you remember the song "Have You Ever Been Lonely?"

Today is Friday, just after work and seeing as how it's Friday, the picture changes and when the picture changes, Loretta, Laverne, Elaine and Dolores go to the show. You oughta know. Today a cowboy picture is playing and something else, I can't quite remember. Boy, those good old cowboy pictures. Hop-along Cassidy is the name of the character that plays tonight.

Well, you still sound like the same, good, old Slabby, old pal, you remember how we used to wise crack each other? I don't know which one was worst. Slabby, you weren't trying to tell me that you had a little place in that big heart of yours for me were you? Well, I feel the same as you do. The way you talk about coming home sounds as if you didn't know what the word meant and it's not something you eat either.

Well, my aunt is hollering for me to sit down and eat and I'm wishing like "hell" to fill this page with my thoughts of you, but you'll have to be satisfied with my saying that I miss you and wish you were home now so that we could find out what's what, so I remain,

Thinking of you always, Loretta

November 4, 1944

The USS Signet arrives in Pearl Harbor. After loading provisions and stores, she shoves off with a small convoy for San Francisco.

Dearest Loretta:

It sure was great to hear from you again, sweets, but how come the old address? It wasn't delayed long 'cause I just got back into port. We just stay in a few days and then wham, I start accumulating more salt out on the seas. I'm sure going to tell you some whopper of a sea story when you're sea daddy gets back one of these days. But it'll have to be under a pretty moon or else, "I ain't talking I don't know." Savvy?

That sure was a whacky dream you had, what in the hell was I, best man? That sure hurts me way down deep and that's on the "legit." I bet you really looked pretty darn beautiful in satin and lace though, but if I'm not the guy with the ring I'm going to start "oiling my shooting irons." All kidding aside though, as far as me figuring out that one, you've got me stumped but and how. So in the meantime, don't go taking any drastic steps until I get back and that had better be a promise.

What have they got in full blast around the corner now, it seems that they have opened a Bunte candy factory around there the way you mention that all the babes are working there? Maybe it's a reasonable facsimile to Kelley's ice-cream parlor or am I just taking wild stabs at things?

You can bet your right arm that I would get a big kick out of helping you with those household duties. That's, of course, if I wouldn't be obliged to get up in the middle of the night and "walk" the cute little brats to sleep. That, sis, I can't see for love or money. Well, at least not money. But I still say it would be a lot of fun, no matter what the outcome may be. You can cook, can't you? Well, who in the heck would worry about something to eat in times like that, eh?

What's the matter with Laverne? Is she as whacky as a Jay bird in the springtime? I can see her point if "Monk" got a fractured toenail or some approximate injury, otherwise I can't see it "Scoot." As for myself, if I could have a split fingernail and get sent back, it would be a little bit of alreet, but under no other conditions. That is, of course, pertaining to injuries 'cause in case the papa gets a fit and makes with the shotgun, I want a pair of pins under me that can make it across the country in three seconds flat.

That's a hot one about me getting along with two infantry men, do you know any more jokes like that? Monk is a good kid and I never did have any trouble getting along with him, besides if I ever got back to Chicago I could get along with the snakes in Lincoln Park Zoo if I had to. (You didn't know I could type, did you, neither did I as a matter of fact, it just sort of snuck up on me.)

This sea duty isn't so bad though, the evenings are always so nice and usually with such a picturesque sunset that if your pretty little peepers ever started gaping at it, your blinkers would probably shoot out the back of your head so fast that they wouldn't have time to bring the eye-balls with them. On the other hand, though, the water situation is really horrible. I now have a faint idea what the Sahara desert feels like on a torrid day. There is one consolation, though, and that is whenever it rains I can always make a quick spring to the fantail and indulge in a little cold water shower (but why can't it rain hot water)? Yes-sir, the Navy sure changes your life around a bit in more ways than one.

When I get back in port though, don't you think that those nice warm showers aren't appreciated, yea man. Then again, I always get a letter or three from you and what could be any sweeter, I ask you. "Chosef" dropped me a line today and says what a sweet creature you're turning out to be. I knew that a couple of years ago and I'm still wondering, "Is you is or is you ain't my baby" (It's a cute number and I mean that both ways)? That had better be affirmative, eh, sweets?

A radioman's rate aboard ship is pretty good duty (by the way, I made second class this month), except when it comes to those rugged Midwatches (watches at Midway Island), and I mean rugged. Of course, when you're stranded on some island, then they are really horrible. An eight hour Midwatch with about twelve cups of coffee to keep any rigor mortis from setting in. But when you hear some of that sweet stateside music by Glenn or Benny (Goodman), then you come to a conclusion that all of your hardships aren't in vain. Now, if you could accidentally stow away, then I would know that heaven has dropped in on me for a little visit.

Say, what do you think of those two mellow numbers, "Milkman Keep Those Bottles Quiet" by Ella Mae Morse and Freddie Slack and that other catchy lulu, "Is You Is or Is You Ain't My Baby." I could cut a rug to those numbers until my "gunboats" gave away or else the deck, same difference no matter which way you look at it. Yes sir, sweets, we sure are going to have a good time when I get back, so please be a bit patient a little while longer.

How is your two beer diet coming along these days? Speaking of beer, I have had only indulged in that aromatic beverage once in the past month and that was out on some island in the Pacific. It sure was a beautiful island and then the beer to match, my, my, what could one ask for. (Am I kidding?)

61

Well, Lor, don't forget to keep on writing as often as you can and if not, then more so 'cause you know I'll be thinking and dreaming of you about twenty-four hours a day. *Adios* for now and *hasta la vista*. (You didn't know I took up Spanish in school, did you; that's of course besides space.)

Just loving you more and more each day, Sal

November 5, 1944

Good Morning, Honey,

And how are you on this bright sunny day. It is now about 8:45. I'll be going to church in two hours. Yes, I said church (one of my good habits, you know). I don't know, but for some reason I feel especially happy today, maybe it's because you're coming home soon. You see, I still haven't given up hope.

Boy, these Sunday mornings are what I wait for all week. Just think, no work today and I mean no work. I just lounge around the house and get fat. You should see how fat I've gotten. I weight about 155 lbs. now and there are still a lot more Sundays before you get to see me. Boy, you're gonna have some "armfull" when you get in (did I say arm? I meant arms.) But you'll still love me anyway, won't you, Honey????

Say did you ever hear that song "Together"? It's really "mellow" in fact it kinda gets me and that's pretty unusual.

My sister and Laverne went to Hines Hospital again today. I'm going to go during the week. I didn't want to go today, just in case some of his family decided to visit him. He's pretty sick now. Gets a fever quite regularly. He tells me all about this home town. It seems his girl married a Second Lieutenant while he was overseas. She sent him an invitation to the wedding anyway. He hasn't gotten over it. Not quite, anyway. But he will.

I was reading all your old letters the other day. I still have the ones from "way back when." There's quite a few of them, you know.

Do you think I'll ever get a picture of you? Meaning now, since you're on a ship. Why don't you borrow the Admiral's camera and something and take a few.

It's really getting cold out here lately. It seems funny to hear that you go swimming almost every day, while out here the chimneys are smoking, people wearing their winter clothes and you again swimming. I bet at night out here, it's daytime out there, or am I getting too smart for you?

My uncle is asking me for a game of checkers. Do you think I ought to? After all, at 39, I still think he is a little inferior for my mentality. With you, it would be different. I'd ask my three year old cousin to play with you. And don't go getting a "big head" either.

The radio is now playing the "Indian Love Call" swing version. Sounds pretty good, too. Especially when they beat the drums, then come in with the clarinet. It's Tommy Dorsey's orchestration. By the way, what is your favorite song? I haven't any special one yet. Do you like the way Sinatra handles his songs or are you a Crosby lover. Me, I'm for Sinatra. And I don't swoon either.

Well, as the paper is coming to an end, so must this letter, I remain,

Yours, Loretta

P.S.I really only weigh 123 lbs. but it doesn't make any difference does it?

November 10, 1944

Dear Sal,

Just received your letter, say, did I make a mistake in your address again? So now you're a real sailor. Meaning that you finally got yourself on a boat (or should I say "ship") and I can hardly wait to hear some of those sea stories as well as the ones while at port.

Say, you got that dream all wrong. I didn't say I liked that sailor that was my husband, in fact I didn't even know why I dreamt of him, I only met him but twice or thrice. What did you mean by "Don't go taking any drastic steps?" As if I knew what the word "drastic" meant.

The girls worked one night on that part-time job. I made a mistake on "around what corner it was," but anyway they were working on picture frames.

You asked me if I know how to cook??? Well, the answer is yes and no. Yes, I know how to make spaghetti, and nothing else. Of course if you'd be satisfied with eating spaghetti five nights a week (we could always visit my relatives the remaining two days, I have enough of them) I think we'd get along—but good.

Laverne is right across the table from me writing a few lines to George. My uncle is just giving her a "shot" with a beer for "wash." I'm next. Oh, boy! Well, Slabby, here's to you. "NaZdrowie." Guess what? I can now "safely" drink three beers. And who knows, by the time you get home, I'll probably drink you "under the table." Some fun, eh? Ah! Remember the "good old days." I was fifteen and you were nineteen. You were the wolf and I was Red Riding Hood. (My sister was Grandmother.)

Oh Boy! Slabby, "I Wish That I Could Hide Inside This Letter." Sure would make up for lost time. What am I telling you all this for, just goes to show you what liquor does. I hope you're not the drinking type. Boy! That "Italian red" you gave me really "hit the spot." That was the first time I ever indulged. It seems as if you started me off on everything. Meaning you were also the first fellow I kissed. Some kiss it was, eh?

Laverne and I are going to confession in a little while. Today is Saturday, you know. At least we make a "clean" start. We want to go to the three o'clock Mass. Do you think we'll make it?

Well, I see you're finally getting up in this man's Navy. Yep. That Admiral better watch out.

Say, when you're on ship, can you just dive off the deck and swim in the ocean? Some swimming "hole" that would make. The fellows from work asked me to swim with them at some indoor pool, but I don't know, I don't want to be the only girl going. After all.

Quote "Well, Sal, don't forget to keep on writing as often as you can and if not, then more so 'cause you know I'll be thinking and dreaming of you about twenty-four hours a day. *Adios* for now and *Hasta La Vista.*" (But I didn't take up Spanish in school. Just space."

Well closing for now and,

"Just loving you more and more each day," Loretta

November 17, 1944

The USS Signet arrives in San Francisco and stays for five days.

November 18, 1944

Saturday Nightclubs

Hiya, Sweets,

Well, Lor, how are things treating you nowadays? It had better be on the cozy side or yours truly will be having three or four nightmares tonight and boy can I kick in my sleep.

Guess what, Honey, take a deep breath and hold it. I've finally hit the "Promise Land" and is it nice to be back in these good old dear sweet States once again. You realize, it's the first time I've been back here in eighteen months and when I saw that gorgeous Golden Gate smiling at me so sweetly I just couldn't help but return the compliment. I was so damn excited that my toes started curling and goose pimples started racing over me like a forest fire on a rampage. But I ran into a little depression when I asked for a thirty day leave, which I think I deserve, and was flatly refused. Boy, was I a desolate character when the skipper disapproved of it. Well, "you can't have your cake and eat it too" is an old saying but I never thought it would apply to me in that manner. I guess the main reason is that we'll be leaving "Frisco" tomorrow, but you can bet your last pair of silk panties, oops I mean stockings, that I'm going to try again to get home for Christmas and New Year's, by hook or crook. Well, we'll have a time or will have a time of our lives, yea man. You're following me of course, I hope, or else I'll be throwing snowballs at you. Boy, is that word "snow" strange to my ears. I'll gladly leave you wash my face in it as many times as your sweet little heart desires and there will be nothing but smiles coming from me. Say, there is snow back in good old "Chi" this time of the year or have I been away too long that I don't know Eve from Adam?

You know the last time I was in Frisco (I think it was about the time Lincoln was running for President.) I didn't give a hoot for it, but now with all of its pretty lights aglow it really looks "purty." It has Oakland, Richmond, and a lot of other towns, all on a hillside to pretty it up.

I had overnight liberty last night and I bet you can't think of the first thing I headed for (that question was too damn easy)? Yes sir, I went to a sweet bar with another "sparky" aboard ship and had a double shot. It just about killed me, but oh it was good. Well anyhow, one drink ran into another and about two o'clock in the morning I was blinder than a bat in rabbit season and before I knew it I was all by my lonely on a highway in Vallejo. It was colder than a penguin's nose in January, and boy do I wish I was by your side to keep warm, ugh, ugh. I don't think I would be tight if you were with me. I might be a little "happy" but not like that last July. Well anyhow, there I was in Vallejo about twenty miles from Frisco trying to catch a ride when a bus finally came along and I got on that. I must have been sleeping for about five minutes and then all of a sudden the bus comes to a sudden stop and woke me up (anyhow it opened up one "blinker") and me like the nitwit that I am just walked up to the door and got off. When the bus left I decided to open up both eyes and that's when I really felt like passing out 'cause there I was stranded out on the highway still fifteen miles from "Frisco." How in the hell I ever got back to the ship I still don't know, but I guess someone had a prayer for me that night. I got back about five in the morning and after a few hours of sleep, reveille blew and there I layed (laid) in my "sack" just listening to the pounding and rushing of trains going through my noggin'. No kidding, it felt like some "jaybird" was making little rocks out of big ones and was using my head for a sledge hammer.

Time out, there is a mail call, so I had better rush down below to the galley and see what the "scoop" is. Three minutes and ten and three tenths seconds have elapsed (that's what you call precision time.) I'm back in a flash with the "Gash." Why you sweet little chick, I could kiss you about a hundred and fifty times, 'cause I just received three letters and that luscious box of candy. It was really nice of you, Honey, in fact I could shed a few tears without much strain I'm so happy, but I'll save that until I meet you again. That bow is really cute, in fact I'm going to keep it as a souvenir, so help me. That candy is really delicious, how about nibbling on a few pieces with me before the rest of the crew dives into it, huh? I sure wish I can get to see you (I'm so excited that I can't seem to remember to space the words anymore) over the Christmas holidays and then you can say that heaven has decided to pause on Talman Terrace for a while.

I've been listening to the "Radjio" all night in the radio shack (including the Hit Parade) and how I wish you were with me so we could dance until the roosters started crowing. T.D.'s (Tommy Dorsey) "Boogie-Woogie" and "We'll Get It" and a lot of nice sweet ones like "Stardust" by the same maestro; "I'll Walk Alone," G.M.'s "I'll Never Smile Again," and last but not least, "Together." Well, Honey, I've still got a lot to tell you, but my "blinkers" say no and I can't argue with them so I'll write you again just as soon as I can possibly can.

Here's hoping I dream of you tonight and you do likewise.

Oceans of Love, Sal

P.S. How in the Hell did that airplane get aboard? (Referring to the airplane stationery artwork on the last page of his letter)

November 19, 1944

Dearest Sal,

Am writing to you again after a week absence. Although I haven't heard from you for two weeks. I know, I know, "just be patient Loretta, I'll write to you every time I reach port, after all, don't you know I'm fighting a war." So what's the use of telling you to write more often? You know it's hard for me to write a letter without something to go back on. So I'll just have to tell you what I do. Here goes ... Tuesday, 11/13, went to work, got home from work, had to rush and get dressed to go dancing at good old Pilsen Park. Had a pretty hilarious time. You should've seen the boy I was dancing with. Boy! I'm telling you. Here, I'm getting along fine with him, he turns me around and throws me out to "jive" and when I turn around again I didn't see him. I didn't know what to do at that split second, hey, he's on the floor doing the split. Boy, I just stood there laughing. Laverne was standing along the side, she was watching us and when she starts to giggle, I joined in. That's all, brother, that's all. I finished the dance with him though.

Wednesday, 11/15, went out with the soldier I met the night before. Had a pretty fair time. He's not my type, though. Meaning, he's the serious kind. And that's not for me. Kissed him goodnight. Can you imagine? I don't think I'll go out with him again, though. He's going back Friday. He wants me to write. No can do.

Thursday, 11/16, this was my visiting day at the hospital. Do you remember when I told you about that Wisconsin boy that had a touch of Malaria? Well it seems he went out on a pass, comes back and then starts accusing everyone of being spies and that he's going to kill 'em all. Now he's in a room all by himself. Door's locked. No visitors. We're going to the hospital on Thanksgiving. Bob Hope & Company and Kay Kyser are giving a show up there. Lucky we.

Friday, 11/17, today the picture changes at the Ogden. Was there sharply at 6:15 p.m. Remember when it was 11 cents all night on Friday. Now it's 25 cents before 6:30 and 35 cents after. But they still have those good old cowboy pictures, oh yes, we can't forget the chapter. It's a new one. *The Black Arrow.* Oh boy!

Saturday, 11/18, am going out with my ex German boyfriend. Had something to tell me. Won't repeat. I came home early at 1:00 a.m. Told him I had to get up early and go mushroom hunting with my uncle. Met the girls at 2:00 a.m. at Lea's tavern (our hangout). They waited for me. Boy, we had one swell time. Guess what? I smoked my first cigarette. Never again, though. The girls are still laughing at me. Did I say "smoked?" I meant swallowed. Met the milkman on our way home. Ain't I getting terrible? I have more fun with the girls anyway. Fellows get too serious. I'm too young for that. Until you come home anyway.

Sunday, 11/19, day of recuperation.

Thanksgiving starts the holidays and no Slabby.

And so Dear Diary, I close for now.

Loving and still waiting, Loretta

November 20, 1944

Monday Night $

Well, Sweets, how are you:

Didn't I tell you that I would write you as soon as I had another chance and that was less than two days ago, so I guess you can start calling me "honest Abe" from now on, or some other reasonable facsimile? I must have read your three letters about three hundred times. That just goes to show you how much I really am in love with you. That feeling had better be mutual or else I'm going to change that name of the song you were listening to the other day ("Licorice Stick," Shaw's "Indian Love Call," to "Indian War Call").

Speaking of Maestro Shaw, guess what? That wasn't quick enough. I'm afraid I'm going to tell you we're going to stay in Frisco two more days, and tomorrow night when your one and only has liberty, Artie (Shaw) will be tooting his stick in Oakland and how I wish you were with me to enjoy ourselves to the fullest extent. I hope you don't get burnt up 'cause Sunday night and tomorrow night are the first dances I have attended in eighteen months and I want to get some of the "Savage" out of me before I see a nice sweet kid like you again.

Sticking to the Shaw subject for the moment, do you notice that quite a few of his old recordings are beginning to become very popular like "It Had To Be You" and "Don't Take Your Love Away From Me." The latter one is really sweet and that's exactly the way I feel about you. So if you hadn't ever heard the recording (It has to be Shaw or you won't get the real affect of how I feel for you, so don't forget) do so before another minute elapses and just make believe that I'm holding you in my arms, "Chubby."

Sticking to favorite melodies for the moment, no doubt you have heard of "I Dream of You" and how I go for that number. Every time I hear it, I can feel my lips pressed against yours in a long but sweet embrace. I'm telling you, Honey, I'm so anxious to see you again that I'm afraid I'll have gray hairs if that lucky moment doesn't happen quicker, in fact it had better be faster than that.

I'll try and send you some pictures as soon as I get the chance, but it's a little tough right now 'cause I only have liberty at nights and most of the photographers are closed by that time. We don't get liberty until four o'clock, seeing that we have to work all day like true "Swab Jockies" just shining the ship until it looks something like a mirror. So some day when we manage to get that little bungalow, don't go holding it against me just because I spent some time in the "Navy" and make me hold "Field Day" every day. If you do, I might get a bit angry and join the Foreign Legion. Who in the hell do I think I'm kidding now, I've spent two years in this outfit and it only seems a little bit less than twenty so don't go taking advantage of me and work me to my skin and bones.

I've just listened to Horace Heidt and his musical bums playing "Together," but they burned me up. They didn't sing the lyrics. Consequently, I could only visualize kissing you about fifteen times. Guys like him should be shot for doing these things to us, but wait a minute, he just excused himself by singing the words to "I'll Be Loving You Always," so we'll leave him go at that, that's if you haven't any complaints coming. I'll be by your side if things don't agree with you, so don't be afraid to "harp" a little.

You know what, Honey, the last time I was out to sea, which was only four days ago some dirty bitch "heisted" my wallet and it had all those nice pictures of you, so pardon me if I used the wrong language, but I was really burnt up. It also had in it at the time, pictures of all my buddies from the corner including the baseball team (The Flying Victims) with good old Hoban and Monk in it and last, but not least, pictures of my bro and the rest of the family. If I ever catch the guy I'm afraid that yours truly is going to be held for murder and then all of our sweet plans will be all in vain.

I didn't mind the God-damn jerk taking the forty bucks that were in it, but he didn't have to throw the wallet overboard with all of those invaluable pictures in it. Well, I had better get off of this subject in a hurry or else I'll rattle like this throughout the whole letter and there's not much use in crying over spilt milk.

My bro almost got a leave, but he seemed to get into a little trouble and got shipped to the Philippines instead. I wish the hell, we could both get a leave together because if I deserve a leave, he "rates" three of them seeing that he's been in New Guinea for about two and a half years now and hasn't even seen the States in that time. I suppose you've heard that my sister has joined the Waves. I wish I was home at the time and she would have went to "Boot Camp" with a broken neck. I hope you don't ever get any of those silly ideas. By the way, how much chubbier is my sis Marie getting. You see her once in a while, don't you? How is Stella's bro? I seem sort of nosey but I don't think it's out of place in asking you or am I wrong?

Well, Honey, make the sauce just right and I'll take you up on a couple of spaghetti dinners when I get home. I'll close for now, so keep going to church, you cute rascal, and send a few more photos if you have any.

Love and then some, Sal

P.S.

I didn't put my address on but keep writing to the same ship

November 23, 1944

The USS Signet heads to the Hawaiian Islands with a small convoy.

November 25, 1944

The USS Signet, a few hundred miles out of San Francisco, drops depth charges on what may be a submarine.

November 26, 1944

Dearest Sal,

Just received your letter and you're back in the States. Boy! Was I happily surprised. How'd you do it?

Here, I first write you a letter saying that you weren't home yet at the beginning of the holidays, and the day after I get this happy message. I'm sorry that you didn't get that long-earned leave, but then it's probably best 'cause your thirty days would have been up before Xmas and New Year's, and I wouldn't want the New Year to start not knowing where and with whom you are with. Or out on the sea thinking over the time you could have had.

See it's all for the best. But make sure you get home soon before the New Year is up!

Say, didn't you let the family or anyone else know you had arrived in the States? I told Carmine you were back and he was surprised. I also saw Lorraine (She's a blond now, you know) and gave her the glad tidings. She says she's going to start preparing for your home-coming. You and her used to be pretty good pals, huh? By the way, do you ever hear from Laverne? You also used to "hit it off" pretty good with her too. Remember? The strolls through the park and such.

You mentioned that if we had any snow as yet, but funny as it is, Thanksgiving eve, it started to snow big, white, beautiful flakes. It was really pretty. The girls and I celebrated that evening. You know, Thanksgiving, your letter, the first snowfall and such. If your ears were ringing then, you'll know the reason why. Between "Dolores and her Eddie," "Me and my Slabby," "Laverne and her Donald (crossed out Donald and inserted Monk)," and "Tillie and her Donald," boy, we had one swell time. (Always do, the girls are finally getting smart, now when we go out together we all come home together. Before, they used etc. (Too much explaining.) You should hear the conversation, my goodness, especially when we're about to drink our "coke," it goes like this, "To Eddie, To George, to Don" and last but not least, to Slabby. Crazy, eh! Say, you better watch out, take it easy with that fire water. After all, one of us has to be sensible. And me, I'm tired of being sensible.

So you finally got the candy. I didn't know if I should've sent a spoon or what.

Say, where do you hear all those sweet songs? Once in a great while I'll hear a "ditty" that'll set me to thinking. But you know the old saying, "Anything for the service men." Well, almost anything. Well _____ anything. (Ahem!)

You didn't put your address on the envelope, and if that's because you were going to be changed again, I didn't write, but I'm writing twice today.

That's classy stationery you got there, fella.

My sister's boyfriend proposed to her. They're getting married as soon as he leaves the Army. I think he's getting a M.D. (medical discharge).

I saw Kay Kyser in person at the hospital. Soldier took me. Crutches and all!

Well, Honey, I'll be closing for now, have to write you the other letter.

Love xxxx, Loretta

November 27, 1944

The USS Signet meets the other half of its convoy, which comes out of San Diego. All continue to Pearl Harbor.

Dear Sal,

Am writing to you from 1323 So. <u>Fairfield</u> Ave. —not Washtenaw, Dopey!

I was really surprised to hear from you so quickly, "Abe"!

Say, the way you talked about those songs and the notions you get make me wonder if I haven't missed something while you were still available. Huh!

Hope you had a nice time while A.(Artie) Shaw was entertaining you. How are the jitterbugs out there? Slick?

In talking about the future in your former letter, you mentioned "a little bungalow," well I just wanted to know if you've decided how many windows it has. That's very important. (For the window washer, of course, Slabby.)

I'm sorry to hear about your wallet, but please, and don't think I'm sprouting wings either, don't ever use such "cussin" in my letters again. Understood? (Guess, that's telling you a thing or two, eh?)

By the way, if you want a picture of Scully, Sonny or Roy, I'll send them to you. Just write into Miss Loretta in care of station I.O.U.? Also enclose 50 cents for mailing charges. That is all. Thank you.

I imagine your brother should have gotten his leave long ago. Say, what's the matter with you boys? Why don't you write in to your Commander In Chief and pour out your little tale. I'm sure he'd help you. But first tell him you know me.

I was a little startled when I heard the news about your sister. Won't she be in a higher rank than you when she finishes "boot?" Don't worry about me joining the Navy. Not unless they have girl sea scouts.

Your sister Marie is turning out to be "quite" a young lady. (Look what's talking.) Although she has a few unnecessary pounds., but she's still growing yet.

Stella's brother is still living. I haven't heard much about it, but don't you know you can't kill a Pole? Especially a "drunken one?"

My sister's boyfriend "popped the question" to her last Saturday. So it's wedding bells for her as soon as he's discharged. If I'm not mistaken, did I tell you about this in my last letter? Sure I did. See, what you do to me.

I got paid today. $10.50. That's good compared to Dolores. She got $4.80. Hard workers.

Well, Honey, don't forget about the pictures. Are you still working on that long-waited leave?

The girls and I went to Leo's, Saturday. (When I got home I found your letter waiting for me in the drawer. A mistake in the address made it travel throughout the neighborhood, I guess.) We met the milkman. We know him good now. I'll have to take you to Leo's when you get home.

Henly was there all ready. It really is a nice place. Right in the midst of Polish town.

He also took my brother there on his last furlough. He O.K.d it.

Well sugar, it's time for me to be signing off for now. So be a good little boy. Brush your teeth in the morning. Take a little exercise in the afternoon and be in bed at 9:00 (alone) at night.

Okay Honey, Goodnight. X

Sleep tight and such.

Will write soon.

Your one & only (I hope), Loretta

Chapter 11, December 1944

December 2, 1944

My Dearest Slabby,

As I sit here, with your picture in front of me, at 10 o'clock in the morning, I'm thinking of you and missing you terribly. I know it might sound a little "corny" coming from me, but that's the way I feel. I'm telling you, I don't know what's come over me, but lately all I've been thinking of is you and you and you.

Maybe it's the couple of drinks I had at Rita's house. But to tell you the truth, here's the way it goes. My sister, Tillie, Laverne, her sister Elaine (that's the whole mob) and I have all someone that we have a special place in our heart for, in the service. We can't get to them, sooo we go by Rita's house, either she has some wine (terrible stuff) or we bring "something" over and we have one swell time. And I mean one swell time.

Did you ever see a girl cry for someone she liked, or shall I get bold and say loved. It's not a sad sight. But there she is shedding a few tears, knowing that it's not going to bring him home any sooner, but she feels good after. The way some fellows talk about a letter meaning so much to them, well it means just as much to the girls back home. Say! Am I getting dramatic on you? Well this happens only once in a lifetime. Once. But to let me finish, I rushed the girls home from Rita's to write you this letter. We all had a drink on you. Don't mind how this letter sounds, but I'm writing just what comes into my head. And right now I'm thinking how come after all these years; I'm beginning to think of you. We really never had any special time together. You never told me that you liked me, and yet I miss you. (I think maybe it's your letters.) But anyway, I always did have a soft spot for you in my heart and that comes straight from the heart.

Boy! I can hardly wait for you to come home. And our first kiss. I hope it will be something special to you for I know it will be to me. And this goes double for me. Quote "you have heard of the song 'I dream of you,' and how I go for that, number." Every time I hear it I can feel your lips pressed against mine in a long, sweet embrace. I hear that song every day at work and how I think of you.

There, I just kissed your picture.

It seems that anybody I meet doesn't interest me. I always find fault with them. You know something, I'm afraid to close my eyes (I had four wines, by Rita's house), but that wasn't enough, no, not for Loretta, I had to go upstairs by my uncle and have two "shots" before I wrote the letter. Tomorrow, well, that's today, I think I'll stay home with the rest of the girls and throughout the whole evening, I'll think and reminisce only of you.

Here is a poem I thought would express more clearly my feelings towards you:

All the love in Chicago, Loretta

I'm gonna seal this letter now, 'cause I know I'll destroy it, tomorrow if I read it over again.

December 3, 1944

The USS Signet arrives at Pearl Harbor and spends the rest of the month in the Navy Yard.

December 5, 1944

Dear Sal,

Well, I'm playing nursemaid again to the five little angels, and I'm telling you it's getting me down. (I thought I'd have a nice quiet evening at home and write you this letter.) So here I sit, right next to the radio, The Ink Spots are now singing "Somebody's Rocking My Dreamboat" —mellow. But that song doesn't apply to us, does it? Noooooo!!!

Before I forget, how'd you like that snazzy little letter I wrote? The latest one. Bet you didn't think I had it in me. Neither did I.

The four "Snowballs" are now giving out with "I'm Still without a Sweetheart Because I'm Still in Love with You." (The title makes up practically the whole song.)

Artie Shaw is playing at the "Chicago" (Theatre). Say, is he your favorite band? By the way, what's your favorite song?

I think I told you that we have music where we work. Well, we finally get popular music. Did you ever hear the song, "There Goes That Song Again." That's pretty "cute" but I heard it eight times in a row (someone forgot to change the record) and I'm tired of it already.

Hildegarde is now singing "Always." She's got a different style. Sings with a slight accent, huh?

I finally got my graduation pictures out of the studio after a year and a half. The ones with my cap and gown. I was sweet sixteen on those pictures; in fact I was almost sweet seventeen. My, isn't that wonderful?

I was talking to Scully on the telephone. He was surprised to hear that you came back into the States. He also is planning on your homecoming. So you'd better not disappoint us! He told me he has a steady girl. That I want to see for myself.

You know it took me almost one and a half hours to write this letter. Started out with the Ink Spots, went on with the Pepsodent Show, listened through Hildegard and am finishing off with Johnny Mercer's, "If I Knew Then." Of course, I had about umpteen interruptions.

It's snowing again.

Say, what about that picture of you? I haven't any as yet. But give me time.

Well, I'll be chasing this "mushy" "love" letter until next time.

So hurry home, Loretta

December 6, 1944

Dearest Loretta:

Well, Honey, I was sure glad to receive your letter but and how. You know I can't see how you and I can go wrong after this "mess" is over, so don't forget to be good.

Do you realize that I got one letter from you today that went to so many different places in the Pacific that it come to me with three ribbons and four stars on it? Sooooo, next time don't go putting on my old address or else I'll be receiving letters from you three years after the war is over.

I wish I could be home for the Christmas Holidays, in fact sometimes I think I'd be willing to depart with my respect. One never knows where he will be a week ahead of time in the Navy, so I'll just have to pray for the best. You and I would sure have a sweet time together and I'll bet both legs on that, whether it's New Year's Eve or July 18th. So, Honey, have a little patience, there's a time limit to everything.

Say, what are they calling you back around the neighborhood now, "Miss Fearless Fosdick?" You are getting brave you know, if I may quote you're latest letter, "Well almost anything, Well — anything (Ahem!)." If I'm around New Year's Eve, I'm going to hold you to that promise. Ugh. Now I'm getting bold—well, damn it, I can't be reluctant.

I just received a letter from Monk the other day and the old Irishman is doing alright for himself. He's seeing quite a bit of Europe and how I wish I was in his shoes. The people over there got a little book learning but over there they "just ain't no gottum."

By the way "Cokes," how many times have the other girls carried you home in a wheelbarrow? You can tell me. I'll forgive you. Be sure you always come home with your girlfriends or else you'll be calling the guy on this end of the letter, "The bald-headed man with shoes on."

I haven't been to a show in a month and a half now, but I don't miss them much. Of course, if I had a sweet chick like you to take with me, it'd be like pulling teeth to keep me away from one, but there's no such soap in these islands.

Been rather busy all day cleaning the "shack" and painting the deck. But a nice shower (fresh water) makes a new man out of you (at least for a few hours anyhow).

Well, Sweets, I have to write my bosom buddy Cowboy a letter, so I'll close for now.

Love and Everything, Sal

P.S.

The only chick I write to around the corner is you and that's all I care to 'cause you're plenty good enough for me.

P.P.S.

How about a studio photograph when you get the chance 'cause I haven't a single picture of you now.

December 8, 1944

Hello, Sweets:

Say, you can really get hot under the collar when you set your mind (Notice I didn't say what mind) on doing so, but I love you just that much more when I see a little fight in you. But the way, you hopped on me in your last letter reminded me of the good old days—I thought I was in front of juvenile court.

Oh hum. Say, that Leo's Place—that isn't on 21st Place and Cermak or is it around 21st and 25th ? I used to visit a couple of nice places right around there but I suppose that isn't it. Anyhow, if your Bro okayed it, it must be alreet for an angel like you to attend it.

By the way, how is your Bro making out? I never really got a chance to buddy around with him, but I still remember what he looks like. (I had better put the stop margin up on this "mill" or else I'll be finishing this letter on the next mill.) He used to play quite a bit of basket ball at St. Agatha or have you got me all twisted up? It's probably the latter, 'cause you're always on my brain. It's a good thing I just made "brain" singular or else I'd probably have a book from you on arguments about that point, and don't go coming back with "if you had another brain in your head it would be lonesome," or I'll bash a rollin'-pin over your head, you sweet thing.

Say, those pictures were really welcomed like a blast furnace up in Eskimo-land, so help me. You know you really are getting pretty handy with "wallets." I still remember that picture of my bro, although I can't remember exactly where it was taken, either in our mansion or McQuillan's bungalow. I believe that arm belongs to either Mrs. McQuillan or my sis, El. Now you can set your weary brain to rest for another decade. Don't aim that thing at me, it might go off.

Haven't been swimming in at least two months now, can you imagine that? It seems funny that I haven't mentioned that word after using it in my letters for the past year. I had to get it in somehow seeing that it's such a clean word (Nix on the "it just depends where you are swimming at.")

The "Radio" is now giving out with "What Are You Doing the Rest of Your Life," but if I went and asked you something like that you would probably start making with some smart crack so I guess I'll fool you—I just won't ask you—not now anyhow.

In your future letters, don't forget to knock out the "I hope" whenever you put "your one and only" or I'll have to drop a ten-ton boulder on that fragile "noggin" of yours. Am listening to a program direct from Chi and is I or am I in my glory—yea man.

Seeing that you're meeting the milkman so many damn times, I'm beginning to wonder if your theme song is, "Milkman Keep Those Bottles Quiet." I wouldn't put it past you.

I've been running ragged all day today doing this and that and that and this then what happens—bang—they slap a mid (midnight) to four in the morning watch on me and that I think is pretty "chintzi." Oh well, I can take it 'cause I'm rugged—I mean rugged.

Thanks for those three "resolutions" on how to be a healthy and successful lad. I sure got a kick on that last one. You know, you're sure getting to be a witty girl but I hope you follow suit, especially on that last one. And if you don't, they'll be calling me just like the "Jack" mentioned on the program not more than an hour ago, "Droop of the Loop." You don't want that to happen do you—what you do?— $@*'*?/** yeah here comes the period.

One of my buddies from Chi is still out here. Met him the other day and he's expecting a leave as soon as the next war starts. Sort of a pessimist, but really a nice looking lad. He hails from Maywood and once we get back, he's going to take his chick out and I'm going to grab your hand and off to the races we'll be. You had better start saving your energy now, I'm warning you.

Well, Honey, my "peepers" stopped peeping and my "blinkers" ceased blinking, so that leaves me only one alternative and that is obtaining a bit of shut-eye. In the meantime, don't forget to wait, sweets. I'll be back before 1950 or else I'm handing in my resignation.

Loving you always, Sal

P.S. Send all the pictures you can of the boys and, last but not least, of yourself—just mark it on the budget. I'll square it away later.

December 10, 1944

Dearest Sal,

Well, two weeks have passed and no letter. You know, I have to keep reading your last two letters, over and over again for inspiration. (Besides look at your picture, too.) So don't mind if this is short.

Yesterday was Saturday and today is Sunday (ain't I brilliant?) Seeing as how yesterday was Saturday, the mob gave their business to Leo's. Yep, we had some time. I don't know, but do I look like an understanding person or something, but anyway Tillie and I were sitting at our table when this matured jitterbug comes up and asks me to dance, but you know me, look before try, (that's all I needed was one look.) I said no. So what does the hep-cat do, but does us the honor and sits down at our table. Of course, we didn't want to say anything as yet (after all he looked like he needed a rest) he offered to buy a drink, well you know how it is—we're from Chicago—so we took it. And that's when he starts pouring out his sob story to me, mind you, to me—not Tillie. He started by telling me I remind him of his beautiful daughter (I thought he was throwing me a compliment until I saw her pictures.) Well, anyway, he finished relating his story to me by telling me his wife didn't love him anymore. And before, when I mentioned it was a sob-story, I meant it, for then and there he made with the tears. Can you imagine? And when I glanced over at Tillie, she was laughing. I looked at him and he was crying. Boy! Was that a turmoil. What was I to do but to kick Tillie to stop giggling and tell this character how sorry I was, that he should take his wife "out" more, what a nice looking daughter he had, don't worry, etc. By that time, Dolores came "down" from her boyfriend's house. He lives right on top of Leo's, and after she visits with him she comes down and goes home with us. Not right away, though. So when Dolores came and Laverne and Elaine, I guess that was too much for the "I feel so sorry for myself" person and he parted our company (whew!). After that, when we were all gathered together, we start having our fun. That's why I like to go out with them. No one cares about anyone, just be friendly to everyone. Almost everyone. Say, let's drop this boring subject and let's talk about something more exciting.

Well, we had our first blizzard of the year. I got up this morning (don't tell anyone, but I missed Mass this morning) at 12:30, got dressed, went out and pulled my little cousin on the sled, had a good old-fashioned snowball fight with a couple of girls, went to Kelly's for a Sundae, came home, undressed and I went to sleep, woke up a little while ago, ate, and decided to write you this letter. I thought I wouldn't have anything to tell you about, but here I am still scribbling away.

Yesterday, they played the song, "I Dream of You," and I just closed my eyes and there you were, dancing with me, (I don't think the other fellow minded playing second fiddle to a memory.) He was an old friend anyway. And you better do likewise... that's an order. I heard that song, "Don't Take Your Love From Me," it was really mellow. Say, Slabby, are you really serious when you ask me (in your round-about way) to wait for you? Or are you making conversation?

Well, it's closing time for this letter and for my eyes too. I guess going out and getting a "bit of fresh air" was a little too much for an old fogy like me.

So goodnight for now, sweets, and "I'll Be Seeing You,"
Loretta

P.S.

How'd you like the classy stationery?

December 11, 1944

Hello, Honey:

Well, angel, I guess you know that I just received that luscious letter dated the 2nd (yeah, it's December) and I must have read it fifteen times in the first hour. It sure was a nice sweet one and I hope it's at least as half as serious as I am and I'll be plenty satisfied.

I hope you don't mind too much that I'm knocking out this letter on a "mill," but I've a handwriting that probably takes about six men from the intelligence office to decode, so I figure it's much more readable with this mechanical instrument I'm using. Besides, I've only made one mistake so far so don't squawk.

I've been laying around port for the last few days and have really been busy. Whether you're out at sea or in port, they always seem to keep you busy, pretty disgustful, isn't it? I've got the twelve to four in the morning tonight (yes, again) so I'll be thinking of you while I'm not busy copying code.

Time sure has been flying since I've got aboard this ship. I hardly realized that it's December of '44 already until I accidentally took a gander at the calendar. I've been in this

"Navy" over two years now and I sure hope I don't see five—Ugh.

Went to town the other day, but there isn't much to do in this part of the Pacific or in any other part of this ocean. I'd rather be out at sea myself, except for the conveniences of showers, movies and other smaller items in the same category. Well, getting back to the "beach," all there was to do was to drink beer with a couple of other "swabbies" and think of you. We only get liberty to 1830 in the evening so you can see that I sure make a bold try of it.

I haven't seen my buddy from Chicago in four or five days now so I'll have to see what I can do about it in the very near future. That'll give you a slight idea of just how busy I am—when a guy can't get off his ship to see a bosom buddy of his, well then—just period.

That sure was a nice poem your sweet little self sent me and now I can say "At Last" by "G.M.," in person. I'd gladly bet you a quarter that I could memorize it by heart before I see you again. What, you mean to tell me you're afraid to lose a dollar—tut-tut.

I probably won't be writing for awhile once we pull out but that can't be helped 'cause after all we don't carry a mail plane with us just for that occasion.

Sometimes I wish we did 'cause I think I could very easily talk the pilot in accidentally giving me a ride to Chicago or pretty close to it—strictly pipe dreams, well I can dream can't I? Anyhow, don't forget to keep writing four or umpteen letters a week and I'll make up for it somehow, sweets, I guarantee that.

You girls sure have one swell time together shooting the breeze, drinking "champagne" (I'm not French so don't look at me that way if that beverage is spelled wrong) and playing pinochle. I hope it goes like that 'cause I don't see nothing wrong in it. What ever happened to that Dutchman that use to go with your sister—you know the guy that said he might join the Coast Guard? He sure was a funny character to figure out.

Say, when am I going to get a few more pictures of yourself and don't be afraid to put a little snow in it? I'd sure like to see you with a background of heaps of snow and trees— what, it don't snow in Chicago?—I haven't been away that long. Do you realize that I haven't one single picture of you now and that is getting awful drastic or don't you think so?

Thanks again for that awful nice letter and in the meantime take care of yourself and I'll do likewise.

Well good night for now and sweet dreams.

Loving you always, Slabby

P.S. You weren't really going to tear that letter up were you? I'm awful glad you didn't.

December 13, 1944

The USS Signet is dry-docked and given a new paint job, which starts a rumor about big operations coming up because the new paint is a different color than the current one.

December 15, 1944

Hello, Honey:

That's the way I like to see things ride, getting a letter from you every other day. Just like eating Swiss steak and that can't be beat.

Getting back to your previous letter for but a moment, I'll have to say you sort of somewhat startled me. I hope you never regret the part about not tearing it up 'cause I know I would of if you had. I was always waiting for a letter like that 'cause I knew it would bring us closer to another and that it did, yes-sir, that it did.

I read in the paper the other day that quite a blizzard hit Chicago and other surrounding parts. I bet you went right out in it and didn't come back in until you caught pneumonia. What, you did? Remind me when I see you again to take you over my knee and spank the blazing daylights out of you. I think I could handle you unless you have taken some Jiu Jitsu practice lately. We use to have some good times in old Douglas Park together, remember? I'd sure like to be back there with you again, but this time it would be ten times as much fun or do you disagree with me? What—starting an argument already? Wait a minute and I'll run down the ladder and get my dictionary and then watch me "slay" you. Aw, the Hell with it, I don't feel like arguing, not with you at least, maybe some other time. Hey—what am I saying?

The crew went down to the baseball field the other day and we had a nice game. The first time I've played in about three years. There is only one setback and that is as follows: There's a kid from Tennessee aboard, you know where that is don't you—where the "revenuers" are treated like dogs, and he decides to take off his shoes and play. Seeing that my "Civil War Gunboats" are a bit troublesome too, I decided to follow suit. Well, after seven innings of fun (I really mean torture) my feet had more holes in them than my head ever had or will ever think of having—it might be going to extremes, but that's the truth. Those "boulders" sure made a mess out of my paws. I should have known better than to try to compete with a mountain boy, but you learn something every day so why "beef?"

I sure saw a good show the other day, *Sweet and Lowdown* with B.G. (Benny Goodman). First one in a couple of months and it was really mellow. When I heard that "Jersey-Bounce," it was just like old times—but definitely mellow. That "Making Believe" is also very nice.

Well, Sweets, be good and save all those kisses for me 'cause I certainly could use them.

All my love, Sal

P.S.

How about that photo?

December 17, 1944

My dearest Sal,

Just received two letters from you today, you sweet boy, you. But, you know, Honey, there was something in those letters that didn't set me up in the usual high spirits. Maybe it was the fact that in the first letter you told me about three times "to be good," and in the second one about fourteen times. And that hurt—'way down deep.' Say, you don't think that I have "holes in my head" do you, or do you???

You know, if you're taking the wrong impression, when I tell you I go out, I won't tell you anymore. And another thing, you can now go and stand in the corner for two hours and think what a lazy boy you were for writing only three pages.

Boy! Was I disappointed to hear that you won't be home for Xmas and possibly New Years. Just when Willie is on leave and Tommy is coming home in five more days. Yep, you three Navy men sure would have had some time. Me, too. Rooski from Washtenaw is in on furlough. He was in the M.R. but was transferred to Infantry. Dolores' boyfriend is pretty sick now. They think he has an infection. She doesn't know if he'll be home for Christmas or not. If not, all the girls are going to the hospital with the good old mistletoe. But not me, no. I'm gonna sit home and read my comic books 'til they come back, and then I'll go out with them and drink "cokes," and if someone asks me to dance, do you think I will? No!!! I'll just tell him I broke my leg and it's against the doctor's orders. But I won't mind, I'll just bring along some of the joke books and if things get too boring I'll excite myself with a game of Tiddling Winks. But don't forget, you'll have to do likewise. Say!! Did you read the latest "Captain Marvel." He's got a new partner. A girl. (I guess he's not so dumb.) Well, I guess this is enough for my night life.

My brother finally went "over." He sent me handkerchiefs with the Signal Corp Insignia on it. My Christmas gift. He had a big sign "Do not open 'til Christmas," but Dolores just stood and nagged and nagged until I opened it. (Yeah, she had a shotgun in my back.)

Say, Honey, how are you getting along with those Frisco Belles? Is there still a Barbary Coast? Where's that picture you were going to take? Or is it on the way?

Well, Honey, I guess my dreams of seeing you will never come true. So if I sound a little downhearted, you'll know why. But, Slabby, I want you to hurry home—like mad. The radio just get finished playing "I'm Confessin' That I Love You." This is a new style radio, just start thinking of something and pronto! —They play a song that fits the occasion.

Well, I'll have to be closing for now and I'll be expecting that picture besides a few hundreds letters. So goodnight, sweets.

I remain your one and only, Loretta

Dearest Loretta:

Well, Honey, I just received another letter from you and what a "Lulu" it was. I know you're not related to Shakespeare in any way but then again when I read your letters I begin to have my doubts. You must have a little English blood in you, or else he had a little Polish in him?

Do you mean to tell me that you haven't received a single letter from me in the past two weeks? When I read that part in your letter I could seem to see the "scoop" and began burning like a forest fire. Then all of a sudden it dawned on me that the Xmas rush is on and that could logically be the only outlet. I have written you six or seven letters in the past two weeks so leave me know when the first one hits your area. But if it don't, you and I will have to tangle with the egg that took Farley's place in Washington.

Say, what did that egg think you were, a Dorothy Dix or something?

Them guys are a pain in the neck, you should have kicked the guy in the shins instead of Tillie. Just the same though, you seemed to know the right answers in straightening that hombre out. I suppose in reality, it was a hint to make me "fly

89

right." Well, don't worry 'cause I've been flying right for some time now. What you don't believe me? —Alright, I'll stand on a stack of Bibles fifteen feet high then.

I sure wish I was around that blizzard, not only because I love you, but snow is also a vigoring sight. Especially when those nice big crisp flakes come floating down. I bet I could walk around the whole park five times if you were by my side to keep me company. I'd probably catch pneumonia, but wait a minute, now how in the heck could I catch pneumonia if you were next to me? After all, we wouldn't go through the park to play checkers. If you answer yes, I'm going to break your pretty little neck in about thirty different places.

I haven't gone ashore in the last five or six days now. What I wouldn't give for a couple bottles of Miller High Life, a cozy table, two chairs, with one of them being occupied by none other than yourself, and last but not least, a nice mellow orchestra. No reveille, no nothing, just you and I and the music. I'll have to make a note of that right now so I can dream about it tonight.

I'm not beating around the bush when I say I love you, and ask you to be patient until I get back. So, Honey, don't forget what I'm saying and we'll be together someday. I think of you and you only, day in and day out, and don't ever forget that.

Loving you always, Sal

December 18, 1944

Hi Ya, Sweets,

Just received another letter from you today. Say Honey, take it easy. If I keep getting letters like the last one, I'll be too shaky (or something) to answer them. Boy, wait until you come in... I'm saving all my love for you. Seventeen years of it. I won't kiss or even look at another fellow (well, maybe, just look or dance with them,) but that's all, and when I dance with 'em, I'll be thinking of you.

But you wouldn't want me to stay home... so I'll go out to dances. And I can't always go to dances, so if someone asks me to go out with them, it's okay if I go to a show. But I won't let him put his arm around me because I know you wouldn't like it but then, I can't be rude, or seem "cold" to him, so I'll just let him. Okay! There, I knew you'd understand.

Say, Sal, in your last letter you mentioned the song "At Last." That's one of my favorite songs, you know. You know what, let's you and I have a favorite song. You mentioned a couple that you like and then if I agree with you it will be ours and ours alone. Dramatic—huh!

Well, I'm home today with the rest of the family and what a family. They're sure having some fun, but as you know, I'm still reading my joke books. (No, I'm only kidding.) My uncle wants me to quite writing and dance with him. The old "Pijouk" (Drunk). Here I have your letter in front of me and trying to concentrate on you. My sister Dolores just came into the room.

(Dolores writing)

Hello Slabby, if you can't read the writing, blame the liquor in me. Too bad you can't be with us now, me with my boy friend and you with Loretta, boy, some fun we could have. We could see who drinks who under the table. Well, I better stop, Loretta wants to write some yet.

(Loretta returns)

That was my sister. She is feeling the same as I.

I'm telling you, Slabby, the only time I get affectionate is when I have my two beers. So I say to myself, think I'll write Slabby a letter. Just a minute. See, I was interested in the letter then my five cousins come in and I had to chase them all out—including my sister.

Say, Slabby, I know this is a crazy question, but have you got hair on your chest? Just curious, that's all.

I think I'll be closing for now, before I stick my neck out—so good night, Honey—and have a nice dream on me.

Loving you forever, Loretta

Hello, Honey,

That's the way I like to see things ride, getting a letter from you every other day. By the way, how does Swiss steak taste?

It seems "that letter," I wrote made quite a "hit" with you. Well, I'm glad I didn't tear it up now. I didn't know what you'd think about it, that's why I was a little hesitant about mailing it. You see, I'm not such an "iceberg" anymore. Not to you anyway.

Maybe it's the fact that you're about 4,000,000 miles away from me, but I don't think so, do you?

Say, I'll take you up on that "spanking" —some fun! (What am I saying?)

Ah! Yes, I remember, good old Douglas Park... How could I forget? Spelling games and such. Remember the basket ball games at the boathouse? The baseball games at the ball field. You were shortstop. Right next to Scully. The both of you sure made a pair. Always kidding around. That's when I first noticed you. There was a ball lined right at you. You just got finished talking with Scully and you's were laughing about something. Well, anyway you missed it, slipped right through your fingers. Clumsy. Here the rest of the girls and I were laughing. We were saying, "It's just like Slabby to miss it, and sure enough. You missed it."

Well, today is the first day in three weeks that I missed work. Now, ain't that something? I got up at 1:00 this afternoon. Received your "Gorgeous" Christmas card, the photo of the lifeboat you stay on. I think they call it the USS Signet. I'm not sure though. Now don't fall "over" but I got ambitious today and I scrubbed the kitchen floor. On my hands and knees, too. That was the first time I did any sort of housework in over a year, except maybe I washed dishes once about six months ago. That's all, though. Somehow work and I don't agree. But definitely. Good thing you've had some experience in housecleaning 'cause we're going to need it for that bungalow in Oak Park we get in the future. I know you won't mind. I'll still be the cook... you little spaghetti eater, you.

I was really surprised and sooo happy to receive that card from you that I could have shed a couple of tears. And coming from me, it means "something" extra special.

Well, Honey, I guess it's time for me to close this letter, so keep writing and I'll send you a photo soon.

Well, Sweets, be good and save all those kisses for me 'cause I certainly could use them.

All my love, Loretta

P.S.

How about that photo?

December 19, 1944

Hello, Sweets:

Seeing that I have "Time On My Hands" (not very much though), I thought I'd drop you a few lines to leave you know that I'm still kicking and then some.

You know, Honey, it seems that you've been wandering through my mind continuously for the past three days. I don't mind it a bit either, but it would be a lot nicer if you would take your shoes off. All kidding aside though, I really have been thinking quite a lot of you lately. I always have, but just a little more lately. Maybe because it's nearer the Holidays and a guy's mind always does a Hell of a lot more day-dreaming than usual. Anyhow, it's you, you and no one but you.

I saw *Buck Private* the other night and it really brought back old times. When I first saw that picture I was a civvy and it happened in the old Ogden. We sure had a good time in that "social gathering" spot every Friday night, didn't we? The whole click would be there and would that joint be in a turmoil about a half hour later. Just about everything went sailing through the air, but the light from the movie projector, and that never did work except on Sundays.

I use to try and get your "goat" by foolish pranks such as taking a "snap" at that luscious crop of hair. You use to "burn" so pretty like, that I just couldn't resist an opportunity. I realize I was rather rude but I'll leave you make up for it when I get back. You can take the largest baseball bat you can lay your paws on and smash me over the "noggin" once or thrice. That ought to balance matters. Hey—young lady—that gleam in your eye is a bit too sparkling. So take it out. After all, I wasn't serious about the bat maneuvers.

I had liberty today, but I didn't go into town. Just slapped on my "whites" and went over to my buddy's barracks and dragged him out of his "sack." We then proceeded to the beer garden and guzzled beer and listened to some nice snappy jive all day. The beer was horrible, but the music did more than make up for it. He's from Chi too and we've been practically with one another off and on ever since we joined this outfit. So if we both get back together, we'll sure have one swell time. He'll grab his chick and I'll strangle you and we'll cover every spot form eighty hundred west to the lake-front and forty-five hundred north to a hundred and five south.

We'll be going out for a pretty long time this next trip so don't get angry if you don't receive mail too often 'cause it'll be pretty impossible. I'll try and write a letter every now and then while I'm out at sea, that is whenever I have the opportunity so don't forget—don't get angry 'cause the only time the mail goes out is when we hit a port. But, keep on writing regularly like you have been doing in the past and you'll never regret it when I get back home.

Well, Honey, I'll have to come to a sudden halt mainly because someone will be "blowing" out the lights in about sixty seconds so take good care of yourself and save those pretty lips for me—"I'se coming."

Loving you always, Slabs

P.S.

The lights have already been blown out so leave me know how I do as a double for an owl in putting on the address.

Just more love.

December 22, 1944

Dear Sal,

Here's two pictures I thought you'd might like to see, mostly the one of the hoods from the corner. Do you recognize the background? I can't find the picture I had of Wiggler, but I'll keep looking.

I met Tommy on the streetcar as Dolores and I were going downtown. He still hasn't changed any. When was the last time you saw him? Dolores, Elaine, Tillie and I didn't go to work today. Laverne was the only one that made it. I still don't know how!!

Continental gave their annual Christmas party yesterday. Had some fun. (And I didn't drink.) But we were out 'till late waiting for Tillie and a fella to come back from eating. Some wait.

I have some Waltz Time program on the radio and oh, brother! Hurry home. Are they playing the sweet songs. I can just picture you and I on that dance floor, with the lights so low, and in your sweet embrace, and the band playing "Always." We'd be "Out of this World." Or do I sound like I'm out of this world and in a little one all by myself?

So goodnight, Honey.

Love, Loretta (The Dreamer)

(Enclosed is a drawing Loretta made of a woman going up the steps and her handwritten message: "She's going to speak to the Admiral about getting you a leave!")

December 23, 1944

Dearest Sal,

This is a little message to let you know that I haven't forgotten about you if you haven't received my card, but "dopey" me, I didn't put enough postage on and it was returned, so I cut out the verse (I couldn't get another envelope to fit) for I thought you'd like to know what it said. It's a little "late" though.

So, Honey, as the days roll on, and Christmas draws nearer and nearer, I want you to know that I miss you more than ever, and that you'll be on all my thoughts every second. But how I wish you were home, now.

Love, Loretta

(Card)

A Christmas note to tell you the things my heart would say
that my love for you grows deeper and more tender every day
that I long so much to give you every joy your heart can hold
nor just at Christmas time, Sweetheart, but as the years
unfold!

Forever yours, Loretta

December 24, 1944

Christmas Eve
(But no Adam)

Hiya, Honey:

I guess you know I wrote you a letter early this morning
and I said that I'd write you one tomorrow but I was too
anxious so I'm "making" with the ink tonight instead. Not
mad are you? If you are, I'll break your leg in about eight
different places just to see if a crutch and you can get along
together.

The way you've been receiving mail from me and of
course vice-versa, I think it would be a good idea to charter a
special plane just for ourselves. The pilot would just have to
call us by our nicknames and besides, after a few trips have
elapsed, I'd be a cinch for a perfect stowaway and gee, Honey,
would I'd make a bee-line for your arms, but in nothing flat.

You know I miss you more than anything in the world,
except my family, and that shouldn't be too hard to
understand after all they treated me "white" all my life.
Anyhow Honey, I can see big things ahead for us, so I hope
your patience can hold out a bit longer 'cause I know mine is
practically made of steel after all these years.

Tell Dolores that I could read between those few lines she
wrote and boy she was hiccoughing like Hell. She must have a
cast iron stomach or a pipe leading to the basement.

Say young lady that was a very "poisonal" question you
threw at me, but you know I wouldn't keep anything from

you. Consequently, the answer is affirmative but bundles and bundles as you shall see some day. But now, may I ask, just why did you ask? If you don't answer, I'm not going to leave you ride in my kitty-cart anymore. And don't ask me if that's a promise or I'll break the other leg.

I have been listening to the records up until ten o'clock, but they "blew" the lights out just now so I came up to the radio shack to finish this letter. Well, we only have about ten good records left and that isn't very much so something (I think) should be done about it immediately.

"Boogie-Woogie," "My Blue Heaven" and "Perido" by the "Duke"(Ellington) are my favorites amongst the ten. I still get my heart all aflutter though whenever I hear "Taking a Chance on Love" by B.G. and "It Seems To Me That I've Heard That Song Before" by "Able" James. My favorite amongst popular songs is "I Dream Of You" and you can say that again, Honey, and when I'm awake then I just think of you.

I suppose as I'm writing this letter that you're well under the weather by this time back in Chicago and I don't mean that there's a blizzard floating about either. I can't blame you a bit either 'cause if I was in your shoes I'd be about twice as bad and, boy, would we have a barrel of fun, that's if you had enough initiative to bring a barrel. Don't forget to have one on me and that goes double for New Year's Eve.

Imagine, it's been Christmas Eve all day and I haven't even had as much as a beer all day and not a damn prospect in sight. So help me, I'd even be glad to ring out the bar rag. Anyhow, it's better than last Christmas Eve 'cause I had to spend that joyous holiday out on the Midway Island with nothing but sand in my shoes.

Well, Honey, I'll have to write Dad a letter, so here's all my love coming through for you to save until that certain day when I come struggling down Ogden Ave.

All the love I possess, Slabs

December 25, 1944

The USS Signet spends Christmas day at Pearl Harbor. Most of the Christmas packages have arrived, so the crew is in good spirits.

Good Morning, Honey:

Well, I got up awful bright and early this morning, anyhow, I got up early if you want to argue. It must have been the yuletide spirit that made me take such drastic actions but deep down in my heart I feel pretty sure that the boatswain's tugging of my arm really did the trick.

You know, it's pretty damn hard to realize that it's Christmas "out here." No snow, no Christmas trees being towed around and no Salvation Army band anywhere in sight. What a lovely Christmas this will be. Well, this is only my third Christmas away from home and if the law of averages holds true, I ought to be home before I see The Fourth.

So Cowb and Beaver will be home for the Holidays? Well, I always told myself that it'd pay to be Irish, even if it was just for the sole purpose of inheriting that everlasting luck that they can't seem to get rid of. They both deserve it though, but I still wish Cowb would give me a little "info" on "Who's Who In The Navy." I'm suppose to "wire" him as soon as I hit Frisco and notify him that I'm heading for Chi, but I'm afraid he'll have to wait awhile longer.

Say, Honey, do you know anymore jokes like "How are those Frisco Belles treating you?" I left the States over a month ago, and our stay there was such a short time that it feels like I haven't been back since I first went overseas. You'll have to pardon me for about three or eight hours 'cause I'm heading for the dental office for my semi-annual checkup.

Umpteen hours have elapsed—I'm back in a flash with the cash but not the "rash"—of my teeth. Well, it wasn't so bad. He only drilled two teeth and fixed them up in the same day. Of course I could use a blood transfusion to amend for the three quarts of blood I lost when he chopped my gums into little pieces, but otherwise everything ran smooth. I couldn't kick—they had three pharmacist mates pinning me down—so how could I? Well anyhow, there's one consolation, and that is I won't have to see another "ivory carver" for another six months (I hope). They're really good "eggs" though, just so long as you don't get to know them better.

You know, also with those two luscious letters from the sweetest and nicest thing between the Atlantic and Pacific, I also received a nice box of candy from Henly. It arrived just a day before Christmas Eve and that I would call, perfect timing. So don't forget to thank him for me and I'll drop him a line later on at the very first opportunity I get.

Say, Lor, I guess I was a bit selfish when I told you about three hundred times to be good, so you'll have to excuse me, and I won't utter another word that resembles the phrase. I'll have to think of something else, you see, Honey, I love you more than you'll ever realize, so I get a bit too jealous now and then, mostly now. But anytime you want to go out and have a good time, don't leave me stop you 'cause after all there is no sense in both of us suffering the consequences of war.

However, when I get back, we'll make up for all the time we lost and probably double it. I just can't wait until I get you underneath a nice mellow moon once again—and oh, young lady, you had better lookout. And I'm not a kidding.

Well, Honey, I'll drop you another letter tomorrow so until then I'll remain—

Thinking & loving you Forever, Sal

Dearest Sal,

Well, Honey, I see you just received another letter from me, and judging from it, I guess you don't approve of my friends. Well, not that character anyway.

Anyway, it's good to know that you've been writing more letters than I've been receiving. But lately I've been getting 'em quite regularly to my surprise.

As you can see, today is Xmas Day. I just got up a short while ago. And to my astonishment, my uncle came in and said, "Loretta, here's two letters for you." Boy, then I surely knew that "Santa Claus" was not a fable. Yes, Honey, they were from you. That's the best present I received. It still would have been better if you would have been here to hand them to me. But then, if you were here, I wouldn't need 'em would I?

It snowed again last night and was it "nice" outside. I was going to go to 12:00 Mass last night but someone (could it be me?) changed their mind, but however, we didn't get there. Boy! Was it crowded on the streets about 12:30-1:00 o'clock. You'd think it was 8:00 a.m. at night, everybody was singing "kibitzing" around, throwing snowballs, and last but not least, the mistletoe.

I had to deliver the gift my brother got for his girl, she's Italian, you know. (One of your "Pizons.") Her last name is Rizzo. Well, anyway, Laverne came with me, we get there and no sooner got into the door than before we knew it we each had a shot of Italian sweet white whiskey. But it can't beat that Italian red you've got hidden in your cellars.

Say, I don't think I'll be of much help to you when you go running through the park during that blizzard, after all, they don't call me "iceberg" for nothing. But seeing it's you, I'd probably melt just enough for a little kiss and then freeze up again—(or would I?) Encouraging, ain't I?

The radio is now playing "Auld Lang Syne" and is that or isn't that a sweet, memorable song? Boy, I'm gonna really miss you on New Year's Eve. You know, sometimes I get to wondering how you've changed (if it's possible). Do you think that I've changed, judging from my letters, of course? You know what I mean.

The "Andrew Sisters" are now singing "In the Navy"— Nice, eh?

Boy, that last paragraph was just what I wanted to hear. It made me so happy. Now, I can tell everyone that you're my boyfriend. You know how it is. I just wanted to be sure. Say, have you got any idea as to when you'll get home? And don't go pulling that 1950 business on me again. You know, it's been over two years since I last saw you and I thought that as soon as you got into the Navy and went "across" the war would be over and here it's still going on—what's a matter, aren't you eating your Wheaties regularly?

Willie was over the house a couple of times this week. We—I mean "they"—(okay! so "I") had beer, danced a little, talked awhile, and the last time when Laverne and Elaine were over, they kissed him "Merry Christmas."

You know, come to think of it, I kissed him too. I had to be sociable, but don't worry, I didn't forget about you, so I kissed him again and made believe it was you. But I'm telling you, don't you go trying it. Now! I'm only kidding, you have my permission to "go" with all the girls you want, just as long as you come home to me. (I guess you can see who's gonna be boss.)

No—now to be really serious, now get serious, "I want you so, more than you'll ever know."*

So, Honey, I guess you know how I feel about you— maybe you're going away was good for us—anyway, I'll be older and more settled down (not too much though) when you get home.

I'll probably even be serious minded.

So until I further write—I remain yours, Loretta

*Taken from the song, "I Dream of You," as if you didn't know.

December 27, 1944

Hello, Honey:

I haven't very much time to write very much on account of the lights will be "blown" out in about fifteen minutes, so don't start climbing on my back if this isn't the habitual four pages. After all, Sweets, a couple or three are better than nothing, considering the time I have.

Good old Carmy sent me Goose's new address and I shot out a letter to him so fast that the plane on the stamp bent its props from the sharp acceleration. I haven't heard from him in over a year, and now he's in a Naval Hospital in (San) Diego.

I suppose you're just about straightening up and flying right after a hilarious Christmas Day. I could hear you mumbling in your sleep all the way out here. All you were saying was "more Vodka, more Vodka." I'm going to have to teach you a thing or three once I get back, and don't ask what, or I'll bounce a pillow over your head (boy am I getting "soft").

We had a fairly nice dinner out here on Christmas and a beautiful breakfast to boot. I had a half dozen sunny side eggs plus toast and some good "Jamoke" (for a change) to boot. But in reality, it would have to do some mighty fast traveling to pass up a dinner that I could have had back home.

I might be home just about when the snow is through melting, so you had better check your bathing suit and see if it doesn't need oiling or something. Yea man, I can see us now Lor, so hold on to your breath, we'll be going for some "joyride" pretty soon.

Well, Honey, I hate like Hell to fold up now, but the lights are ready to go out and this is the last chance I'll have to write for a few months.

Loving you forever, Slabby

December 28, 1944

The USS Signet heads south to Maui and spends a week there in maneuvers and minesweeping practices. Several liberties are taken in the town of Lahaina. Crew rumors abound that they may be going to the Philippines or China Coast.

Dearest Sal,

Well, I haven't received a letter for three days now, and I'm telling you it seems like ages. Right now, I don't know what to say—but I guess in a little while, that single brain of

mine will begin to function and who knows, this might even
turn out to be a sweet, touching letter. Right now, I'm going
to try my hardest—I know it shouldn't be difficult, but seeing
as how I didn't see you for such a long time, words seems to
fail me. So let's pretend—let's pretend that you'll be coming
home next week and that it's summer time and I'll be so
excited. Right now, I'm telling everyone that my boyfriend is
coming home at last, and of course they seem a bit enthused.
Not much, because their "dear" one is so far away.

And I have so many plans to be fulfilled. Such as going to
the beach at night and looking at that great, big, beautiful
moon—star gazing, and most naturally, those kisses. Ah!
Those xxxxx. (That's what I mostly keep dreaming about.)
You haven't been to Riverview for quite a spell, either, have
you? It'll be nice, won't it? But I can't forget about dancing of
course, not that we'll go to some nice dance hall and "beat it
out" on a few numbers, but I'd trade all the "fast" numbers
for one sweet, slow melody with you holding me ever so close,
and whispering "sweet nothings" into my ear, and I know that
I'd feel likewise, for Slabby, you have touched my heart, (boy!
am I getting melodramatic) and I mean really "touched it."
You "might" be happy to know that you're the first one I
really ever cared for, outside of puppy love, of course. Oh, I've
had a lot of "crushes," but it's you that I think of when I wake
in the morning 'til night falls, it's you that I want to be with,
so Slabby, I guess you got yourself a "gal." (Poor you!)

So, as time grows short and the two beers I've had begin
to wear off, I'll have to be closing now and erase all my
thoughts of you until I get undressed, anyway, but don't think
I'll forget about you. No, not me. I think I'll have a nice
dream on you, so sweetheart, I bid you goodnight and have a
little dream on me (Excuse me, I meant nightmare).

Love always, Loretta

Caution: Destroy After Reading

December 31, 1944

Dearest Sal,

Well, Honey, it seems as if this will be my last letter for the year, so don't go getting' mad if the next letter is dated '45. I just finished washing my hair and am going to put it "up" in a little while, have to get ready for the "big night," (you know how it is) Boy! I can hardly wait. The radio is now playing "Poor You," but I don't think that song pertains to you. If I know you, you're probably getting ready to "chase out the old" and "ring in the new" year with a date with a "gorgeous" blond and just raring to hit all the spots that side of the Pacific. By the way, Honey, how did you spend last Christmas and New Year's Eve?

Did you even think of me at all?—I bet not. Not after that long intermission anyway.

"I'm Making Believe" is playing now and I'm telling you if I keep pretendin' and making believe I won't even believe it's you when you do get home (and don't ask me what that is.)

Say, Honey, don't mind if when you get "in," you're about 4 feet shorter than I. After all, someone has to grow—and those 30 lbs. I gained isn't (excuse me I meant "ain't) going to help any either.

Boy, am I trying to think of something to say now. Wish I was like you and just rattle off a letter—1-2-3 (or am I wrong?)

Tillie and Laverne are still having their birthday parties, but my sister and I aren't going, although they'll be expecting us. We're sort of breaking away from the mob. After all, she has her boyfriend and I still have??? And we can't be running around so "free like" can we?? I know you wouldn't care if I did or not, but I like to think that you'd get jealous—I think that's the name for it.

Say, when is that picture coming up? I'm still waiting, you know. If I seem to be drifting from one subject to another, you can blame it unto my three cousins and two sisters that keep on interrupting my train of thoughts. Well, what do you know, they're leaving. Mind readers—that's what they are.

Ah! We're alone now. Now don't come near me, Slabby. What am I saying? Just pretendin' again. Wish we were alone.

Say, has Tommy got the same rating as you? Just curious.

Well, sweets, I guess I'll have to get along without you on New Year's Eve, but I'm telling I'm really gonna miss you. But I'll ring in the New Year with you. Explanation. At 12:00 on the dot I won't kiss anyone. Just you. In a matter of speaking, of course. You know, I get "mad" when I think of all the time I've wasted when you were "free."

Say, Sal, how old are you going to be on your next birthday? It's July 4, isn't it? Oh yes, one more thing, what made you join the Navy? Not that I have anything again it— just "nosey". You know how it is.

I'll have to be closing now, so my dear one—I know it'll be a little late, but Happy New Year!

And in the coming year, I hope you get everything you're li'l heart desires.

Can't send you all my love this time. The Post Office is complaining, too much weight. So here's just a portion of it.

Love, Loretta

How'd you like the little poem?

Part Three—1945

Chapter 12, January 1945

January 1, 1945

Hello, Honey:

Happy New Year, sweets, and may this one reunite us together again "for better or worse" (preferably the former, without any doubt whatsoever). How's that for starting off the year with nothing else but a letter. Well, that's about all I can do out here, although I wish I could think of something to remedy the situation. About ten minutes of 1945 has already passed and can you imagine I'm soberer than a judge could possibly ever think of being. Well, it isn't my fault if they locked up the paint locker and thus removed my last chance of having any intoxicated drink. Maybe you don't know it but this now makes my third Christmas and New Year's Eve in a row that I've been soundly sober. What a Hell of a habit to get into, don't you think?

First one in "boots," second one on Midway, this one on the sea and now I'm hoping on the fourth one will be back in "Chi" in '45 but still alive. After all, I just have to get out of this monotonous habit or I'll be swinging at bats in my belfry.

I just wonder what you're doing about this time, oh well, what I don't know, won't hurt me (I hope).

I just received three letters from you just about three hours before midnight and was I ever happy, Honey. Those pictures were like two quarts of Haig & Haig to me, and the way you said "especially of the two hoods," was really flabbergasting. Of course I was happy to see their friendly faces again (what did they just get through drinking, a barrel of wood alcohol?), but not one tenth as tickled as when I saw that chic picture of you again on that bicycle and in a bathing suit to boot. My, my, ain't that lovely. But what's the idea of saying "do you remember the bicycle?" You're just a natural born "kibitzer," you sweet angel.

Say, don't go throwing the kisses at too many of my friends or else they'll soon be my enemies. By the way, do you still remember that number (very mellow) from a few years back called "Jealous"? Very "neat," indeed, and that applies to the receiving end of this letter also.

I just got off an eight to twelve watch and what a way to end a year, don't you think? I should really be getting some "rack-time" since I have to get up very early today, but I'd willingly give up almost any amount of sleep ("without strain or pain"), just to be nearer to you in some way or another.

Before I forget, you never told me that you were such a talented artist. I sure liked the way she fit in the dress. Don't be afraid to send a few more sketches in the future 'cause I just "gobble" them up.

I'm sure glad that we more than made up after that silly parting the last time I was home (that was just about when inauguration of Lincoln was taking place, I believe). But "you can believe you me," that you're in for the time of your life when "We'll Meet Again" ("Woodchopper Herman's" arrangement), and I have reason to believe it'll be not so far away.

Well, Honey, my "blinkers" are blinking a bit too much so I had better put them out of commission for a few hours.

Con Amor, Amor, Amor, Slabby

January 2, 1945

Dear Honey,

I just received two luscious letters from you today—the first of the New Year. I'm so happy to know that you were a little jealous of me. Boy, it sure makes me feel good. Say, if you really want, I won't go out anymore 'til you come home. After all, if you can wait, so can I. Say, Honey, there's one little thing that worries me. I know we haven't seen each other for a long time and are you sure you're in love with me... or a lot of memories? But I guess, "Time Will Tell," but I hope I'm not disappointed, and you either, for that reason. But, let's forget about such trivials for the present and let's talk about us.

"Us." It seems so funny to say "us." I don't know why, but I can't forget that long intermission. And I hate to keep reminding you of it. But as you see, I write what comes into my mind—and that little incident keeps poppin' up. I can still picture how you looked that night and I still remember what you said when you left. Boy! You sure must have hated me. Let's forget about that. I'll try and dismiss it from my mind. Say, isn't it funny the way we both start writing to each other again. Although, you did write to my sister first. I never did quite forget about you.

And, at first, I figured to myself why should I write first? After all, seeing as how your address might have been changed, not mine.

I decided I wouldn't write until you did. So as weeks rolled into months and soon a year had passed, I got to wonderin' how you were getting along—if you changed any— maybe you had a steady girl—maybe you were Captain or something—so I wrote. And then my sister gets a letter. Can you imagine—after I go through all the trouble of asking everyone if they had your address. To tell you the truth, I wasn't gonna answer your letter, that is until I received it, and then I changed my mind. I don't know why, but after all that time, I began to miss you. And I really mean, miss you. I was sorry that I didn't treat you any better when you came in. And I was hoping that time would—for just a little while— show you that I wasn't kidding when I said I missed you. And now as I think about it—I just get mad—that's all. Just mad. Well, now you know my side of the story, how about pouring yours out to me? I'm dying to know how you really felt. Okay!

So, Honey, I guess it's closing time for now, but I'll be back in a day or two. Incidentally, these are the first letters I received in over a week. Whatsa matter are you slippin'?

Well "goodnight" "dear"!

Forever yours, Loretta

January 4, 1945

The USS Signet heads back to Pearl Harbor and spends a week loading stores, spare parts and extra gear to get ready for sea.

January 6, 1945

Saturday Morning

Good Morning, Sweets:

You know I tried to write you a letter last night after the eight to twelve watch, but "no can do," the eye-balls were out of focus. Well, the letter this morning ought to suffice. After all, what's a couple or three hours amongst friends? Did I say friends, that's this "mill" for you, I tried to get it to make with "sweetheart," but it just "ain't got no edumacation."

Being out six days, I was expecting about four letters from you but all I received was one. Boy, you're really getting mean (or is it wicked), but after I read that sweet letter, I knew that it was worth its weight in gold, or at least it was equivalent to ten of the best letters I ever received, and that is coming from down so deep that I feel the oil gusher sprouting already.

Did anyone ever tell you how very nice you can pretend? You can really flabbergast a character like me with those mighty potent words you've been using. You know, I couldn't have thought of anything sweeter than you. Just thought if I was locked alone in a room for twenty-four hours. Say, have you ever been out to the O'Henry Ballroom, about fifteen miles out of Chicago on Archer Road? It's only open a certain part of the year, but if I hit about that time and get home, we'll have to make a few trips out that way. I know you'll like it, it has a nice crowd and the lights are always blended together in such sweet harmony, but they're the "soft" type, mind you, so young lady, you had better look out, 'cause when I get back, you're in for a big surprise. Don't say I didn't warn you.

And without any doubt, we'll have to take a couple of cracks at the Sherman Hotel's "Panther Room" and pray that Goodman or Herman are there "making" with the "Licorice Stick." Of course, if Les Brown or Charlie Spivak are there I won't "Beef." We can't help but having the best time of our lives once we get together, even if we went to the Ogden just for old times sake. By the way, what's keeping that "institution" together these days? I surely thought that it'd be a heap of ruins by now. But, I'm willing to bet money that just as soon as I take one glance at it, the roof will collapse, pronto like. The same thing always happens whenever I go to church too.

Say, Honey, I'll have to "knock off" for awhile 'cause I'll have to get ready for liberty. I'll be with you as soon as I get back from the "breach," so I hope you don't mind waiting (I'm getting wackier than a jaybird in rabbit season).

Time waits for no one, and consequently I'm back by this "mill" again in a matter of not more than twelve hours.

I was going to have a couple of photos taken but the shop was too busy, so I decided to have a few drinks and by the time I got back, the place was closed up tighter than a clam, but I'll have some taken on my next liberty and that is a promise.

Just before I came into the radio shack to finish this letter, guess what I saw? Yea-man, it was *Orchestra Wives.* This makes about the fifth time I've seen it since I've been in the Navy and darn it, it seems to get mellower each time. When old Glenn made with "At Last," I could feel goose pimples blooming all over me. You still like that number, don't you, Honey? "Serenade In Blue" had me rocking on the edge, too, but when they gave out with "I've Got A Gal In Chicago, Ill," (I mean Kalamazoo), I really flew out of this world in no time flat. I wasn't the only one either. It had the whole crew "jumping" from the warrant machinist down to the seaman fifth class. Those are the kind of shows I like to see, and not these obnoxious propaganda pictures that seem to be flowing out of Hollywood like water over a dam.

By the way, what's the "scoop" on Maestro Miller, has he been captured or killed or what? You see, I was out at sea when that brief flash came over and never did get it straight so how about helping your "worst half" on a not too difficult a matter like a good girl (I should have underlined good, but I'll leave it go this time). If something did happen to him though, I'm afraid the "Heinies" are really going to catch hell 'cause he is, without a doubt, the favorite band of the servicemen and that goes double for me. You had better not take any chances and buy up all of his records that you can, and then we'll dance to every one of them on my leave.

I'm listening to some very mellow music right now and I'd gladly give a toe-nail up to have you dancing here with me. On the second thought, I'd might be able to part with two of them (mighty big of me, eh?). You know I'm only kidding about the latter part, 'cause in all reality, I'd give almost anything to be with you tonight and every night, but at the present, we'll just have to be a little patient for the time being. They're making out with Benny Goodman's "Jersey Bounce." What in the Hell are these guys trying to do, torture me, 'cause if they are, they're doing a swell job of it.

Well, Honey, I hope you don't mind if I come to a sudden halt 'cause I'm only using one eye-ball now and that's just about ready to go out. I guess you know I still love you more than ever and I'm going to have a dream on you whether you like it or not (be agreeable, will you, Honey) so good-night and sweet dreams, Honey.

Loving you forever, Slabby

January 6, 1945

Dearest Sal,

Well, Honey, here I am back again. It seems that all I do is (right) write to you and what do I get in return. —two letters a week. But don't think I'm complainin', 'cause I'm not. Just letting you know how things are. It must be hard for you to write a letter—seeing as how you don't go anywhere or do anything out of the ordinary (that just depends upon what you call the "ordinary").

Say, Honey, I didn't think I was askin' such a "poisonal question," and what did you mean by the remark "as you shall see some day"—(I hope). You'd probably think I was silly if I told you why I asked "the question," so I'll save that until you get home. Which I hope will be very, very, soon. You know, I'm getting mighty anxious to be with you again. And this time, I'm telling you it will be different, but, and how. Gee, Slabby, if I only knew what to say now, how I could tell you how I feel about you. All I know is that I "want you so" —it's funny but those words keep poppin' in my mind every time I think about you. I guess all this waiting we're doing will turn out for the best in time to come. I know it will, at least I hope so. And when they play "I'm Making Believe" over our recorder at work, I'm telling you, it's all I could do but keep my mind on what I'm doing—that song was just made for me it seems—'cause when I write you a letter, I'm always in my bedroom with the doors closed (for no interference)— "So here in the gloom of my lonely room."

And then, I picture myself with you at your house, "dancing as we used to do." But I didn't get down to "Kissing My Pillow." I think I'd rather wait for the real you—oh, boy!

Gawsh, Honey, that was a sweet ending you had to your letter, "all the love I possess," are you sure you haven't been distributing it around that side of the Pacific? No answer, eh? Just what I thought.

The radio is now playing "I Dream of You." Time out while I reminisce of you and of what's to come when you get home. Boy, was that song mellow.

Well today is Saturday night—12:20, and as you see, I didn't go out tonight.

I thought it'd be nice to stay home and devote my thoughts to you. We just had a little poker game here. My aunt, uncle and Laverne, and yes, I even got her to stay home. Well, anyway, I came out ahead of about fifteen cents on the game. Laverne and my aunt were the losers.

Say, Honey, you "supposed" wrong in your last letter about Christmas Eve. My word of honor. And that's better than a stack of Bibles. You can also include New Year's Eve, too. Ain't I reformin'—It looks like I'm reforming before I really start. Uh!!!

Am enclosing a little poem that I thought you'd like to receive. You know, from me, to you.

Forever yours, Loretta

January 9, 1945

Hello, Honey:

Well, here I am again, Sweets, trying to keep "tab" with those three or four letters I promised to write you each week. I believe I made a resolution like that on New Year's Eve or didn't I ever tell you before? I think it's a pretty good one, so why don't you follow suit?

Say, you "Pretty Little Busybody" (Vaughn Monroe), I never heard so many different questions in all my life. What are you figuring on becoming, a star reporter or something?

Speaking of good old Cowboy, him and I are practically in the same rackets, that being communications. He being a signalman, will work with flags and blinker lights, while we work strictly through radio, di di di da. How did the happy-go-lucky Irishman look on his leave, or was he "blind" as usual through the entire leave?

You hit the nail right on the bean when you took a "flyer" at my birthday.

Well, I'm twenty-two now, so if you'll sit down in the corner and start thinking for a minute or two, you'll probably be able to figure it out. If you run into any difficulty, just leave me know and we'll both try and work it out together.

You know, Honey, I might be home sooner than both you and I think. The way my heart has been pounding lately though, I'm afraid I'll probably die of heart failure before that happy occasion arrives and that would be simply pitiful. You know everything I want in the coming year is "you" and to be with my family once again. So pretty yourself up, I'll be home sometime before my next birthday, I guarantee you that.

Next time you start telling jokes about the gorgeous blond I probably went out with on New Year's Eve, I'm going to boot you right in the seat of your pants. Do you realize the first white women I've seen in a year and umpteen months are the chicks I saw on those three liberties I had in "Frisco" in November? By the way, does your birthday still fall on the twenty-third of March or did you have it rectified just to show up the President and his Thanksgiving Day schedule? It'd be just like you to kibitz around with something like that.

I think we'll flip a coin to see who is boss when I get back and I guess you know I'm going to use a two-headed nickel regardless of how much you may squawk.

Take that surprised look off your face. I know what you're thinking.

I got that picture of your bike hanging up in my locker and is it a beautiful "bicycle." Yea Gods, what am I saying? I must gaze at it at least fifteen times a day and I don't mean the bike. I can hardly wait until I am able to get in your arms again.

See what you're doing to me, I'm saying everything vice-versa, topsy turvy and what not. If you keep spinning me around, I'm going to fade out like a light in blackout season.

Am I ever listening to some mellow music right now. Who it is, I don't know, but he's giving a Glenn Miller kick to his introductions and that is plenty "alreet" for me. It's the kind of music that makes your knees buckle and your ankles spin around like a revolving door, even though your feet are actually a bit reluctant to move. I wish we were "Together" to enjoy it, but I guess "you can't have your cake and eat it too." But there'll come a day soon, and then will we make up for all this lost time.

Why I joined the Navy, I'm beginning to wonder. Cowb, Goose and I use to go all over the States of Illinois and Wisconsin when we were young between the ages of twelve and seventeen. Well, I always got a big kick out of traveling and we figured on joining the Navy when we got out of high school (that was 1940), but somehow we just let things ride (and I am glad).

Now that I am in, I'm pretty sure I've seen all of this cruel world I want to see, especially out here in the Pacific. They can make little corals out of all of these big corals (the smaller the better, just as long as anyone can't live on them) as far as I care.

Well, Honey, I haven't much time to get some shut-eye before I go on watch, so I'd had better hit my "rack" now if I want to see you in my dreams tonight. You had better be there or Mayor Kelley is going to hear about it and I guess you know he's pretty "wicked."

Love & Kisses, Sal

P.S.

How about "making" with the photo.

Dearest Sal,

Just received your letter today—and boy! Here's I was complaining in my last letter 'cause I didn't get one from you for one week—and when you told me that this was your last letter for a couple of months! Well, honest, Slabby—I won't complain anymore.

Oh, Honey, before I forget—now, don't get scared if any of your "pals" start sending in their "best wishes" for a happy wedding, but I showed Laverne one of your sweet letters and the next thing I knew is that she told George that soon there'd be wedding bells for you and me. (Heavens only knows who else she saw.)

Of course you remember Laverne. Well, I just saw her last week and brother did she spread out—but and how! "Catty" of me—eh?

You know, there's some new fella from the neighborhood that looks exactly like you—with the exception, of course, is

that you're cuter. And boy am I tempted... but don't worry—
"There Will Never Be Another You."

I saw Scully and his girl. Scully got fatter and his girl is
pretty sharp, too.

Sonny got a nice slick chick for himself. But between you
and me she looks about three years older than him, at the time
I saw 'em anyway.

Henly's is okay. The latest one I mean. He changes his
like the weather. (I'm taking about his girls, dopey.)

And speaking of the weather, we had a cold wave of 8
degrees below this morning and was I tempted to stay in bed,
but all I did was look at your picture which is on my dresser
and zip—I was up and out and almost at work before I began
to feel the cold.

Speaking of pictures, the one I have is exactly 1 year, 11
mos. and 5 days old and you were in boot camp then. How
about sending one with those newly earned stripes? After all, I
wanta show off, too. The rest of the girls do.

You say you'll be home soon, the snow is melting. I'm so
anxious and excited, then summer will come and summer will
go and I'll probably get another letter from you saying, "Don't
lose patience, but "I'll Be Home For Christmas"—Yeah! In
your dreams all right. And soon 1955 will come—You'll be 30
and I'll be 29 (catching up). But don't worry Honey, I'll still
wait—But then you probably won't wait—you'll probably go
ahead and marry the first "white" girl you see. And I don't
mean the one who's sitting on your lap while reading this
letter.

Goodnight, Honey.

Yours, till? Loretta

January 10, 1945

Dearest Loretta:

Well, Honey, I was sure glad to hear from you so "pronto
like." You can sure keep my morale way up in the
stratosphere by sending those sweet letters of yours out this

way. If you keep it up, you're going to have my heart drawing flight pay and that wouldn't burn me up a bit. (I'm not money hungry either.)

You know, I'm going to leave you in on a little secret, whether you want to believe it or not, it's entirely up to you— but Cowb and I always used to go out together on those weekend nights (long, long ago) and when we use to pass up that unforgettable lamp post in front of the empty lot, we always used to see you joking around with the rest of the mob. I always used to tell him what a pleasant girl you'd turn out to be in another year or two, and there would never be an argument from his angle. You were always smiling in the most pleasant way and so happy-go-lucky that a fellow couldn't help but like you.

Then a few years passed by unnoticed. Most of the guys joined up (that's when the "war" came) and not very many were left. Cowb and Goose left not very long before, and as I didn't figure it was my time to leave at that time, I was figuring on having a nice girl to talk to, etc.... Well, right away I started running to your house and we always had a little fun just "kibitzing" around but still, you didn't seem to really understand what I was trying to put across in my humble way and I was beginning to get a little "disgustipated." When I figured by going along with Dolores might make you slightly jealous, I was sadly mistaken. What I was supposed to do then? I couldn't figure it out to save my soul where it is most unusually warm, so I sort of gave it up as a bad case of day dreaming. Well, more or less I did, and when I joined the Navy, I began thinking of you all over again. I wasn't counting on you, but still I kept thinking about you and I thought maybe we'd get things straightened out on my leave that was coming up, but that really "gummed" up the works didn't it?

I don't think it was entirely my fault, after all, when a guy has only three days home, he is already thinking of that gruesome day when he has to leave long before it is up and that doesn't make him feel too happy. Why I didn't go and see you the first day I was in, I don't know, but all I thought of was Al's Tavern.

Somehow, I felt as if we were still on such understandable terms, but when I tried to make a bee-line for your house, I just couldn't find enough courage to head that way. You know that isn't like me, but maybe that's probably because you were the first one I really fell in love with.

I can't blame you a bit for not wanting to go out with me that last night, especially seeing the condition I was in. I guess I didn't choose my words very well that night, and I don't see how you'll ever forgive me, but if everything always ran smooth, then this world wouldn't be so much fun living in it would it?

Well, Honey, that's the straight dope up to there, and then when we stopped writing to one another. I never really felt too good about it and as I had more time to think, I begin saying to myself, if I wasn't so stubborn we'd probably be able to patch up everything again if I would only drop you a line. Once again, I couldn't get enough courage to write directly to you so my next bet was to drop your sister a line and see if we couldn't get together "thataway."

I guess you know the rest. As soon as I wrote to Dolores, you had previously written a letter two days before. When I come to think of it, it sure seems funny, but not in the humorous sense of the word, but that we were both thinking of each other about the same time.

Now to get off that subject for awhile (I'm pretty sure I explained it as best as I can). Right now, I'm listening to Maestro Benny giving out with "Jersey Bounce," it seems that they can't write songs like they use to, but most of them aren't so bad. How do you like "Deep Purple" for our favorite song of the week? I'll leave you pick out the next one, old or new, makes no "dif" or does it?

You probably won't be hearing from me for about a week, so don't get mad, 'cause you know it's not my doing. I'll try and write you at any opportunity I may get, but I don't get too many of them.

When are you going to send some more of those sketches again and a few pictures to keep them company? After all, I want to see how my "goil" is coming along, or aren't you going to snitch?

Before I close, I want you to know that I really do love you and it's not my mind that's telling me but something else, and I can't seem to be able to wait until I can get back to that good old Cicero suburb again and be with you once more. Hope you don't mind tonight if "This Time the Dream's On Me" (Woody Herman specialty). So until next time, Honey, I remain,

Yours & only yours, forever, Sal

January 10, 1945

My Dearest Sal,

I just received that luscious letter dated Jan. 1. Was that a sweet beginning or wasn't it? Are you sure no one helped you with it? Hey! Stop throwing those fishes at me.

Yeah, I know how it is to be sober on New Year's. Well, to tell you the truth, I don't even know how it is to be intoxicated. (If it wasn't for the "censor," I'd say "drunk.") I'm waiting for you to come home before I really start "indulging." I'll try it anyway, but in the meantime, I'll stick to my occasional two beers.

I can just imagine what your thoughts were about me when you asked, "I just wonder what you're doing about this time." Well, Honey, I can truthfully say that my thoughts were a few thousand miles away 'way up to little you. I was hoping that you'd be thinking of me at twelve, but I really didn't expect you to be writing to me. It made me soooo happy to know that you were.

I'm glad you liked those pictures I sent. Nope, the two characters weren't even slightly inebriated. That's their natural looks. Whats'a matter, are you forgetting so quickly? And about my picture. It's a little better than two yrs. old. (I think my bicycle was older than me.)

Say, Honey, do you mean to say that you were actually jealous just because I gave one of your buddies a Christmas kiss? Or were you just kidding me and trying to make me feel good? You were. I know you.

Well, Slabby, I'm glad you recognize talent when you see it. (Yeah!)

You know, Honey, you mentioned last "July" (here I go bringing it up again). You remember when you asked me to go for a walk because you wanted to tell me something (Now don't go straining your brain to try and think of the incident.) Anyway, what was it that you wanted to tell me? I'm still curious.

When I got your letter yesterday saying you weren't going to write for a couple of months and then I "gets" this letter today, well you sure made Yours Truly very happy.

Well, today is Wednesday and I missed going to the Ogden. *The Song of Bernadette* is playing anyway. That doesn't exactly interest me, and at the present, neither does this letter interest you. So I'll have to be closing for now and wait for a little inspiration. Your picture is wearing out from my looking at it—so I'll be expecting a new one soon, see—that's an order.

Missing you more & more, Loretta

January 12, 1945

The USS Signet returns to Maui for another week of maneuvers, sweeping and firing practice.

January 13, 1945

Saturday

Dearest Sal,

I just got home a little while ago from work, and I had to "get in" this letter. I haven't got much time, but I just couldn't go out without writing to you first. I'm going to the Aragon tonight, and I have to work tomorrow (double time). So you see, I'll be pretty busy.

I can't understand why you haven't been receiving my letters, I write almost every other day. If not more often. I guess we'll have to blame it on the sharks again. Eh!

I just received another letter from you, today. Now I can go to the dance with the best of spirits. And don't worry, I won't come home in "high" spirits either. I wish you were here so that we could go "together."

I was never at any of those places you mentioned, although, I've heard about 'em. Isn't O'Henry's Ballroom "open." You know what I mean—dancing outside. Isn't that near Lemont and Joliet? I hope you do get home by summer. I'll be old enough then to go to all those places.

You know Laverne and Dolores were teasing me today about you. They were talking together (but just loud enough for me to hear) about you. Laverne was saying she remembers when you took her for a ride on the bike with a little stop over at Douglas Park and you kissed her.

Then Dolores comes up with "yeah! I remember when I took a walk with him through the park. He used to sing that song, "I like cake, that's no mistake, so Honey, come on and knock me a kiss." And he used to roll his eyes real "nice," boy I used to have so much fun with him. And once I was kidding around with him and he carried me through the whole school yard."

Now that was only part of the conversation. When you get home, I'll let you finish it, you sweet boy, you. But as I imagine those were only mild tales. I think I'd prefer to hear some of the "rougher" ones.

Have to be closing for now, Honey.

Loving you more and more, Loretta

January 15, 1945

Dear Sal,

Here's that girl again! Back with more idle chatter about each and every one (crazy, eh!) Boy, now I know how they got that saying "Blue Mondays." No kidding, Honey—"Jealous" is now playing on this radio. You know, that is a pretty sweet number. That, of course is due mostly because you suggested it. You know you've opened my eyes (and ears) to a couple of other mellow numbers, such as "Don't Take Your Love from Me."

Do you remember that song "After You've Gone?"

They're beating it out now!

Say you and that "mill" are getting along fine, just keep it up. And how! You know... if I use any "potent" word, that's just to keep up with the fancy ones you use.

How long of a leave will you get when you get home? Gee, I hope none of our plans "fall through." I really miss you more and more each day, but you seem soooo far away, as if I'll never be with you again.

Say, how often do you get liberty? I thought you were always stuck on your ship, but now I see how it goes. Looks as if I'll be humming that song "Jealous." You mean to say that you could've gotten pictures taken before and you didn't. My!! Now you just go right back in that corner again for another two hours. You bad boy, you. Shame ...

I remember *Orchestra's Wives* from way long ago, and I always did have a special liking for that song, "At Last." In fact it used to be my favorite. I agree with you on your choice of pictures.

I know just as much about Miller as you do, but if they're any special records you like, I'll be glad to get 'em for you. We haven't any recorder as yet. They've been rationed, you know. So I haven't been exactly "up-to-date" on records and such.

So, Honey, I guess I'll have to be signing off for now, have to get ready some of my clothes for work. So, sweets, I guess this is goodbye for now until tomorrow, probably.

All the love I have (and I'll even dig 'way down in my reserves.), Loretta

January 16, 1945

My Dearest Sal,

Gee, Honey, I think that was the sweetest letter any girl could have gotten. And that comes straight from the heart. I think I'm the luckiest girl in the world to have such a thoughtful boyfriend as you... I'm so glad you told me just what you thought and felt because that's the way I like it! No "beating around the bush," just come "right to the point" and if ever anything (which I hope will never happen) comes between us, I want you to tell me right off. And of course, I'll do likewise. But Honey, I guess nothing ever will, it took me one whole year to realize how I've missed you. Maybe that's why I never took anyone serious (meaning the fellows I went out with). It's funny, but I never felt right with them. And you are the first one I ever told that I cared for you and really missed. (Okay, I'll say it), I guess that means I'm in love with you, Honey, so the song for the week will be "You Are My First Love," and that little melody applies directly to you and especially the second line. It might ease your conscience just a little to know that I "was" a bit jealous 'cause you took a special liking to my sister, but that's the way I am. I never stand in one's way. I figured you knew what you wanted.

I wish I could write how I feel, but I don't think I'd be able to think of the words fast enough, and by that time the emotion I have would wear off.

So, Honey, I guess you know how I feel and want you to know that I'll wait for you forever—so hurry home. I don't want to spoil the family's record (with one exception) and become an old maid—Gee, is that a funny word to write and a matter of fact, to even think about.

Honey, I'm really missing you more and more every day. See those same words are "popping up in my mind" again. I want you so, more than you'll ever know," etc.

Love to the bestest of persons in the world, Loretta

January 18, 1945

The USS Signet returns to Pearl Harbor for last minute preparations.

Dearest Sweetheart:

Well, Lor, after being out on a not too calm sea for a while, we come back into port, and what do we find but Santa Claus—I mean the mailman—waiting for us at the dock. "He" handed me eight letters and I guess you know that I didn't put up a "beef," especially when three of them were from lovely you. Yea-man, Honey, and every one of them was luscious, just like peaches and cream.

While out at sea, I bet I read all of your old letters at least three times if I read them once. That "literature" I receive from you is priceless to me and I wouldn't trade it for anything in the world unless it was the chance to be alone with you on the highest mountain in the world. Just think, Honey, waking up in the morning and see Heaven gazing at us through the kitchen window. My, my, would I be in my glory with a "Heaven" in the "mansion" and the original one not over two hundred yards away. There wouldn't be many arguments between us I know that now, besides, don't try and tell me that rolling pins were made to mash spuds. Instead of taking your "daily dozen" you can "make" with the exercise by brushing my "noggin" with that hypocrite of a rolling pin. I'd just love to get pounded by your sweet delicate hands (you haven't taken up "judo" lately, have you?) so we could make up and love each other that much more. You got me so excited that I'm afraid you'll never be able to read the rest of this letter the way I've been making with the errors the last few minutes. I guess we'll have to come down from that mountain for awhile, but just for awhile, Honey. You're not mad, are you?

I just heard B.G's, "Jersey Bounce" a minute ago and still the goose pimples are rising. What a few sweet letters and a nice mellow band don't do to me—/*%—. I'm telling you, it's worst than that ancient Chinese torture. Listen to them guys will you—they're giving out with a nice mellow arrangement of "Together" (and that does apply to us). If I sign my next letter as "Loving You Always," "Rigor Mortis" don't holler too much. After all, I'm only human—well that's what it claimed on my birth certificate, so don't go giving me any arguments.

I sure thought a lot of you when I was out at sea and just bouncing to and fro on those waves (yeah those "waves" are small letters). Quite a few sick swabbies but not your old "Iron-guts" Slabby. At noon, I would just be on the fo' castle stripped to the waist with a hot blazing sun playing havoc with my back. I would just lay there thinking of you until the hot sun and a nice fresh breeze from the sea would put me to sleep. About an hour later the famous old boatswain mate would tap me lightly on the shoulder (with a nice big juicy crow-bar) and tell me to "turn-to."

Before I forget, Honey, that sure was a nice poem you sent me.

I'm guarding every one of them with my life 'cause I sure admire your taste. I'll get some pictures for you this week or my last name isn't ___. This will be my last chance for a while, so I'll just have to get some.

Closing for now with all my love.

"Yours forever" Slabby

January 19, 1945

Hello, Honey:

I just received two more letters from you today, Honey, and how you keep my heart beating just for you and only you. Keep the good work up, sweets, and for every letter I receive and have received, there will be dividend of five kisses per. I don't know whether you could exactly call it a "dividend," but I'll try and make those letters pay off if the kisses aren't worth the effort.

I have so many letters from you in the last two days that it'll be impossible for me to answer and comment on some of those luscious statements and questions, but you know me, I'll die trying.

Well, I finally have sent a couple or three pictures out your way. Yep, I did it today, nothing very special, but at least you'll know I'm still living (you'll probably change your mind when you see the pictures though). Now I can "get on your back" and gripe, "when am I going to get a photo of you and some snapshots."

You know, I only have one "snap" of you (it's mellow—oooh) and it was taken two years ago, the one with the "bike." It gives me a lot of inspiration though, but as you say "my daily glancing at it is wearing out the features," but in my case (thirty-eight glances a day), I'm afraid something awful will happen. After all, you only have a bathing suit on.

By the way, Angel, you've no doubt heard Gene Krupa's, "Flamingo." Well, that is one of my favorite melodies and if you ever get the chance to buy that record, do so by all means, just for me. It must be by Krupa and no one else though 'cause he had an awful good band then (about "40") and an awful mellow male vocalist. I just can't think of his name to save my soul in—maybe you know his name. Well, anyhow, if you can get the record, just put it in your "cedar chest" until I get back. Then we'll either go to my house or play it at yours, whichever one you suggest. Oh yeah—you can bet your sweet life, we'll dance to it. You didn't think we were going to play checkers while a sweet tune like that was "maneuvering."

Why don't you get one sweet record for yourself to play when we get together again? Don't leave me know what it is though, just sort of surprise me. I know your taste for music (and a lot of other things) is similar to mine so I have no worry in your selection being an awful sweet one.

Well, my pretty little Polish girl I went "ashore" today for the first time in a week and a half. Say, young lady, you got the wrong impression of me going ashore so often 'cause I don't. And when I do, have no fear of me going out with a "smooth one" 'cause if you'll notice that one picture, you'll see that there isn't one "skirt" on the whole street and that is Main Street.

Pardon me for dreaming for a while but Tommy Dorsey is on the Spotlight Band (Friday night). He just played, "Song of India" and is now giving out with "I Dream of You." Oh, Honey, how I wish you were here with me so we could dance together. I'd squeeze you so tight that you'd probably need a pull motor to revive you. You wouldn't mind though, I hope.

Well, he finished the program with "We'll Get It" and not later than five minutes, on another program, comes Artie Shaw's, "Summit Ridge Drive." Gee, Honey, they can't do this to us—keeping us separated like this—it's unconstitutional, I tell you.

Well, I guess that lousy beer I had this afternoon has given me a slight headache, so I'll have to knock off. But I'll be back tomorrow, and I guess you know I still love you more than ever. So as Bobby Sherwood is ending, "The Elks Parade," I'll have to do likewise with this letter.

Love & A Flock of Kisses, Slabby

P.S.

The last two records I mentioned are very mellow indeed, have you ever heard them?

January 20, 1945

Hiya, Honey:

Well "Irish," as yet, no mail has arrived aboard so I can't say for sure whether I'm going to get any mail from you today or not. But even if I don't, I'm still writing that daily letter to you whenever I'm in port.

They really had me going today. I never worked so hard in all my life, not even when I was in an outgoing unit in Idaho where they had me carrying boxcars on my back all day and unloading coal-cars at night. Well, it makes you feel pretty good when you're through, though, and underneath a warm shower. Yea—it makes you wonder why in the _____ you ever joined this outfit?

Going back to the five letters I received from you in the last two days, I will say again that I wasn't jealous when you said you kissed my buddy, Beaver. All I did was lose about two nights' sleep and about thirty-thousand hairs out of my "noggin." So next time you think of trying anything like that, you can proudly say to yourself that "I'm the one who made Slabby balder than an eagle." I'll bet you'll be mighty proud you, you, you witch you. (I was only kidding about that last noun, you sweet kid, and you know it).

Guess what we had for chow tonight? That's a good enough guess. It was spaghetti and meatballs. Even the way these Navy cooks turned it out, it still tasted pretty fair. By the way, you can cook a good dish of that Irish desert, can't you? So you can, well, well, I guess you'll have to cook me a dish when I get home on my thirty day leave. It better be good, mighty good or else I'm going to take you over my knee and give you the darndest spanking of your life or would you rather have me take you to the shores of Lake Michigan and feed you to the sharks? What, you mean to tell me you rather be fed to the sharks than enjoy a good spanking by me? Boy, you are wicked. I'm not kidding.

I was working in the radio shack all day today and naturally had the radio on throughout that period. If I didn't hear, "I Dream of You," at least ten times, I never heard it at all in my whole life. From Tommy Dorsey to Guy Lombardo (that's really going from the top of the ladder to the bottom in a hurry, isn't it?), they were all taking a fling at it. I bet you can really warble the lyrics of that number in a way that would really make my head spin. You bet your life I'll give you a try just as soon as you get my leave all fixed up. You are working on it, aren't you?

Now it's my turn. Where you just a little jealous when Laverne and your sis started shooting the breeze in the kitchen that day? I sure hope you were, but as you know, those days are gone forever and the only one I'll ever think of is you and none other but you.

The way you're taking in those poker chips, it's a wonder the girls don't tag some "moniker" on you such as "Diamond

Lil." I can picture you now after I come home from a hard day's work and find the "sugar-bowl" empty—I'll know where it went—yes-sir, Diamond Lil. I'll know where it went. But go ahead and have fun 'cause I wouldn't want to see you lonely, not too lonely I mean.

I haven't seen a show in all my days I've been in port now just because I've been writing a letter to you each night. But I rather write a letter to you in preference to any show Hollywood could ever put out and I want you always to remember that.

It's true that we've been away for quite a long, long time, in fact it seems more like a lifetime as each day goes by. But when we get "together" again, will we make up for it or will we make up for it. That isn't no lie either. I'm going to hold you so tight in my arms that you'll be gasping for breath and probably be yelling for a cop at the same time.

That O'Henry ballroom isn't an outdoor dance-hall, but it sure has a lovely terrace outside and the inside isn't so bad either. Besides, if it is pretty warm then, what would be better than to go for a swim in the quarry, or if you wouldn't like that there is always good old Lake Michigan to keep up our morale.

Well, I'll close for now, Honey, but I'll be with you in your dreams until the next chance I have to write.

Love but plenty of kisses, Slabby

January 21, 1945

My Dearest Angel:

I just come down from the open bridge a few minutes ago after trying to enjoy a flock of dull movies. But no soap, I just couldn't see them "scoot." They were really disgusting. Of course if you were with me I could have enjoyed "That Ace of Cowboys," Roy Rogers, but fate is pretty wicked that way. It was slightly chilly up there so I had a nice "wampum" blanket to keep me warm. But I don't think I would need a blanket to keep me warm if your sweet little self was there, but then again, on the second thought, it wouldn't be bad at all, it would just make us that much snugger.

Funny thing about these shows are that there is a different one showing on each one (I mean ship 'cause they are all right next to one another) and sometimes it takes quite a bit of strategy to figure out which one you're going to see. I usually see about four of them at once and then when they're all over I don't know what either of them was about. Yea, it sure is a great life, isn't it?

By the way, in your last letter that I received two days ago, you mentioned something about writing me the very next day. Well that was dated on the fifteenth and I should have had another one by now. I'm pretty sure that PBM mail plane didn't crash into the sea and all the sharks have gone south for the winter, so what's the catch? Oh, so you don't want to tell me, boy you are really getting wicked.

Boy, these days seem so long lately that I'll go nuts if I don't see you pretty soon. I really miss you, Honey, a hell of a lot more than you'll ever realize. When we're out at sea, it's pretty hard to write on account of we're so busy and the sea refuses to keep the tables on an even keel. So about the only chance I get to write to you is when we're in port and that isn't too often and what I said the last time, I really mean it this time, if you get what I mean. That's why I was praying that I would get a letter from you today but I have better negate that before I go giving out with the ditto marks of that previous paragraph.

By the way, if you ever start feeling blue, all you have to do is drag out Lionel Hampton's orchestration of, "On The Sunny Side Of The Street." If that doesn't put you in the right spirits, then my name isn't Goldberg—what am I saying, I mean—well you know what my last name is after all these years, I hope.

For awhile I thought I was going to have to "knock off" this letter until another date 'cause all they were playing was this here "Wahine" music and if I haven't some nice sweet music to listen to, I find it more difficult to "knock out" a letter. But along comes that *Stardust Serenade* program which has as its theme song, Glenn Miller's, "Moonlight Cocktails," and I guess you know, then my knees start getting week and bam, I'm in the mood to write again. Old Woody "Hoiman" is the maestro for the night and there is no strain or pain to listen to his type of music.

Did you have a good time at the Aragon Ballroom? Did you go alone or did you call a taxi? I mean, I had to think what sum (that last word was abbreviated accidentally like) guy would whisper into your ear while my back was turned and that beautiful star-filled sky was passing over-head. Well I can't blame you too much for going out and having a good time but don't forget, "I belong to you, you belong to me." So please don't try to forget it, stardust. Old Woody is giving out with "Woodchopper's Ball" and I'm sure you remember that mellow hunk of music. I knew you did.

Say, are you all prepared to grab that bathing suit of yours out of the trunk in a minute's notice 'cause after this trip I'll be heading home and it'll probably be warm enough to go for a moonlight dip, yea it will, Honey. If we accidentally go during the afternoon when the sun is blazing like a blast furnace, we'll see if we can get you to bring a little snazzy lunch or something. I'll bring the blankets, pretty decent of me—What? I know what you were about to say.

Here I thought I had all night to write to you and blooyey—in comes our communications officer and throws a bushel of work at me. Don't forget to drop him a line and tell him to take it easy on me.

So, Honey, I'm awful sorry but I'll have to close for now, but "We'll Meet Again" and when we do—holy mackerel, look out for your hat 'cause you're in for a wild time. Good-night, sweets, and I'll be thinking of you every minute I'm out at sea and I always think of you when I'm in port if that had you worried for a minute.

All the Love That My Heart Will Hold, Sal

January 22, 1945

The USS Signet leaves Pearl Harbor with a large Navy convoy and again heads west, destination unknown to the crew.

January 24, 1945

My Dearest Loved One:

Well, Honey, the last time I wrote to you was about three days ago and seventy-two hours. Sure is a long time.

By the way, I believe this is the first letter I've written to you while out at sea. I'll bet a million that it isn't going to be my last, not if I can help it. You still won't get it any faster 'cause it'll stay aboard ship until we hit some port where it can be flown back by plane. Anyhow, it's strictly the principle of the thing, isn't it?

I guess you know I'm going through quite a bit of difficulty in getting this letter through. The ship isn't rolling very much, in fact it's just a lazy roll, but still enough to hamper my writing. It's just like catching a high fly ball in the wind.

I'm here on the fo'castle as I'm knocking this out and watching a beautiful sun "sink" into the ocean for markings of another day that we've been apart. At least there is some consolation for my thoughts and this is that it is more easy to visualize your lovely self in comparison with the gorgeous sunset. Yep, Honey, it's going to be a great day when we get together again. It'll seem mighty good again to be coming home just about the time the roosters start gargling their adam's apple. You can stay up that late, can't you? What! *!-*?

It sure is peaceful tonight and I hope it stays that way. The waves are closer to ripples than anything and it looks sort of pretty to see how nice and easy the bow of the ship cuts through them.

I was listening to some short wave music the other night and it was coming direct from Chicago.

Boy, did I take it all in, but when he mentioned how cold it was back there I sort of started thinking for awhile. This is my second winter out here and it's always warm. Now if I come back to Chicago during the winter, rigor mortis would probably set in my sun-beaten body and I guess you know that wouldn't be very healthy. Of course, there is one outlet and that is if you were waiting at the station to greet me, all of the snow would melt in its tracks. That would be very nice indeed. But even then, I don't think it would take me very long to get used to twenty below, especially if I had you next to my side.

Well, it's twilight out here and as the moon is coming into view, I'm afraid I'll have to leave the fo'castle for the time being. Showers are open tonight and as we only have them open once every ten days while out at sea, I had better get in line now. It would be pretty dreadful if I missed tonight and had to wait another ten days. I'll be back as soon as I get through with "making with the soap."

Well, Honey, I'm continuing this letter in the mess hall for lack of light on the fo'castle. After that shower, I feel like a new man plus a few good numbers being played on the phonograph is really doing the trick. Hurry over, Sweets, but take a plane. The "weather-beaten" phonograph is giving out with "Cootie" William's, "Things Ain't What They Use To Be" and what a mell-ooow piece that is. You should hear those "saxes" blending together, Honey, and would you be sent out of this world on a rocket.

Well, my sweets, I have the Mid tonight so I had better get a few hours of sleep. Goodnight for now, my only one, and don't forget to keep waiting.

Loving you always, Slabby

P.S.

Where are those pictures?

January 27, 1945

Dearest Sal,

Gee, Honey, I didn't know I had such a handsome lookin' beau. You know, the more I keep looking at your picture, I think that any second you're gonna come out with some wisecrack and "bust" out laughin'. By the way, what were you thinking of when they stripped you down for that photo?

Boy, "youse" were a bunch of ferocious lookin' "swabbies." What were you lookin' for that that bright sun was trying to stop you from seeing? Come on, now, tell all ...

If I'm not mistakin', I think that's you leaning on the railing. Lazy—

You know, Honey, you should've seen how happy I was to see those pictures. "You'll Never Know." I went to the Ogden to show all the girls how lucky I was. There, I met Tommy and Henly. I also showed it to them, they were kidding me about the way you signed it. Oh.

Yes, Tommy said it was just like you to get on a minesweeper—that's dangerous isn't it?

Oh, oh, here I go again, but as I was walking out of the show with my little sister, I met Tommy and Henly. They asked me where I was going besides home, so I couldn't very well refuse their invitation, just for old time's sake. Well, first we went to see if Laverne was home. She wasn't, soooo, we three went to the corner tavern. (They wanted me to go to a different place, but I was dressed in a skirt, sweater and bobby socks and I was afraid that I'd look too young) so we went to good old Fred's.

I had a lot of fun dancing when I wasn't talking about you with Henly—tricky sort of a person. Well anyway, we stayed there till 12:30 (Henly left us after he took us home.) Tommy dropped in for a cup of coffee. Oh yeah, I warned him ahead that I didn't know how to make it, but I tried... and how ...

I'm telling you that that coffee was so strong that it almost knocked me off of my chair. Tommy said it was good, but you know politeness and such. I guess you'll have to teach me how to cook and especially make coffee. Well, I very seldom drink the stuff—that's why I never learned how to make it. Anyway, he stayed 'til four. I didn't go to work today either. But Honey, you can have all the Tommy's in the universe just as long as I get that one little sailor called Salvatore.

Loving you forever, Honey, Loretta (lucky)

January 28, 1945

My Dearest Sal,

Gee, Honey, how I miss you tonight. I just got home a short while ago and I don't know—but you kept poppin' up in my mind all evening. (Not that I mind either.) I keep seeing your face before me, maybe it's because I carry your picture where 'ere I go. But, Honey, how I long to be with you once again. This time I know it'll be different. I just know ...

I heard the song, "I Don't Wanna Walk Without You," today and that sorta set me to thinking about you more than ever before and then the orchestra comes in with "I miss you more than I can say. Miss you, since you went away dear. Daytime, night time, nothing I do can makes me forget that I still love you. Kiss you, in my dreams. I kiss you. Whispering, darling, how I miss you. Tell me, do you ever miss me as I miss you?"

Tell me, Honey, do you? Gee, Sal, why does it have to be you that's so far away?

Yesterday, my sister and her boyfriend took me out with them last night. So that's "one" we owe them, eh? I had a swell time kidding around with them. Her boyfriend still has a broken leg from the injury he received in France, but he managed to dance. Did all reet, too.

Say, muscles, you'll probably hold me sooo tight that I'll lose me voice and I wouldn't be able to call a cop and that would be terrible wouldn't it?

Gee, Honey, you should get to all the shows that you could possibly get to. After all, I'd feel a little guilty if you missed your fun while I still had mine. Can't you write your letters while at sea and just mail 'em when you hit port?

You know, Honey, you're just lucky, just plain lucky. How did you know that I could make spaghetti and meatballs? In fact, that's the only thing I do know (about cooking I mean).

Looks as if I'll have to be closing for now but I'll be with you tomorrow.

So, goodnight my love, Loretta

January 29, 1945

Hello, Honey:

Well, I'm back again, gorgeous, and after a lapse of only three days. Not bad at all, I would say or aren't you going to leave me "say?" I didn't think you would. Boy, are you "wicked," you "Simon Legree."

We had "holiday routine" today so I "hustles my bustle" up to the fo'castle and fell asleep in a nice hot sun. I must have been asleep for about two hours and when I awoke I was "well done" but only half of me. Yep, when I got up, one half of me was as red as W.C. Field's nose and the other half was just natural. I'm beginning to think the sun was hitting me on a wrong angle. I don't think I'll ever get a tan again like the one I had on Midway. Maybe it's because the ship doesn't anchor out at sea whenever a guy wants to go swimming. Then again, I don't get much of a chance to roam along our "enormous" decks during the day-time and thus absorb some of those ultra-violet rays, because I'm either on watch in the radio shack or else "turning to." They're both about the same difference. Well, this is getting mighty dull but quick, so I had better change the subject.

After that "turmoil" that I went through up above, I came down to the mess-hall and they were showing the first movie that we've seen since being out at sea. It wasn't too bad although I only saw the latter half. *You Can't Escape Forever* was the name of the "gizmo" and how true, how true.

Seeing that I had quite a bit of time to myself today, I read through all of your letters. Yes-sir, Honey, if I only read a Bible as often as I read your letters, I would be a preacher by profession. You sure write some very neat letters, besides just being gorgeous. I guess that's one reason why I am so in love with you, you have the brains and looks to boot.

Last night after twilight, I was sitting out on the "fantail" just chewing the fat with a couple or three other guys. And what a pretty full moon there was. Can you imagine, it was the same moon that "goes" past Chicago every night? And here I am out at sea, wasting all this precious time when I could just as well be back home with you, and we wouldn't be playing "checkers" either. I presume you follow me or did you take a detour while I wasn't looking? I thought you would, "Simon." I doubt if I'll ever get this letter finished because of a certain "foreigner" that we happen to have aboard. He hails from a town in Mongolia and he just won't get off my "back," no-how. Some guys just haven't any book-learning that's all. He claims he's a censor and with that brand new pair of scissors he has in his hand, it's pretty hard to doubt him. He's a good egg but he doesn't know what a hint looks like. You don't mind if I "break in" a new axe over his thick "noggin." I'll only take a minute.

Well "Irish," I'll be going back on watch in about ten minutes so as a wash woman brings her clothes to a line, I'll just have to bring my line to a close. I'll have to have a dream on you tonight but in the meantime be "gud."

Loving you always, Sal

January 29, 1945

Dearest Sal,

Well, Honey, this is your one and only writing to you again. And how is my handsome Navy man getting along? I'm feeling fine today and I hope you are in the same spirits. I feel so happy today (and I don't mean slap-happy either) that I don't think that anybody could get me "mad." The only exception of course is if you stopped writing to me completely. But that could never happen to us, could it? I don't think I would be able to stand a broken heart at eighteen. (See how my mind wanders?)

I'm eating Chop Suey now, don't mind if you find a couple of spots here and there. Mostly there. Guess what, Honey? I'm learning how to cook. Yep, my aunt finally thought it was time for me to start thinking of doing household duties. Tried to argue it with her, but, anyway. I made supper, yesterday. Yep, made pork chops. Came out pretty good, but I still hope that you don't forget any of the "special" training they teach you there.

I suppose you know that Tommy got an extra ten days. The lucky boy.

Gee, with that radio playing, I feel like dancing now.

Say, Honey, how's your swimming getting along? Learn anymore fancy dives, yet? Well, you better get ready to teach some to me when you get HOME. I'll probably break my back in the attempt, though! But I'll be game enough to try. Yeah!

Now to change the subject to the direct opposite. We're having a cold wave out here. It's now 'way below 0 degrees and still going strong.

Excuse me while I get a glass of milk—back again—My aunt's telling me now that if "I keep on taking snacks like I do now, I'll get fat and Slabby won't like you anymore." But don't worry Honey I never get fat. Noooo! It's a fact that I still weigh the same I did two years ago.

Have to be closing now, Honey. Goodnight, pleasant dreams.

Loving you more and more, Loretta

P.S.

Any similarity to this handwriting and the Palmer Method is purely coincidental

Chapter 13, February 1945

February 2, 1945

Hello, Honey:

Well, how is the only girl of my dreams getting along these days? They're not working you too hard I hope or have they just got you carrying boxcars on your back? Yeah, you sure lead a soft life, that's all I have to say.

I can hardly wait until we hit port so I can get some more mail from you. And if I don't have a stack of them about ten feet high when we get there, I'm going to be throwing rocks at you the rest of "our" lives. So you had better comply or else learn how to duck exceptionally well.

I wish this ship would stop rolling for awhile so I could write at least a half-way readable letter. But "she" won't listen. I'm ignored completely. She just keeps rolling to and fro. Maybe you know some magic words that will put her in her place. But I suppose the only words you know is when "Shorty" short-changes you, and then you start making with the vulgar language to remedy the situation.

Well, today we had a break, I should say natural break but I'll leave it go this time seeing that it's you. Anyhow, old "Father-Time" let go with the rain clouds and so naturally most of us had a nice fresh water shower on the "fantail." It surely felt good and if things like that keep on happening, I'm going to start going to church and give "thanks." You sure do a lot of things backward in the Navy and the above is one of them. Imagine if I was home on a Saturday evening just praying in the living room for a sudden cloudburst so I could step into the back garden and take one's customarily Saturday bath. It would be wackier than a Jaybird rolling up the white line on Lincoln Highway. I hope this life I lead has no after effects on me once I'm in "civvies" again. I guess time will tell.

You know "Irish," as I was reading over some of your letters today, I seemed to get a vague idea that you're beginning to get a little impatient in waiting. I know it's a tough world, but you'll never regret it if you just keep on waiting awhile longer. My time is up and I'm liable to go back anytime before July rolls around. So, Honey, buy a few more comic books and a checker-board to amuse yourself until your wandering "sea daddy" gets back home. Then you can scuttle your comic books and checker board for good. You know, Honey, that I'll always love you, so don't forget to wait.

Well, Honey, I've been "baking" in this hot sun on the fo'castle long enough so I had better go below and get in the chow line. After all you wouldn't want me to look like a Ubangi when I got back? You would, well that's a ___ "altitude" to take. Remind me to kick you in the seat of your pants when I get back.

Loving you more than you'll ever know, Sal

February 3, 1945

The USS Signet and the rest of her convoy arrive in Eniwetok. They keep their provisions and load more aboard.

Hello, Sweetheart:

Well, gorgeous, we just hit some port today and I guess you know that I received four luscious letters from you. But to tell you the truth, I was a little disappointed. I thought for sure I'd get at least seven letters. How come you treat me so "wicked," Irish, or don't you love me anymore?

Say, Honey, Laverne must have sent that letter to the "Wiggler" by rocket because he already asked me what the "set-up" is. I haven't answered him as yet but give me a little time and I will.

It sure is romantic out here tonight with a beautiful starlit sky and a pretty half moon to keep it company, but where oh where are you at? I keep looking around every nook and corner but still your lovely face is nowhere around. How come, Honey, boy, you're "Mean To Me." When I get back, I guess you know you're going to catch it. Think that over awhile.

That sure was a neat poem you sent, Honey. I'm beginning to wonder if you're going out with a poet now or what. All I know is that you're going to make a certain guy very happy one of these days. Let's hope the war ends tomorrow and then it'll be two days from now. I carry all of your poems in my wallet and at the rate they keep flowing I'm afraid I'll have to discard all the "mazamu" I normally carry and feed it to the sharks. After all, what's more important, those precious poems or that useless "greenback"?

Before I forget—didn't you say you would like to argue every now and then—well what's the idea of this salesman taking you home? I bet he was a traveling salesman to boot. I know—he was the "fatherly" type. Who are you trying to kid? Okay, when I get home in a few more months and if you find out that I'm balder than an eagle, wearing fog-horn glasses and my feet don't match, don't go saying that it's my fault. You'll be to blame, entirely. Yeah, you will. By the way, who's this guy that "took" you home on New Year's? If you tell me he's your uncle, I'm going to boot you so hard that you won't sit down for a week. What, you don't even care a bit, well that will be nice and ducky like.

Here's a small snapshot of one of the "circuit-worms" aboard and coming to think of it, that's what I am too. He's a nice egg, and you have to travel pretty far over this universe to beat him.

Well, Honey, I'll close for now and have a dream on you. But if I'm disappointed, I won't mind too much, for the past two weeks I've had a dream about you practically every other night and were they mellow—oh man.

Always loving you, Sal

P.S.

Unless that salesman gets in the way.

February 4, 1945

My dearest Sal,

Gee, Honey, this is the first chance I've had to write to you for two days now. I haven't heard from you for ten days now and it seems that when I don't get any mail from you, you seem so far away and I hardly know what to say to you. I try reading your old letters but the print's almost all worn out now and besides that I know 'em practically by heart anyway.

I'm listening to Art Kessel's "Memory Castle something"—anyway they're playing all the songs from a few years back such as "Temptation," "I'm In The Mood For Love" (Yeah!) "Shoo, Shoo, Shoo, Baby," etc. It's really "nice" though. While we're at it, did you ever hear the song "A Little on the Lonely Side?" That's the song I'm kind' sweet on now. And if you ever get the chance—look for the recording of "Cocktails For Two" by Spike Jones only.

Now, Honey, let's get back to you. When you coming home? I miss you so much now. Probably when I do see you for the first time I won't know what to do or say, so I'll leave it all up to you and let actions speak. By the way, did you change any? Judging ("When They Ask About You" is playing now) from your letters, I'd say you got a little more "naïve." I mean it. I still can't get over you telling me you're gonna use a two-headed coin to see who's to be boss. But that's okay, I think I'd like someone to be a little forceful for a change and not let me have my way all the time. But not too domineering. Just reasonable, that's all. Just reasonable. And since we're on the subject, do you think that I've changed any?

Ooh! Listen Honey, Artie Shaw's playing "Frenesi" (I think). Boy, do I feel like dancing now. In fact, I can hardly sit still.

Well, Dolores and Laverne just dropped in so I'll have to be closing for now. We're gonna have a little poker game just as soon as I awaken my aunt out of her deep slumber. So, sweets, just pray that I don't lose my only quarter, eh?

And before I forget, I just better get a letter from you tomorrow or else beware (skulls and cross bones drawn)

Lovingly, Loretta

Dearest Loretta:

How's the sweetest girl east of the Mississippi about this time of the year? You're taking extra good care of yourself or have they still got you carrying boxcars on your back? Just give me the word, Honey, if they are and I'll make them regret it the rest of their unnatural lives . I'm "rugged," I am. (I should have spelled that with an "A") so don't ever be "afeard". What—you don't want me to take any drastic steps—okay—I'll save my last two teeth for another similar occasion.

Boy oh boy, Sweets, did I really have a swell time this afternoon. I went swimming with the rest of the "Swabbies" aboard in a nice blazing sun. Can you imagine me out here getting a nice tan while you're back home (still waiting, I hope) colder than an Eskimo's nose in a blizzard? (I wonder how cold an Eskimo's nose is under the above situation? Don't forget to leave me know). Well anyhow, I spent all my time diving off of the boat deck into the bay. The water was really mellow, Honey, and I wish you were with me, but we'll have just as much fun "together" when I get back. On either the good old quarries or the beaches of Lake Michigan. Maybe you have found a new swimming hole, but mind you, it must be secluded. Is that a promise? After all, we do want to be alone on those romantic nights and all to ourselves.

We're no longer in the Hawaiian area and am I glad. That's the worst ____ hole anyone can be stuck in and that's where I've spent half of my time overseas.

We're pulling out of this new bay very soon, so once again, you won't hear from me for awhile. God only knows where we're headed for, but I'll be back in your lovely arms after this is over. It won't last too long I hope, 'cause I don't think my morale could last. Well what do you know, I'm beginning to become the sarcastic one now. Well it's all your fault, you "meanie" you.

Went up to the flying bridge to see what was showing on our fo'castle. It was an "icky" so I'll wait for the second one to start (of course I'm talking about the movies) and in the meantime, I'll finish this letter. While I was up to the open bridge (I should have said open bridge the first time but I'm so in love with you, I can't think straight) I saw the prettiest sunset I've ever seen in my life. With a beautiful purple blending amongst the low hanging clouds. I doubt if its artistic viewpoint will ever be surpassed until I see you in the "flesh" again. Yes-sir, Honey, I'd throw the whole flock of these lovely sunsets in the trash can if it would bring me any closer to you, but I don't think that'll work. Well, anyhow, I'll tell you a lot of nice sea stories when I get back, but only under one condition. That is, you'll have to cuddle up to me ever so close so I can just about whisper them in your ear. Gee, Sweets, you have me so "excited" that my heart is pumping like an engine going up a steep climb.

Excuse the new stationery, but I ran out of the other rather abruptly like. How do you like it or don't you?

I'll be with you again, "Irish," at the next opportunity, but in the meantime, I'll just keep dreaming of you.

Always loving you, Slabby

Hello, again:

Say, you gorgeous little doll, if you don't think I'm in love with you (and I do mean madly), then give me a logical answer for this second letter to you after writing the first one only an hour ago. Stumped you, didn't I? Now do you believe when I say you're the only one for me?

Did I get a little hot under the collar on that letter I wrote you on the third? If you think I did, then I'll apologize

149

now, if not, then no apology is necessary. Or do you still want me to get on my knees just for spite?

You know, in that letter where you were telling me about your first dance. Well, when we get together again, I'm going to have you repeat the same thing over again. You're going to have a tough time though 'cause I'm going to kiss those pretty lips of yours about every third word you utter. I can just picture you telling me all about in your cute little way. So every third word will have to be spoken through your nose, now how do you like that?

Speaking about "our" song of the week, does the second line go thus, "And My Last One?" You see, it's pretty hard to pick up music all the time where we're at now and I can't say for sure whether that's right or not. You had better not bawl me out 'cause when I get a hold of you I' going to take you over my lap and I'm not going to leave you up until an hour later.

Speaking of mellow numbers, I know you remember Dick Jurgen's, "A Million Dreams Ago." So how about that one for this week. I really like it and I hope you do too. What—you want to argue?

I managed to listen to the Hit Parade Saturday night and where may I ask is, "I Dream Of You?" I only heard the three top tunes and it was neither one of them. Something has to be done about it very pronto like, even if you have to dream of me three times a night and vice versa. Well there was one consolation in that "Together" was third.

Say, by the way, how is Tommy's mother getting along? I hope she pulls through. But when a person reaches that age, there isn't anything that can be done except leave fate take its course.

So, you think he's falling for Dolly? Will I give him the razzing in my next letter. I got a letter from him yesterday and answered it at the same time, but I forgot to give him the "bird."

Well, Honey, before I close for now, I'll have to ask you when am I going to be getting some pictures of you (any kind—I'm desperate) and also some more sketches? Good night for now, angel, and "This Times the Dream's On Me."

Loving you forever you sweet hunk of eloquent woman,
Slabby

February 5, 1945

After fueling and loading provisions, the USS Signet heads west. Word is passed that the crew will pass within 200 miles of Truk, the Japanese superfort. Lookouts are on high alert.

February 6, 1945

The crew of the Signet has its first air alert. All the ships in the convoy go to general quarters, but the planes are friendly. Word is that the next port will be Saipan in the Mariannas.

Hello, Sweets,

Well, Honey, I still haven't heard from you, but here I am, trying to keep up my end of the bargain.

Guess what? Okay, that's good enough—but I didn't go to work again today. I don't know how they could possibly get along without me, even when I do stay home, I get numerous calls from the foreman asking about orders and such. It's really getting to be monotonous, "rally," it is.

I went by Dolly's house last night for a quiet evening—which instead turned out to be just the opposite. Well anyway, Scully calls up at 9:00 o'clock and said they would be right over (they: Goose and Henly) for a little party. They did. But and how. Scully was on the "outs" with his girl. It seems he took her out on his birthday, which was last Saturday, to the tavern where he use to 'tend bar. And as you can probably guess, he met some of his friends and one drink let into another. Scully got "stewed." She walked out. He called her up. She told him, "When you're fully awake, call me up." Click. Serves him right. So that's that. Well, anyway, we all left Dolly's house and went to the "Spot." There we met Tommy and his date. Boy, Scully sure had it in for Tommy. Oh yes, before I forget, the way Scully talked about when you come home, You, Goose and him are gonna go "out" from the time you get in 'til you go back. So it looks as if I'll be lucky if I see you at 12 o'clock midnight on your last day. Oh no... wait... that's right, Scully gave me some consolation, he said you would be with me for two days at the most. And by the way, how much do you pay 'em for speaking so kindly of you? Everybody, especially me, thinks that you're "tops," swell feller, nice guy. Now come on, you can tell me. How much?

So, my loved one, I guess it's time for me to be closing soon. Not that I want to. But I'll be with you again tomorrow. I haven't been playing the radio, so I guess I can't get sentimental without listening to some mellow melodies, but, Honey, I want you to know that "I miss you sooo, and I do care for you more than you'll ever know."

Love and here's some of the xxxx we've been missing,
Loretta

P.S. Where are those letters?

February 8, 1945

Say, Honey!

You could have knocked me over with the smallest of feathers when I got home a little while ago, for there, awaiting me, were four wonderful letters all from sweet you. And that's mighty fancy stationery you got there, but... seeing that decoration "hula" girl makes me wonder, not that it makes any difference, but did you ever go out with a native girl?

Thanks for that little tip on how to fall out of the blues, Mr. Goldberg, but as you know, I don't know the "bigs" of the City Broadcasting Station, so therefore, I can't have any song I happen to want to listen to just turn on, just like that, you know. But I appreciate you trying to be helpful anyway.

Didn't I tell you who I went to the Aragon with? Well anyway, it was Leona and Elaine and Laverne. We went by way of the new subway. It sure saves a lot of time. My goodness, Slabby, what made you think I was gonna let "sum" feller whisper into my ear? I told you that I was saving all my eighteen years of love for you. Of course, I might get a little practice, now and then, but that's all for you own benefit.

I'm ready if you're ready, Honey—my bathing suit and I are inseparable. I don't even put it away for the winter. I go occasionally at Fillmore's.

The girls had a shower for Rita and her coming blessed event. Your sister was also there. I had so much fun with her. After we had the customary coffee and cake, I helped Dolly with the dishes. Yeah! Can you imagine? Well, anyway, there I stood with a couple of plates in my hands and holding a dish towel and I goes and runs into the parlor where your sister was setting and tells her, "Don't forget to tell Slabby what a good housewife I'll make." But of course I was only kidding. In fact, I don't think I'd make a good one at all. And you'd better not argue with me either. See ...

You know, when I read your letters, I just set this wonderful imagination of mine to work and if everything turns out for the best, all I can see is blissful happiness and love for us both. So, Honey, I'm waiting but missing and wanting you more and more every day.

Goodnight, my sweet. I hope I have a memorable dream on you tonight.

Loving you always, Loretta

Dearest Loretta:

Well, Honey, I realize I haven't written to you in four days, but I guess you know "your worst half" was pretty busy and couldn't find any time to get around to it. I'm still out at sea, but it won't be very long until this letter will be homeward bound, and safe and sound in your sweet little "paws."

All we've been doing the past couple of three weeks is sailing, sailing, sailing. I'm going to have so much salt on my shoulders when I get back that you're going to have to knock it off with a pick-axe. (Listen to me, spread it thick.) Of course, you can always cuddle up to me (but very close) and I'll tell you a few sea stories, but I'm warning you, they're going to last till late in the morning. What did you say?— You're going to bring your kid sister with you—oh no, but definitely. No arguments, please!

You know something, Honey, you've been bothering me something awful lately. Of course, for the last couple of years, you have always been on my mind, but these last two weeks has really been indescribable. Just about every night I hit my sack, "I Dream of You" and oh what dreams, my, my. Then in the daytime, when I'm walking about topside, you are constantly on my mind and I do mean all of you, from the tip of your toes to the top of your "noggin". All I have to say is that I hope you feel just half of that way about me and I'll be plenty satisfied. I guess you get some sort of an idea that I'm really in love with you and that it isn't just "so much conversation" as you may think or am I wrong?

I just had a nice shower and I'm really raring to go, but damn it, there's no place to go except hit my sack and I'm getting tired of that. Now. don't go getting the idea that I'm getting a lot of sleep, 'cause I don't, it's just the principle of the thing (I'll swear it isn't the money). What a place to spend the best years of "your" life (and mine too as far as that goes) way out here in this damn Pacific. But don't think I'm complaining, oh no—not me, I'm just "beefing" in a mild way.

Well, today I got myself a "German Steiny." It's only about a half inch high and if you saw me now, you'd probably—well, I just bet you would. Well, most of the other guys aboard got the same kind of a haircut and you get a vague impression that this is a ship going back to the States (boy, those six letters are really pretty) with a flock of German prisoners. It sure feels nice and cool with a haircut like I now have (I should have just said "head" and that would have been sufficient).

I remember that you asked something about "me" post war plans. Well, I just haven't come to a final decision as yet, but it wouldn't be too bad if you got yourself a nice job in a foundry and I stayed home in the kitchen. And if that wouldn't work out, I don't think you would want me to be a traveling salesman or would you (now I'll find out if you really love me)?

Here it is almost Valentine's Day and I won't be able to send you a darn thing but love. It isn't my fault, mind you, but I'm so far from civilization that it's impossible to get you anything. Say, by the way, did you ever receive that necklace I sent you for Christmas?

Well, Honey, I'll have to close for now. I have to catch up on my sleep and I'll only have five hours of it before I go on watch again. Remember, "Irish," that I still love you and oh, how I long to be with you (oh boy).

"Missing you terribly", Sal

February 10, 1945

The USS Signet and crew arrive at Saipan in the morning just in time to see the B-29s returning from Japan. After leaving her convoy, the Signet goes south to Tinian for provisions and fuel.

February 11, 1945

The USS Signet patrols off Tinian.

Sunday Night

Hello, Sweetheart:

Well, "Irish," I'm going stark mad waiting for some of your letters to catch up with me (maybe I'm running too fast but as of now, I'll have to be contented with reading your old ones.) You know the latest one dates back from the 17th of January and that is over three weeks ago. Of course, I had one from the 20th, but I lost it somehow (after I had already read it of course) so naturally that one doesn't count.

I'm still out at sea, but right near some awful pretty islands. The way those beautiful hills roll into one another, you would swear you were back home going for a ride through the country. It's a damn site better than seeing some poor miserable island covered from head to foot with sand.

I tried writing this letter on the fo'castle (my favorite place whenever I write to you) but the sea was too rough to "follow suit." The bow of the ship would rise high in the air and then go crashing below the surface of the water throwing a huge spray all over the fo'castle. I had a hard enough time "holding onto my hat," never mind keeping the stationery dry.

Well, I guess you figured out by this time I'm down in the mess-hall and if you haven't, well, then you can add one more "trimming" to the list that you're going to get from me when I get back. If you keep this up, will your "what's this" be sore!

The way these lines are going up and down, you'll probably be able to chart the course of the ship. She won't stop rolling for no how.

Now to knock off this "malarkey" and get a little serious.

You know, Honey, I can hardly wait until we're together again (what do I mean "hardly," I can't wait, period.)

"We'll" get a hold of that mellow record, "I'm Making Believe," and dance to it all night (but this time "we" won't be making believe, it'll be the real McCoy in the flesh). And baby, will I hold you close! Naturally, we'll have to tap the wine barrel in the cellar for a few drinks or that would ruin the whole evening, "Two Beers." But mind you, I don't want to catch you trying to "drink me under the table," (even though it would be a lot of fun) like your sister once mentioned in one of your letters. Don't get the idea that we're just going to drink wine and dance, Heavens no! We're also going to give good old Chicago a run for its (I should have said "my") money. You're old enough to hit all the "spots" now, aren't you? (Jumping Jennifer's, what am I saying!)

I sure hope it's warm enough to go swimming when I get back, 'cause we sure will have a lot of fun, especially at those "moonlight dips," and don't ask me, "Remember my bicycle?" They sure have been giving me a continuous razzing ever since I got that picture with that "never dying phrase, "Remember My Bicycle!"

By the way, Honey, haven't you learned how to cook Swiss steak (and it does taste mellow), yet? Maybe one of my sisters could show you, but never tell them you want it well done or they'll burn it like charcoal.

You'll have to keep me up to date on any new numbers that come out, 'cause I can't pick up any Stateside music where I'm at now. I just have to be contented with records aboard that seem to be growing older every day (you can't expect them to grow younger, can you?), but there are a few that will always be "good."

Goodnight for now, Lor, and write to me like the "dickens."

Always thinking of you, Sal

February 12, 1945

The USS Signet returns to Saipan to get provisions.

(Morning)

Hiya, Loretta,

Well, here I am again, Honey, after a short interval of only eight hours. I just got off the Mid and although I only have a couple of hours to sleep, you still find me writing to you. I think the mail might go out tomorrow, so I'd like you to have just one more letter when they reach you. Naturally, I'm expecting four or five letters from you when we got our mail and if there isn't that many, the next time I get "me paws" on you I'm going to "moider" you. That will be alright 'cause then we'll kiss and make up, that's of course, if rigor-mortis hasn't set too far in your lovely little body. And if it has, we'll just have to chalk up one on experience.

How's everybody around the corner, still loafing as usual? I take it for granted that you're fit as a fiddle and <u>waiting</u> for love. (I hope I underscored the right word.)

I got your picture in front of me and Honey!—you "am" luscious. Whenever I look at it, you set my heart all aflutter and then I have to get a hold of myself to take my "peepers" off of you and do some work. When am I going to get some more pictures, or do I have to wait until this year is up? Just as I thought—Boy you are "Mean to Me."

I suppose you're still working at the coffee company as usual. You haven't been getting any more fingers caught in the machinery, have you? If you have, how are you going to be able to count over ten when I bring the pay home once a week? (Okay, I'll leave you club me once or thrice for that remark).

Some guy brought a ukulele up on the fo'castle last night and about five of us started "warbling" some old tunes. You should have heard us. It was awful pretty. Sounded like a volcano in full eruption. It was fun though, in a "corny" way. A guy has to do something to forget his troubles and I can't think of any better way.

Well, Honey, I know you're going to be peeved at me for writing such a short letter, but my blinkers are really closing up tight, but quick. So I guess I'll just have to hit my rack and dream of you.

All my love (and I'll dig down deep this time), Sal

Hello, Honey:

Well, hit me over the head with a sledge-hammer, if I didn't get three very sweet letters from you today. They were really luscious (like yourself) and just dripping with cream.

That's the way I like to see things fly, writing to me three days in succession.

Sooooo (& I do mean so), you were only up to four o'clock in the morning just drinking coffee with my bosom buddy, Cowb? Oh! How I wish I could believe you. It's a cinch you didn't play checkers all that time or was it a friendly game of dominoes? (I'm not kidding either.) I'm beginning to wonder whether you're really in love with me or just trying to make me feel good. Which is it, or aren't you going to snitch?

You ought to know by now that I'm really in love with you, so why do you set me ablaze (and I do mean on fire) like this? Oh well, live and learn.

Now that I cooled off a bit, I can now settle down and write a decent letter (I hope).

It must have been mental telepathy seeing as how you were thinking of that Harry James specialty, 'cause at about that same time that number, "I Don't Want To Walk Without You, Baby," was pounding through my "lonesome brain" like a trip hammer in full blast. Yes-sir, Honey, and you can quote me for the lyrics.

You ask if I really miss you. Oh no, not much. Only about twenty-four long cruel hours each day. You're always on my mind, though out of sight (except for that one picture I have of you) and if things aren't remedied very soon like, I'm going to start rolling up that white line on Lincoln Highway. Boy, I'd give anything to be with you again and nothing is barred—nothing.

Tell your aunt I really appreciate her helping you out in cooking. After all, spaghetti and meatballs aren't bad, but I'd think we might get tired of them after about three years of continuous servings, or don't you think so? Of course, I could always whip up a short snack of "Jamoke" (coffee if you didn't know), and beans. The former is what keeps me awake on the Mid watches and the latter is what they call a balanced diet in this outfit. I'm afraid we would end up in Thompson's restaurant, 'cause after I get out of this outfit, if I had to look another bean in the eye, one of us would have to go. This world wouldn't be big enough for both of us to live in.

159

Those letters of yours sure came in the nick of time, 'cause I won't be able to receive any from you for awhile. With all of those letters, four poems and one picture (wish there was at least four of the latter and then everything would be alright) of yourself. Well, they should keep me contented until I'm able to hear from you again.

If you don't hear from me for awhile, don't start worrying your pretty head off, 'cause I'll be back with you in the very near future. Maybe a little before your birthday, maybe a little after, but whenever that lucky moment for me does occur, look out for your hat, Honey, that's all. We'll more than pay back your sister's beau for his kindness. We're going to ride all over Chi with the throttle wide open. If that day would come tomorrow, it couldn't be too soon to suit me.

Speaking of handwriting, who helps you to decipher my letters? My buddy always gives me Hell about it, but I can't help it if my wrist is broke. You'll have to teach me how when I get back, 'cause yours is really "neat." In return for the kind favor, I'd be glad to pay you back in all the loving you cared for and you had better not tire easily.

Loving you and cherishing you forever, Slabby

February 13, 1945

The USS Signet heads north and then west. Only one hour before departure does the crew know that they are on their way to Iwo Jima.

My dearest darling,

Please, Honey, you can beat me up if you want for not writing to you any sooner. But believe it or not, this is about the fifth letter within four days that I started, but could never finish. I don't know what's come over me. It's not that I go out so much and have no time, as a matter of fact, I haven't even enough initiative "to go out." And, it's not that I no longer miss you. Honey, I even miss you more now, "more than ever." I want you to know that. I know you haven't fallen down on your part, I know you've done more than your share.

I mean, you tell me the things I want to hear, and I still think I'm the luckiest of lucky girls to have someone like you to wait for. Maybe I'm not satisfied with you just telling me through letters, and I probably won't be completely content until you can really hold me in your arms and tell me it's "me" that you want, "me," that you've waited so long for. Oh Honey, do you think that day will ever come? So many times I picture myself coming home from work, to open the door and find you sitting there waiting for me. Or, I imagine myself waiting at the station for your train to pull in. I'm standing there so excited, wondering what you're gonna do or say, and if you've changed any. And there are so many other "things" that run through my mind, which of course I couldn't put down on paper, but I still wonder about 'em. And, honey, I bet there are a couple of things you'd like to ask me.

Oh yes, while we're at it, do you remember way back, when I answered that application. Well, I was reading over some of your very old letters yesterday, and you told me in reference to the application, that you wouldn't take me serious over such a joking matter, but there were a couple of things, you'd like to take into consideration, and that you didn't think this was the time to bring them up, so you'll let it ride for the present. Well, Honey, the present has passed and the future is here. Now, what was it you wanted to ask me?

Now for the local news. Well Dolly and I have become quite the best of friends. We took her out with us last Saturday—Laverne, Dolores, and I. Well anyway, we started to take "her" out, but she ended up by taking us to The Spot for that last beer. And boy, can she guzzle it down. But that's a Polish girl for you. I slept over her house that morning. We really had quite a time for ourselves though. She and I are going swimming today. That's what I like about her. She's so much more active than Laverne or Tillie could ever think of being. I mean she isn't exactly boy-crazy, and such.

Did you hear that Rita is the proud mama of a 6 lb. 6 oz. baby girl? She's gonna call it Sandra Lee.

Well, I haven't been to work for the past two days now. Lazy, eh! I mailed my Income Tax in, a couple of days ago. I should get another refund. Then I'll retire for a couple of weeks. Yesterday, I received the enormous check of $0.54 from one of my former employers. And today, since I got an application from Monkey Wards to do "part-time work at home while my kids are at school," I'm gonna take 'em up on it. My aunt and I will go half and half. Money hungry—that's all.

You'll have to excuse me for now. Time out for lunch.

Back again—this time with a little more energy to finish. Now, I was only kidding. Just looking at your picture and thinking about you is all I need. But then, if I wrote every time I thought about you, I'd be continuously pouring my thoughts out to you on paper and keeping the mail plane on a four-hour schedule.

Well my sister broke up with her second boyfriend. Just between you and me, how are you supposed to know it's the "right one?" I just hope you'll be my one and only!

Well, it looks like closing time for this little leaflet. So, my dearest, I'll try and write again tomorrow. Take good care of yourself and make sure you come home to mama, daddy.

Loving you with all my heart and, Loretta

Dear Darling,

Hello, Honey, hope you're feeling fine, tonight, just as I do. I just got home from the show, a short while ago, and thought to myself, I think I'll write my dear "dollink" a letter. So sweets, here I is.

Now let me see... what could I tell my precious Navy man about tonight? Oh yes, Honey, I've taken your advice. I stayed home all this week and last with the exception, of course, of Saturday.

You know, yesterday I was (as a last resort), reading my little cousin's first grade reader, but soon got tired of See Ann run, See Ted run, See Jane run. So I ran upstairs by my other aunt for some kind of book to read (anything over third grade), but seeing as how she doesn't have a printed library, the selection was quite poor (oh my!).

Well, anyway, I've got a book called "Manhunters, " and I'm still on the first chapter. I just can't seem to catch on to some of the tongue twisters that this piece of writing material specializes in.

And with much pleasure, I was reading over the last few letters that you had composed. The way you described that gorgeous sunset and the stillness of the water, why, Slabby, I believe you have the soul of an Artiste.

By the way, I've been meaning to ask you, but where does the fo'castle and fantail come in on a ship (and don't go callin' me dummy either).

Dolores' former boyfriend called her up today. Seems he wanted to make amends. But if you ask me (which no one is), I don't especially care for the chap. I honestly don't think he's good enough for her. And I don't mean that she's something extra special or some kind of a prize package, but he has his faults.

You should have seen the exciting and eventful week I just had. I go by Laverne's house—she's learning how to bake, so I sat around and watched her bake some cupcakes. Unusual. They come out good. I go to Dolores' house, and she's trying to learn to crochet and sew, so I sat around and watched her also, and besides my going to the show and reading "Manhunters," well all I can say is...

Hurry Home!!!

Goodnight, Honey.

Needing you more and more, Loretta

February 16, 1945

The crew of the Signet gets its first view of Iwo Jima at daybreak. Reveille is early that morning because minesweeping is to begin at 0700. The crew starts sweeping on schedule with the ship at general quarters and everyone

*wondering when the Japanese on the beach will open fire.
The tension eases off a bit in the afternoon and the
sweeping continues without incident. Around 1600, the
Japanese on Mt. Suribachi fire a few rounds at the Signet.
They miss her and her fire support ships put them out of
action. The crew is glad when their minesweeping for the
day is completed and they can get a little further away from
the island.*

February 17, 1945

*The USS Signet patrols a few miles off the island all day.
Those at the patrol station have first-class seats to watch the
bombardment of the island by US ships and planes.*

Sal dearest,

Yesterday I received a letter from you and judging from
its contents, I'd say you were just a little downhearted. And
after just reading the first paragraph, it left me melancholy
throughout the remaining letter. Honey, what made you
doubt my love?

You can't say I didn't warn you about Wiggler.

So the nights are lovely out there, eh? Honestly, I haven't
even had a chance to star-gaze for such a long time now. I
believe the last time was umpteen years back when I was with
you. Remember? But then I was too dumb to appreciate it,
and now I'm "too" smart. Now, just between you and me, the
real reason for me not sending you a photo is that I hate so to
disillusion you, but I appreciate the compliment, anyway.
And, you just keep on thinking about me, and just before it's
time for you to get that leave, I'll send you an up-to-date
snapshot so you'll be ready for anything.

You may as well prepare yourself for two large crates
that will arrive any day now. One will be filled with poems
and the other is a self-addressed empty one for you to throw
all that useless "greenback." After all, why clutter up that
half of the world?

Oh yes, (you see, I have your letter in front of me, and as I read, I write) about that salesman—now believe it or not, here's exactly how it was.

Every year, the Continental Credit Union gives a dinner dance for its members, and since I belong to it, I most naturally went. Laverne and I. (Let's call the salesman, "Jr." just to keep you guessing about his age.) Well anyway, Jr. had previously asked to take me. But me being one that likes to be independent and since, on your behalf, I resolved to no longer go on dates, I refused him in a most friendly way. So Laverne and I went to the affair alone. Well, we no sooner got there when Jr. comes and ask me to dance. Not to hurt his feelings and because I felt like making with the feet, I accepted. But Honey, I had you in mind all evening so I set that single brain of mine to working and with a little maneuvering, I had Laverne and Jr. together. And I was off talking and kibitzing around with the others. I knew practically everyone there, so when Laverne and he were dancing, I was left in my glory— "talking".

Come the dinner and he sat next to me, and soon the conversation was well underway. He asked to take us out, but I specially didn't care to go, but between Laverne and him, I sounded like a deadbeat to hold up the party. Nevertheless, we went to a crazy little Cocktail Lounge for awhile. Somehow he guessed earlier in the evening that I had a boyfriend, which I didn't deny, of course. So I was telling him all about you. How pleasant you were to be with and how smart and intelligent you were. Laverne told him how cute you are. (That'll cost you one nickel, please.)

Maybe you don't know it but he said you don't know how fortunate you are to have such a sweet girl like me waiting for you. (Oops! Almost broke my arm pattin' myself on the back that time).

And as time passed on, it was time to go (12:30 a.m.)

He called a cab and we were soon on our way home. We reached our house and before much could be said, I tapped him on the lips, said goodnight and ran in. Now he considers me a good friend and asks me how I'm getting along with you, etc. He calls Laverne up once in a while, yet.

So, baldy, I guess you lost your last hair. From now on, it's going to be different. But and how.

Gee, Honey, take my word for it—(I hate to go through another five pages and explain to you about the one who "walked" us home New Year's Eve.) It was my uncle. Ah! Ah! Put that foot down. You brute, you.

Say, how about telling me about at least once of the many dreams you have on me. Okay!

Well, it is Saturday night now, but do you think I'm gonna go out? Nope, not me, in a little while I'll start getting ready for my bath, read the Sunday papers and fall off to slumberland. You'll be there too, won't you?

You sure looked different on that snapshot, sailor. My aunt asked me how old your mate was? What should I tell her?

So, my dear one, this looks like closing time for now. I hope you didn't stop writing at sea. Those were the times I felt as if you were closer than ever.

Always loving you, Loretta

Excuse the many mistakes; guess I'm getting sloppy in my old age

February 18, 1945

The crew of the Signet prepares her gear and waits for orders to sweep an area off the north end of Iwo Jima. That afternoon she gets close to the beach during the sweep. As there were several good targets there, the crew receives permission to fire. They fire at several caves and pill boxes, but no fire is returned.

My dearest darling,

Oh, Honey, I could kiss you over and over and over again (and think nothing of it—yeah). You sweet boy, you, I just received five, 5, IV, 11111, letters from you and lucky for me,

I didn't go to work today, for I'm sure the shock of receiving those five, 5, IV, 11111, glorious letters would have proved fatal to poor little weak me and I probably would have been put away for years and years.

Well, I'm glad you finally got your chance to go swimming again. But I still can't see why you want a "secluded" spot for us to go swimming at. I always think, "the more the merrier," and besides, what've we to do by going alone? I mean it, are you sure I can't bring my five little cousins along just for company?

So, I see you said farewell to the Hawaiians. Well, guess I'll no longer see those decorative hula girls anymore (on Sal's stationery). Now, you'll probably have some kind of buxom "Goiman" (German) warrior in its place.

Oh yes, since you left the girless islands, I guess, "Happy days are here again." But I'm warning you, I'm a mighty jealous person to tangle with. Mighty jealous.

Say, Honey, why am I so mean to you? You make me sound like "Loretta, the Terrible." Wellll...

Yep, sweetheart, I can hardly wait to hear some of those sea-stories, but that's okay if you run out of words, just as long as you hold me so close... and I do mean close. Say, Honey, if you think I get "you" excited, well after all, I don't stay home nights waiting for you without some sort of "special" feeling for you. You know, I keep saying to myself, "this time it'll be different." It's easy for me to write and tell you how I feel, and how I miss you, and I wonder how it'll be to really kiss you this time, but Honey I think you're gonna be a little surprised when the day comes for me to "show" you. Now, don't get me wrong, I mean everything I tell you and little things I don't write down, but, Honey, you know how I get when it comes to bare facts. I just turn chicken. That's all... But you'll have to help me overcome this complex, won't you? After all, that's what kept me all yours for so long.

I'll always be loving you, Honey, Loretta

February 19, 1945

"D" Day at Iwo Jima. The crew hopes for a good patrol station so that they can watch the invasion. Instead, they fuel YMSs (auxillary motor minesweepers) north of the island where they are unable to see the invasion beaches. On the Signet's way back to her patrol station, the crew sees a Japanese mine floating by and takes a picture of it before sinking it.

February 20, 1945

Hello, Honey,

Well, what do you know, my wonderful little Navy man wrote two letters within two hours. What do you know? And just for that I love you twice as much now. So there.

Speaking of that letter written the third, I don't think any apology was necessary, but I do know one thing. I won't say what it is, but "Now I Know."

I suppose by this time you've heard that Cowb's mother passed away last week. Tommy is home again, but Willie couldn't get here in time for the services although he's on his way home.

Georgie S. is home on leave just before sailing for home, he tells his buddy and him got into quite a scrap with some Aussies: They loosened all his front teeth and banged his stomach up quite a bit—he was lucky though, his buddy is still in the hospital and expects to be there for six more months.

The words to that song (which was popular last year) go as: "You are my first love, and you'll be my last one. No one else will do. My first and last one will be you."

My, my, you're getting awfully brave and strong lately. Who's gonna take who over who's knee. Ha!

I see you've listened to Hit Parade Saturday night, well then you must have heard Lawrence Tidbit sing "Don't Fence Me In" or "Accentuate the Positive." I'm telling you, he actually makes us laugh with that voice of his.

Hey, you better not mention anything to Cowb about Dolly—I think he or she changed their mind.

Last night, for the first time in about two years, I played volleyball and basketball. Dolly and I. Today, we went and played Ping Pong at the boathouse. See, that's what I meant when I said she's much more active.

Well, Honey, soon I'll be closing for the night but I hope I do have a dream on you. After all, I let you dream of me, why not me of you? Once I had some kind of a screwy dream about you, but that'll have to wait 'til you get home so you can kiss me every two words, before I tell you.

So goodnight my love, sweet dreams, Loretta

February 21, 1945

The crew sees its first air raid. "Our ships at Iwo Jima really took good care of themselves." Several Japanese planes came down in flames that night. The crew picks up a pilot just after dark who had run out of gas and had to land his "Hellcat" in the water just ahead of the ship. "He was sure glad to see us."

Say, Honey,

Take it easy on that temper. After all, you told me yourself, "go out and have some fun," then the minute I do, you go and blow your topper. At least I told you all about it—excluding nothing. And furthermore, I don't think you trust me in the least. Do you? Then to have the gumption to wonder, mind you, just wonder, if "I really do love you or just trying to make you feel good." That hurt—way down deep. Just reading that second paragraph left me speechless. I'm telling you, it shocked me beyond words. And, Honey, I'm so disappointed in you. So.

If you must know, you're really the first one I ever wrote such letters (and again I repeat) the first one I ever fell in love with. Everyone else was always kept at a friendly distance, you're the first one to ever capture my real thoughts and also my eighteen years of love (almost).

169

We have a couple of new albums of records at work. They're all the songs that were on the Hit Parade a few years back: Such as, "These Foolish Things," "The Woodpeckers Song," "Where Or When," "The Music Goes 'Round and 'Round," and I was really happily surprised when they played, "I Don't Want To Set the World on Fire."

There were a lot others, but I can't remember 'em all.

Well I cooled off a little, so I guess I could call you Honey. How are you gonna ride all over Chicago with the throttle wide open with no car, no gas, and with this new curfew they have. Chicago has to pull the sidewalks in at 12:00 a.m. Not that it really matters to me personally, but what about when you get home? Well, well, just have to start out early, that's all, and then end up in my house for coffee and— (now I really got you worried).

I went to the show today and came home with a splitting headache. I don't think I'll go to work tomorrow. I'll go and keep Dolly company. She's not working either.

Be closing for now.

Love, Loretta

February 23, 1945

The crew of the USS Signet watch the Marines hoist old Glory on the summit of Mount Suribachi (mountain on the southwest end of Iwo Jima). They then do more patrols around Iwo Jima.

February 24, 1945

(The letter below is not in Slabby's handwriting)

Friday Afternoon

Dearest Loretta:

Well, Honey, I suppose you're a bit angry with me as I haven't written to you in close to two weeks. But I'm sure you will understand the situation when I tell you this is the first opportunity I have had to write to you. I guess you know that even now I am giving up a couple or three hours of precious "sack-time" just so that I can write to you. But you must promise to send a carload of tooth picks to me when you have a chance. I have just run out of my ration of the above mentioned "gizmos" and I must have something to keep my "blinkers" in focus.

I guess you have come to the conclusion that this is not your "worst-half" that is writing this letter. To tell you the truth, he is one of your "kinfolk." His name ends with "ski," but he still has the nerve to claim he is Irish. But "a friend in need is a friend indeed," no matter what he claims to be.

He is doing a mighty decent job even though he has never had any lessons from the "Palmer Institution," in fact, he has never gone past fifth grade in school. "Just shows to go you" that it isn't what you know, but (and I do mean definitely), who you know. All kidding aside though, Honey, he has really gone through Junior High School (without any strain or pain whatsoever), although he claims it's a God-damn lie.

You are probably thinking that my "marbles" have rolled in the "drink" by this time, but in all reality, I accidentally smashed two of my fingers in a hatchway (and I do mean my right hand). I suppose in about another week I'll be able to use "me own paws."

I've tried writing with my right hand as it is now, but it was all in vain and pain. You would have to at least be a member of "Naval Intelligence" to try and make any sense of the above.

Now that you understand the situation, I can now settle down and I can get down to what is really on my mind (and don't ask me what mind), to say nothing of what's down in my heart (way down deep).

I imagine you are a little disgusted with the last letter you received from me, which was dated the twelfth of this month. I was slightly disappointed when you told me the way you went gallivanting around that night with my old bosom buddies. Of course, it may have all been in fun, but now-a-days, "one never knows, do one?" Anyhow, I have already forgotten it as I know I can trust you.

How are you coming along in those cooking lessons that you have been taking from that dear aunt of yours? I hope you can now cook something else besides spaghetti and meat balls (even though I crave it as I do). After all, when I get that thirty day leave in the near future, I am expecting a good home cooked meal at least once, and by your own sweet little "paws." You savvy, don't you?

I am really missing you, Honey, as you no doubt will find out when I get back to the good old corner, and this time I won't have a rendezvous with a couple of taverns as previously I had committed on my last leave so long ago. This time, it will really be just we two first, and the gallivanting will come afterward. I mean, we will be available for foursomes after the first two nights, and of course, if any of my buddies are home at the time, I know you won't mind my running around with them a few nights.

Well, sweets, I guess you know that I love you and nothing will ever change my mind about you. So as the cramps are beginning to form in my buddy's arm, I'm afraid I will have to close for now, until either my fingers get better or else I can get another secretary to dictate to.

Oceans of Love (and I do mean the whole five), Slabby

February 25, 1945

Hello, Honey,

Well, this is old faithful back, writing again after a short intermission of only a couple of days. See I can't stay "sore" at you... not when they play such lovely music as I'm listening to now. "I'll Get By" just finished playing and how true, how true.

Today is Sunday and after a whole solid week of staying home, I'm just about ready for the "booby hatch." You know it's easy to tell yourself that you're going to stay home, "but" when your girlfriends start coming over with, "Aw, come on

out, just tonight, Slabby won't mind. Don't be a deadbeat."
That's only a little sample of what I'm up against. But don't
worry, your blessed, little "angel" would never think of
breakin' her word and besides I don't think I could really
enjoy myself with you constantly in my mind. Now could I?

Say, are you sure there's an arrangement of "Flamingo"
by Krupa? Dolly and I were out all over lookin' for it. Maybe
you can suggest some place to go. (I'm still talking about the
record. So.)

The top three hits of the week are: 1. " Ac-cen-tu-ate the
Positive," 2. "I Dream of You" (and how!), 3. "Don't Fence
Me In" (See I'm not the only one moanin').

"Smoke Gets In Your Eyes" is now giving out. Mellow.
Oooh listen! "Is You or Is You Ain't My Baby," boy, do I feel
like dancing. Say, at this rate, it looks as if you're gonna have
to teach me how all over again. At least we'll have something
to do between all those kisses I'm waiting for, uh? Boy, how I
wish you were dancing with me now. Harry James is now
playing, "Moonlight Becomes You," and how that song brings
back memories.

Looks as if I'll have to postpone the letter for another
short while—Laverne and Dolores just came over to "get my
goat"—telling me about all the fun they had last night and
such. But that didn't bother me in the least. I think they're a
little jealous 'cause I've got "something" to really wait for.
And I keep telling them better times are coming, you'll see.
The longer I wait, the more fun I'll have. I'll still be young and
full of life while you sacks will be helping each other down the
stairs and probably too worn out to walk 'way over to Ogden
for a movie. (That's when I had to hide behind a chair to
escape the furniture they were throwing at me.) All kidding
aside, if I sound like I don't wanna stay at home, you can add
it to that list of trimmings, which I'm supposed to get when
you get home, Muscles.

I, too, hope it's warm enough to go on moonlight dips
when you get home. I always did wonder what it would be
like. I just hope it's like my imagination says it is.

I was talking to your sister, Marie, with some of the other girls up at the candy store. Well anyway, we—she, and the others got to talking about cooking so I asked your sister what Swiss steak was. I didn't even finish saying what I wanted when she says—oh! That's Sally's favorite dish. We used to have it almost every Saturday, and then she told us how she burned the rice the first time she made it, etc. But she knows how to make it now, so she'll just have to come over and cook for us, and watch the little kiddies, while she's at it. Just 'til I learn how. Okay!

Say, speaking of records, I'd like to send you a couple of sweet ones that just came out, but I'm not sure I'd be able to safely send 'em. Everyone I asked isn't sure either, so you tell me. And if it's possible, then you put down a couple you'd like to hear to chase away those lonesome hours 'til you get home. Alreet!

Everyone at the corner seems to have given up loafing for the duration. I saw Willie and Georgie at Kelly's, and to show you I mean what I say, I refused their invitation to go "out." See. But that was a battle with my will-power, but, and how. I just kept seeing your eyes in front of me with a funny sort of gleam in 'em. How's about it?

I didn't go to work again Saturday. That makes three days out of six. Boy, am I getting' terrible.

If it weren't for this #xo!*! War, I think I would have been out on my ear long ago. It doesn't hurt my conscience in the least, and they do need what little help they can get (and that's just what they get from me). I never did stay long at one place anyway. But this is one exception. I got all of $50 saved in their credit union. Can you imagine? That's just a start though. I expect to get a higher paying job in the near future and throw that sum into the safest bank in Chicago. Ah yes, I have my ideas about money.

Well, let's get off that boring subject. (Boy, do I sound money hungry.)

And how is my wonderful Navy man getting along and when is he coming home?

Boy, it's really torture to listen to all these sweet songs on the radio and not be able to dance with you or be near you (sitting on your lap, I mean). Lately, Honey, the days seem to drag and drag, and it seems if you're coming home will never happen. And during these home-staying days, I seem to miss you even more.

Guess what? I finally had my dream on you. Yep, finally! Say, are you really that sweet? Boy, I sure hope so. Then I know my waiting was not in vain. But, Honey, do hurry home. I guess you know by now that I do love you, and I want to be with you more than anything I ever wanted before. And when you get home, don't think I'll expect you to see me every day. I know you'll want to spend a lot of time with your old cronies, "but"... Do you remember the song, "My Mama Done Told Me?" It's playing on the radio now. I used to like that song.

And so, my sweetheart, as the days when you'll be home and I'll be safely in your arms, is drawing near, my love for you is getting more "violent" and intense. And here's hoping you know how to control it. (Am I kidding?)

Will have to be closing for now before I get writer's cramp and I won't be able to write to you for a long time.

So adios for now my love, always yours, Loretta

P.S.

Were you kidding about that necklace?

175

Chapter 14, March 1945

March 1, 1945

"A Mar"

Dearest Loretta:

Well, Honey, here I am once again, just trying to express to you in writing, how much I really care about you. Since I'm no Shakespeare, you'll have to help me out a bit by using a little of your imagination, and then my thoughts will reach you without any strain. I would much rather be right next to you in reality, instead of spiritually, and then you would really find out how much I love you. Consequently, fate won't permit it for a couple of months, but then look out!

I guess you know that I'm using my own "paw" this time, but you probably knew that when you glanced at the first character. I suppose it seemed a little strange having another guy writing a letter for me, but I just had to, "Irish." After you read this letter and spend about three hours trying to "break it down," you'll probably tell me, "Why in the Hell don't you slam a door on your right hand again so you can have some guy write for you always."

Boy, you are really wicked that way, but I'll tell you what—when I get a home, I'll translate any part you have difficulty with, for you. That sounds fair enough doesn't it?

February surely flew by like grease lightning. It went by so fast that I think I only had a chance to write you about three or four times at the most. I know that you know that I would have written more oftener if I could, but it's impossible when at almost any minute you're afraid that you'll get your (three-four words cut out of letter by the Navy censor).

Since March has already begun, and I have started it off with a bang by writing to you on the first day, I'll try my utmost to "keep em' flying." I'll try and make up for it somehow (I'm speaking about February, of course). We've been out to sea for a month and a half now and naturally the mail situation is terrible. The last time I received any of that precious literature from you was on the twelfth of February and that is a mighty long, long time.

A few days after the twelfth, a fast cruiser caught up to us and gave us some mail by using the heaving line to pass it from ship to ship. It sure is exciting when there is some mail for you in that "batch," but it's about the dullest thing on earth when you don't receive any. I got a letter from Libby and my Unk that day. It sure made me feel good, but I would have felt much better if a letter from you was in that "batch."

(The censor removes a few sentences)

I've been singing for the past few days, "Davy keep that ocean quiet," (any similarity between milkman and bottles with the above is purely accidental) but it is all in vain, it seems. They had better hurry.

(Censor removes a couple more sentences)

I managed to find a few minutes each day during the dull periods to read a very interesting book. *A Tree Grows in Brooklyn* was the name of the "gizmo" and it was one of the best books I ever read in my life. I hope I get a chance to see the picture, but I don't see how it will possibly be able to compare with the book. This must be rather boring to you so I'll change the subject, but to me, especially out here, it keeps reminding me that there still is such a thing called the "States."

You know, Honey, your birthday is only twenty-three days away and I can't even buy a postage stamp where I'm at. I'd really like to get you something nice to remember me by, but what can I do? This war sure is a pain in the neck in more ways that one—you don't know who started it do you? I'll be thinking of you more than ever on your birthday and hope you're able to see seventy-five more of them with each one increasing in happiness. I'd like to spend all of them with you, too, in fact I'll make a note of that right now.

I'll always love you, Lor, and will always be near you no matter what happens. I have to "turn-to" now, but nevertheless, it won't stop me from thinking about you—not just for a day, not just for a year—but always.

Loving you forever, Sal

P.S.

If you get some time send a few pictures out this way, Honey

March 4, 1945

The crew sees the first B-29, crippled from a raid over Tokyo, land on the airfield at Iwo Jima. Every night, the Japanese harass the crew of the Signet, but they don't do much damage. The crew is alert, anxious and tired. The mail situation is bad with no deliveries being made.

Hello Honey:

Well, Sweets, I've found another few moments to write to the love of my life. I don't know what I'm going to write about, darling, but you know me, I'll surely try my best. At least I have your picture by my side for a very helpful inspiration, and you are sweet—yea man!

If they don't deliver us some mail pretty soon, my morale is going to drop below the absolute zero point and sister that am mighty cold—brrrr. To tell you the truth, it has only been about three weeks, and I think I could stand about twenty-four more hours without any mail—but not a minute longer.

Things have quieted down to almost a minimum out here and it's about time. After all, I'm too young to die—well, that's what I keep telling myself—but I won't believe me.

Here's a little ditty I picked up, which I thought you might like to read. You probably have seen it already, but out here everything is behind time, so don't go beefing. We still think the "horseless-carriage" is the most beneficial invention of the year.

Just the other day someone told me that "Indian Summer" was no longer on the "hit-parade." What do you think of that? Just as I thought, you don't think. Don't! Hit me, Honey, I'll take it back.

I managed to play a little cards the last few nights, and after I finish this letter, I'm going up in the mess-hall and teach a few buddies of mine the fundamentals of "Hearts." You remember that "Talman Terrace" past-time, don't you? For Heavens sake, Honey, don't let Scully get wind of my turning instructor in the game of Hearts or else he'll want to pack his suitcase and come out here and teach me the way it should be played. He and I used to be partners back on the corner and I use to get caught with "Dirty Nora" so many times it ceased to be funny. Would he give out a yell whenever we had to bury the beer (that word really tastes good, yum yum) and we only had to bury it always.

Somehow, I was able to pick up some good music the other day. "T.D.," "B.G.," and last, but not least, "G.M.," were really giving out with all those old "goodies." I wish you were here with me so we could struggle out a couple of hundred numbers. It wouldn't be no struggle though, in fact, it'd be much on the contrary. Most of the times there is so much interference from storms, distance, etcetera that you don't know whether they're playing the "Russian Anthem" or "Chinese Chopsticks."

Boy, I bet you never could guess how much I really miss you, Honey. It's going to be a great day when I lay my "blinkers" on you again. You have to promise not to take my breath away to any great extent. After all, I might be short-winded and then what! Well, I'll tell you, you would have a case of rigor-mortis on your hands, and that would be bad for one's disposition, wouldn't it?

We're about due to get relieved out here and head to some group of islands for rehabilitation. I certainly could use some rest and some nice warm sunshine again. After that rest, I might be heading back home (I meant to spell it HOME but accidentally forgot). If not, it won't be much longer.

Before I close, Lor, I want you to know that I'll be loving you the rest of my life even if something does turn up. For my part, I don't see how it possibly could happen. I sure hope we both see alike. Well good-bye for now and write as often as you can.

Yours Forever and a Day, Sal

March 6, 1945

My dearest sweetheart,

Gee, it seems so long since I last wrote that I don't know exactly how to start, except, I haven't heard from you for such a long time that I seem "lost" without your letters. I know this shouldn't be so, but after all, ours is no ordinary love affair—now is it? But if you really want to know the real reason—just between you and me—"laziness," that's what it is, just plain , ordinary laziness (and you'd better not agree with me—see!)

I'm listening to some very sweet music now, that's when I miss you the most I think—when I hear all of that mellow music. It just sets me to thinking and wanting you, "More and More."

Boy, it's really "painful" to want someone like I want you, and not have you or be able to do anything about it either. Just wait. Well, I've been waiting for you like a good girl—meaning: on Monday I play volleyball—just like I used to, remember? Tuesday and Thursday I go swimming at Philmore—and guess what? I've finally mastered the swan dive, can you imagine? And I'm telling you me, it's lucky I come home with no broken bones trying to do that jack knife dive. But I'll keep trying. On Wednesdays and Fridays I watch the fellas from the corner play basketball, and then go to the show. And last Saturday, I went to a surprise birthday party. It turned out pretty good—and oh yes, Sunday, I stayed in Church all day—Yeah! As you see, I've broken away from my old crowd and spend my time solely with good old Dolly—But I'se telling you, you'd better hurry home but quick... this solitude is almost killing me—and I'm mighty sure you wouldn't want to take out a corpse when you hit home (When?)

Oh, Honey, they're playing and singing, "Stardust," and would I like to be with you sitting in our parlor (with one little light on to give a shadowy effect) and just sit with your hand holding mine and talk, "but I dream in vain."

So, nighty nite, my sweet and I sign curiously in love with you??? Loretta

---

Tuesday Evening

Hello, Honey:

Well, Sweets, here's your faithful "beau" leaving you know once again that I'm feeling fine except for a fractured skull, and my morale can't be beat unless with a whip, and now, how about you? Just as I thought, you're always beefing. What is it now, didn't your boss give you a raise or did he go one better (worst is a more pertinent word—but what the Hell!) and fire you.

Of course, you know I was only kidding in the above paragraph, don't you? I'm feeling pretty good both in health and morale. I'll have to take the latter back mainly because of the mail situation. If I don't get some letters from you pretty soon, I'll have to start writing my troubles to Miss Fixit. Wait a minute! Didn't you claim once that you were just as eminent as the previously mentioned character? You've got me stuck—now who am I suppose to tell my troubles to? The Chaplain died last week!

I'll be back with you in a jiff, Honey, so don't go running away. We're having a movie and seeing that we don't have them very often, I had better not miss it.

Well I was only gone an hour, bet you didn't even miss me. Boy, you are really wicked. What am I going to do with a sweet lovely girl like you or have you grown into a gorgeous woman instead??

Getting back to the first paragraph again, it's amazing how I can lie like that and still live with myself. If I find out, I'll leave you know.

You know, Lor, I first took a liking to you so long ago that I can't remember exactly when. As the days rolled by, the last three characters of "like," began to change into love, and it's been increasing ever since. I don't think it will ever stop and it had better not. You're very easy to look at, lovely personality, and it's rather hard to improve your sense of humor. Last, but not least, you have some "living material" in that "noggin" of yours. I guess I've told you this a million times and I'll tell you another million if necessary, so you had better believe me when I tell you that I'm madly in love with you regardless of whether you're really in love with me. You had better be or "alright for you."

The movie was pretty whacky, but that's what a fellow needs out here is some good belly-laughs. Maybe it seemed pretty good because I haven't seen a movie in such a long time, but what's the "diff," just as long as I enjoyed it one way or another, mostly another.

Say, I'm ready to run out of ink. I can hear the pen gasping for "water" already and I haven't any ink in the locker. How about sending over a spoonful by rocket before my pen drops dead on me? Oh well, we'll just leave it die and give it a military funeral in the morning.

Don't stare at me that way, after all, you got me this way, what are you going to do about it, eh? Not a darn thing! It looks like you turned out to be the lazy one and not me as you once commented.

I'm writing this letter all by my lonesome, so if you're not too busy, why don't you drop around and then we can indulge in a nice quiet game of "checkers." Of course, if you want to stay at home, it's alright too, 'cause, I'll be there in a very short time from now. I'd say about May at the latest and then Honey—Look-out! Anything goes! What am I saying? I had better change the subject in a hurry before a rolling-pin comes crashing over my dome and smashes the last brain I own.

Managed to take in a shower this afternoon. It sure seems funny taking a shower about once every ten days, but what can a guy do about it? "Things Ain't What They Use To Be," no siree.

Last night, I was listening to some of the better records that are aboard and did they put me in a reminiscing mood. When one hears, "Rusty Dusty Blues" by Count Basie, G.M.'s "In The Mood," and D.E.'s "Don't Get Around Much Any More"—Boy, it's just like old times. When we get together again, are we going take in all the "Sweet And Lowdowns" all over the city. But until that happy day, Baby, I'll have to be contented with, "I'm Making Believe," and then again, your picture goes a long way, too.

Goodnight, "Irish." I'll see you in my dreams, so don't go disappointing me now.

Loving You Eternally, Sal

March 7, 1945

The USS Signet leaves Iwo Jima and heads back south to Ulithi in the Caroline Islands where the crew hopes their mail will be.

Dearest Sweetheart:

Gosh, oh me, Honey, but did you make me happy as a skylark or didn't you? Three luscious letters from you, darling, and did they send my heart skipping. I owe you so much loving that we'll both have to live to about two hundred years of age before I can even think of getting even with the "debt." Don't go worrying your pretty little head about not getting paid in full, the thing you'll have to worry about is getting over-paid!

This is the first mail I received in about three weeks and it sure was worth waiting for. I like the way you put down things in your own little way. Something new, something blue, sometimes sweet, sometimes neat, but it is always enjoyed tremendously by your "worst half." We're just "naturals" for one another, Honey. That's all there is to it.

The last letter I received prior today, was a letter from you dated the 31st of Jan. The three I received today (all from you) were dated the 17th, 20th and 21st, so I expect there are some that haven't caught up with me as yet. And if there aren't any between the 31st and 17th, I'm going to take you over my knees (yes, both of them) and give you Hell. If you don't think I'm strong enough, young lady, just wait and see that's all, just wait and see! Confidentially, I can hardly wait for that day to arrive. My pulse gets all excited just thinking of it.

I still have all of your letters saved and I'll bring them home with me if you wish and we'll keep them all together. You can hold them all if you desire, and then some day when we get old together, we can look back on them as a glorious beginning. They may be tattered and torn, but what the Hell, that's the way nature treats everyone sooner or later. After all, it's their contents that count, and they'll always be readable, unless you use them to plug up your bathtub.

Well, sweets, we're finally going to get a little rest on some island down south. It's about time we got away from this place and headed for a warm climate. I've just about caught a head cold in the three weeks we've been here, and colds and I don't agree no how. Anyhow, one of my fingernails came off and it's about time, 'cause those creatures are parasites when they get smashed pretty bad. Now, all I have to do is wait for the new one to finish growing. I hope it grows faster than I did and no comments, please.

Do you mean to tell me there is a curfew in effect in Chi now? Oh—nooo—it just can't be true. Who in the Hell is responsible for this, and now that I'll be home very soon, who is the boy that will have to go into hibernation when I get there? It's either hibernation, or his life, one of the three.

You're not kidding when you say, "now I really have you worried."

Boy, those gray hairs are shooting out already. We'll go by your house and have coffee and _____ and what??? Do you realize that I drink so much "Jamoke" on these Mid-watches that I'm beginning to look like a coffee bean? Oh well, mama knows best—so they say. But that clause that follows, "and," had better be very "neat."

Well, Honey, I was pretty darn sleepy when I started this letter, but now I'm only more so. Wish I could lay against your shoulder and travel into dreamland, but that will have to wait until later. Goodnight, Honey, and please have a dream on me tonight, it'll make me feel a whole lot better.

Loving and Trusting You Always, Slabby

March 9, 1945

Still at Sea

Dearest Lor:

Say, Honey, I still can't get over those three beautiful letters I received from you a couple of days ago. Every time I get a spare moment, and they are very spare, I read those beauties over and over again, and they seem to grow more luscious with each reading.

Don't think me mean, but that last letter in which you were soooo angry really made my heart miss a note or three. When we're together again, I'm going to ask you to repeat the same thing underneath some beautiful moon passing through a low hanging cloud. I imagine that you will be so pretty with the rays falling on your brown hair that I'll just smother you with kisses. Imagine—Hell! It has to be a reality and no objections please, because they will only be over-ruled.

(Censor removes several sentences)

Sweets, "What a difference a day makes," or two or three to be more exact.

They're getting pretty generous aboard now. They let us take showers every four days and don't think that I'm one to object. I just got through with one and now I'm up here on the fo'castle writing to the "Girl of My Dreams," and I mean every word of the lyrics.

This is the first time in a long time that I had a chance to come up here and write. It's so refreshing with these nice cool breezes sweeping over the bow that it reminds you of an ice-

cold Coca-Cola or a delicious bottle of Schlitz beer. What do
the two above beverages taste like nowadays? It seems that I
forgot how refreshing they really are. I haven't tasted either
one in such a long time.

Well, Honey, it's almost sunset, so I had better have a
smoke before they "darken ship." You don't smoke, do you,
'cause if you do indulge, we'll smoke this one together. Well, if
you do smoke, it had better not be a corn cob pipe.

It seems that you and Dolly are getting to be pretty good
friends. She's a nice kid and there are very few of the female
species that can top her. I'm afraid I'll have to admit though,
that you're one of them. Now, how much loving have I coming
from you when I get back?

Say, was I with you that night when you traveled off to
dreamland? I must have been because I tried my very best.

Speaking of those lovely dreams I had on you, Lor, I
think it'd be much better if I told you about them when I got
home. A few were really potent and if I told you them now, it
would only take the kick out of it. Don't forget to remind me,
and likewise I'll remind you of that one where you guaranteed
me a kiss for every second word. It had better be an
encyclopedia or else I'm going to be might disappointed.

I'm sorry for flying off the handle like I did in one of
those letters so, "What Can I Say After I Say I'm Sorry,"
huh? I was a little upset at things in general and that's one of
the main reasons.

Remember what you said about an up-to- to date
picture? Well the time has come, Honey, so you had better get
that.

I'm down in the mess-hall again and, sister, it's hotter
than a blast furnace working overtime. Have the mellow
records out now and as the "Duke" is giving out with, "Don't
Get Around Much Anymore," how I wish you were with me
dancing to it. I'd hold you so close that you'd think we were
one, any objections? No, well that makes things perfect!

Well, Honey, I'm going to travel off to dreamland, so I'll meet you there. You very seldom fail to show up and I don't think this is one of them nights.

Buenos Noche, Mi Amor, Sal

March 10, 1945

The USS Signet resides at Ulithi from March 10th to 19th. The crew gets a well-earned rest including a beer party that includes swimming and hunting for coconuts and shells. They get their mail, too – after it had gone to Iwo Jima and back. With the Iwo Jima campaign completed, relaxation periods alternate with stints of work to prepare for their next operation: Okinawa.

March 11, 1945

Lorretta, My Love,

Here I am again, writing a couple of words to the one I love and worship the most in this whole wide world (I guess you know that covers a lot of territory), excluding none, except my family. Just how are you on this glorious (or is it miserable) day, only eleven days plus one from your birthday? I hope you are still thinking of me just, "Once In A While," because, Honey, wherever I may look, you're always in focus, and whatever I may be figuring out, you always seem to pop up. Yes-sir, Honey, you're always on my mind, though not out of sight, and it really is appreciated. When I get back, I'll really show you.

We just have arrived at some pretty islands (every island that has vegetation I call pretty, so don't misinterpret me) and we are going to rest up for awhile. Our mail was supposed to be waiting for us here (that is all the back mail from the twelfth of February), but just before we arrived, they sent the mail up north where we previously were and now we have to wait for it to come down again. Does that burn my topper or does it? I thought surer than the dickens that I'd have about twenty letters from you waiting here, and then they have to pull a boner like that.

Seeing that there is no other alternative, I guess, "I'll Have to Sit Right Down and Write Myself a Letter, and Make Believe it Came from You. It's going to sound so mighty sweet, it's going to knock me off my feet," etc. Do you remember that old Fats Waller number? I thought you would.

Guess I'll have to dream the rest and like it.

We might be here a week for rest and recreation, and then we go gallivanting around this damn ocean looking for trouble. Of course, I might get transferred back to the States before this short rest period is up and I'll be in your arms by April. Gee, Honey, are we going to make up for lost time or are we! Every night will be spent under some mellow moon or else some pretty rain cloud. It doesn't make much difference to me, just as long as it's you that's in my arms. You had better get all the sleep you can while you're able, 'cause I can't guarantee you very much siesta time when I'm "knocking on your door-step and a whistling at your door." Don't say I didn't warn you.

About two days ago was I happily surprised. I was tuning the radio for some jive, then all of a sudden out of nowhere, I picked up some music that came all the way from the Panther Room in the Sherman Hotel. Raymond Scott was the maestro that was giving out with the music. Was my heart missing a few beats every now and then. Say, Honey, you and I are going to have to take in old Benny Goodman's hangout. It's really a neat joint.

That guy with that so called title of "Jr." knew his stuff when he said I was very fortunate. I bet he went to college.

Don't forget, Honey, keep on writing as often as possible, 'cause each and every letter helps show me how much you really care.

Everlasting Love, Slabby

P.S.

Won't you please send a photo before it's too late?

March 13, 1945

How's every little thing around the neighborhood these days? Is the twelve o'clock Lamplighter serenade having any effect on the "peoples" around there? Just as I thought, they still can get all the vodka they want to drink after hours. What a life. Yea Man.

Now that I think back, it comes wandering through my perforated skull that I've been writing you a letter every other day since old windy March began. Pretty good I would say, but you wouldn't listen now, would you? Just kidding, of course.

I had a pretty swell time yesterday, that's of course in comparison with the times I've had since the last two months have elapsed. We're resting up on some islands (nice and warm), for a little while, just long enough to catch our breath, and as I was saying, yesterday, we went on the beach and had a beer party. The "Pebble" was filthy with coconut trees, and scenic, in a round about way, but I guess I never went around that way. I managed to guzzle down about five cans of Budweiser beer, and after the fifth one, I thought I was swimming in Lake Michigan. I'll have to drink beer more often so that good old lake comes flowing by more oftener.

After the beer, I went swimming in the same old Pacific with the rest of the boys, and baby, was that water mellow. Had a lot of fun trying to drown one another, but somehow, after we ducked a guy, he managed to live.

After a while, it got pretty disgusting when no rigor mortis cases developed, so when we slapped our clothes back on and I was about fully dressed, they threw me back into the "drink." I'm still drying out, that is the pneumonia and I. You haven't an extra pair of—wait a minute what am I saying? I had better start dropping coconuts on my head so it'll be use to the pounding which it'll undoubtedly get when you lay your hands on me. I had better drop the subject before I start giving you hints.

Right now I'm listening to *Bob Hope's Circus* and is that guy a card. It's little things like that that keep reminding you that there is such a thing as back home. Don't go getting the idea that I'm down-hearted or something of that sort—it's just that after being out here for so long, it's rather hard to visualize the setting back in the States. Of course mail is the best "pepper-upper," but the trouble is that we haven't been getting any for quite some time.

I have been satisfied with those three letters from you about the 20th of February, but one of them—whenever I start reading it again, I can feel a black eye coming up. You really gave me the work in that one, Honey, but you were right, and I should have known better, but a guy's brain gets more or less contaminated out here, and they aren't passing out any new ones lately, so-oooo.

I seem to be hearing quite a lot of, "There Goes that Song Again." It's pretty neat, but tell me, is it dropping or has it already dropped?

By the way, "coffee and —???," have you been getting any records lately? You know, if you haven't a "Chanute-box" at home, we could always go to my abode and see if the phonograph is still working. If it isn't (and there will be hell to pay), I'll leave you sing and I'll whistle underneath some nice big mellow moon. It wouldn't be too hard to dance to now, would it, skylark?

Just went out on the boat-deck to get a breath of fresh air, and I've notice something very peculiar about this new group of islands we come to rest on and that is there are really trade winds down here. I never felt such a cooling breeze at night in all my life and that even takes in Lake Michigan. It really is nice down here just as long as we don't stay here too long.

I'd really like to have a vacation on a nice snug island like this with you in my arms all the time. No worries, no taxes, no nothing, but love and that would be exquisite don't you think? Go swimming all day and park all night, my my.

Since you're so nice about sending things to me, here is a little "gizmo" that isn't too bad either.

Am closing for now with all the love in the world,

Yours forever and, Slabby

(Poem enclosed)
I never kiss, I never neck,
I never say hell, I never say heck
I'm always good, I'm always nice,
I play no poker, I shake no dice,
I never drink, I never flirt,
I never gossip or spread the dirt,
I have no line or funny tricks,
But what the hell—I'm only six:

March 15, 1945

Dear "Love of my Life":

Gee Honey, I don't think that twelve page letter could be beat if I had to make a call on Maestro Shakespeare himself and tell him to make with the pen. All I can say is that I love you, I love you and (once more) I love you. Our mail is really fouled up and when I get one of the sweetest letters I ever got and ever expect to get until my ticker stops beting (an "a" goes in that last word somewhere), well I guess you know that you're the only one that could possibly be made for just poor me and no one else would do. Sometimes I don't think I deserve the secluded right to be next to your side when this is all over, but sweets, you'll know that I will always be trying my best to make you the happiest woman in the world, excluding none.

I imagine you are lonely, but I hope you don't think I'm a heel when you say you're lonely, 'cause I'm lonely too. If you want to go out and have a good time every now and then, I won't mind too much just as long as you leave your conscience be your guide. I'm not going to preach to you 'cause I know that you're too intelligent to misinterpret me. You know what I mean, Honey. I'll always be thinking of you no matter where your little feet may be wandering, and not only thinking of you, but also longing (and I do mean longing for you.) So,

Honey, save a few thoughts for me whenever you go out gallivanting.

You mean to tell me that you couldn't pick up Gene's "Flamingo," Boy, Honey, am I going to have to take you over my lap for that. I guess it's pretty hard to find all of those favorites nowadays, that is unless you happen to know some of the syndicates that are manipulating in that branch. I don't know if you ever tried a little hinky-dinky record joint on Roosevelt just a little off the street where Central Park Theatre is (see, I still remember some of the streets), but I know I used to pick up quite a few neat records when I was back there. But regardless of the consequence, "Flamingo," should be in your sweet little paws (by Krupa of course) by the time I get back there.

I hope you don't mind me typing this letter instead of using my paw, but Honey I just got back off of a beer party (which you undoubtedly can tell by all of these mistakes), and I'm pretty sure I can make better headway by using a "mill" instead of a pen.

If my sis don't teach you how to make some exquisite Swiss steak, you tell her that I'm going to tan her little fannie, but good. After all, I can't eat beans (boy, that is an ugly word) all my life or will I? I couldn't think of a better cook in this world I would rather have than you and I really mean it.

Seeing that I mentioned a beer party a little forehand, I think it's proper that I should mention the consequences that follow (no matter what one may do, there always seem to be such trifles called consequences that lag not more than a dog's tail behind), this predicament that I got in. Well—and thus ...

After having quite a number of beers in my tummy, and Budweiser at that, we decided to go in swimming. Don't start worrying about females being in the picture. The only thing way out here besides us are coconut trees, and that is a hell of a comparison with the above.

Anyhow, as I was saying. I was flying blind and decided to take a running dive into the incoming waves. Well, I dove alright, but the damned wave went rolling by too fast and when I hit, there was nothing left but some sweet coral. To get the point a little more abruptly like, I just come sliding in on my face and does it look like a meat grinding production or does it? If you saw me now, you would probably be throwing rocks at me the rest of my life. It isn't as bad as I may exaggerate, but I sure looked mighty bloody for a moment.

The scratches will be healed up before you can say, Yebrokoswzlirslinsky. This isn't the first time I banged myself up while swimming on one of these (coral) atolls. Somehow me, beer, and coral don't agree for no how. What do you suggest? I hear you talking, Honey, I'll take the very next plane back. Don't forget to be waiting for me in your best.

The beer party wasn't as bad as the above may lead you to believe, of course I lost a little playing "dominoes." :/:

We are still at these islands resting up after our last encounter and will probably be shoving off for some other engagement pretty soon. I was expecting to be heading back to the States after the latest one, but I guess you have to lose a few toe-nails and then some before they judge you fit to enter that beloved land. Well, if everything keeps on riding smooth, I ought to be coming back in one piece, I hope.

Can you imagine, I couldn't enjoy the movie tonight because of these so called trade winds that keep whistling in your ears and thus prevent you from hearing what's going on? But (gulp) if I had you next to me, it would be too, too divine and the trade winds could howl all they wanted to, in fact the louder the better, I would say. Alreet, dig, dig, dig... /

Say, Irish, I guess that necklace that I mentioned must have been lost somewhere on its way over. It happens every time. I know you would have liked it, because it was pretty neat, but there's no use crying over spilt milk, so we might as well drop the subject and chalk it up on experience.

You know, gorgeous, it's only eight days away from your birthday and I still haven't been to a place civilized enough to buy you a nice present. You know, "something to remember you by." And, Honey, that really burns me up something tremendously. After all, I would like to send something dear to you so that you could always hold it by your side and treasure it the rest of your life, but as I said before, then come the consequences. Of course, I could send you a coconut tree, but ask me one question—what in the hell would you do with a coconut tree in Chicago? Well, I guess that answers that in a hurry.

Gee, Honey, would you mind when I get home if I could teach you all over again the fundamentals of dancing (that's if I still remember)? Of course there is one catch, and that is I would really hold you close, closer than you have ever been held before and we would be swaying away to, "Flamingo," "I Hear A Rhapsody," and "Stardust." How does that sound as the opening numbers to your sweet little heart?

Speaking of records, if you desire to send a few out this way, and it wouldn't be too much trouble on your part, you can take my word that it would be appreciated. As long as you put enough corrugated paper in it and make it secure, they would get here safely. A couple of years ago, my bro sent a few recordings of Australian jive all the way back to Chicago, and out of the whole bunch, not one of them broke. Of course, those people down there are so far behind in the musical world that it ceases to be funny, but it's the principle of the thing that counts. If you do, pick out which ones you think are becoming and that will be plenty sufficient. After all, your tastes are so similar to mine that you would have to be a detective to tell them apart.

Say, where did you pick up all that Spanish "lingo" that you used in this last letter. Pretty soon, I'll have to be calling you my Senorita Hermosa or something, and then what?

A little while back, I used to be able to pick up some sweet music from these islands that we would keep passing up, and the sweet "downbeats" that they would produce really made me homesick. I guess it's the first time I ever used that in any letter I ever wrote, but I have to admit, it's the truth. They would always seem to play more than any other pieces, "I Dream Of you," "I'm Making Believe," and "I Surrender, Dear." That last one might be a little aged, but it sure is mighty "neat." I seem to be a little puzzled up to when I'll exactly be home, everything seems to be so vague now, but when that time does come, I'll hold on to you forever and squeeze you so tight that you'll feel like next to kin of a lemon. So, Honey, if you keep on waiting, "I Promise You," it will not be in vain.

Boy, it's getting late and I had better hit my rack after what I've been through today, so you'll be there in my dreams, won't you?

All the love I have, Sal

March 17, 1945

(1945, of course)

Hello, Angel:

"At Last," sweets, they are finally starting to send us some of our back mail. Just received two luscious letters from you today, Honey, that were dated the 6th and 8th of February, and even though they were delayed, they were just like wine, always improving with age. So far, I have three letters from you that were written in Feb, the above two and that marvelous twelve page masterpiece that you made with the pen on the twenty-seventh.

Oops, wait just a minute, (I've been thinking and dreaming of you so damn often in the last few months that I can't seem to do anything else right, do you mind?) I also have three other letters written by you between the 18th and the 21st of the same month. I have more coming from that month, haven't I?

Gee, Sweets, I realized I didn't write to you hardly at all during Feb, but that was an awful busy month for this weather-beaten tub. But, Honey, while I couldn't write, I was doing my share of thinking about you in the day and dreaming of you at night. I didn't get my share of sleep that month, but when I did manage to sneak in a few hours, I always dreamed, and whenever I dreamed, it was always of you, you sweet angel. You were always so luscious and considerate that some how I wonder why you did have to pick on me, of all the people in the world, to be your faithful beau. Well I guarantee you, you'll never regret it! When I get home and we are alone on some beautiful night, I will tell you all about them. Then, Sweetheart, lookout, that's all, lookout!

Lately, whenever I start thinking about you (which is always), my heart and mind just fly away with their selves. I'm telling, Honey, it's the cruelest torture in this world to have you on one half of the world and myself on the other for such a long time. But when we're together again, I'm going to hold you in my arms and don't think for the moment that I'm ever going to leave you go. I'll squeeze you till you're blue in the face, kiss you till your lips are chapped and everything that's in the books, whether it's legal or otherwise.

As for Scully (the kind-hearted soul) giving me to you for all of two days, I can say he hasn't changed a bit. And I can say again, he's all fouled up. He and Goose are two of my best buddies, but I've changed a bit in certain things since I've been out here. A guy gets mighty lonesome on this ocean, and all he dreams of is back home and some sweet understanding girl that he can take care of forever, providing she burns the steak just once in a while to burn me up. I'm almost certain that I've found the right one, "At Last" (you'll have to play that "mellow" G.M. recording at your very next chance and just day-dream of us or if it's time for slumber land, then just fall asleep in my arms, okay)?

At least half of my leave will be spent with you, if you don't think me a bit too arrogant. That's, of course, if your sweet little "egg-beater" desires it that way. And we will have fun, plus all the loving you can stand, Honey, both body and soul.

They're leaving us tell what parts and engagements (and I don't mean with some other girl) we've been in after thirty days have elapsed since it's released to the press. Some of the ports and harbors are, "Lulu," Midway, Kwajalein, Mazuro, (that's where the most beautiful moon I ever saw was. I'll tell you all about it when we're swimming together some night), Enawetok and Tinian.

(Censor cuts out sentences)

I'll close for now, Honey, and meet you all alone at the quarry. Will you be there?

Loving you Always, Sal

March 19, 1945

The USS Signet departs Ulithi on the 19th with the ships of six sweep units and a gunboat support division.

Monday Night

Hello, Angel:

Now, how is the sweetest girl that was ever created feeling these days? That's the way I like to hear things ride, I did hear it that way, didn't I? I hope you're lonely at times though, 'cause you know I'm lonely, too.

Can you imagine, our short recuperation is over already? I'll never forget those islands as long as I live. Now how could I, when I went on three gorgeous beer parties with each one improving as they went along (if such a thing is possible)? Second, I've got a couple of nice scratches on my "noggin" to prove that I went swimming. Third, I hit the beach with a little "mazuma" and came back with an empty wallet, and last but not least by all means, I received a few mellow letters from you that I wouldn't part with for anything in the world. Gee, those "African Dominoes" is really an interesting game at times. It wasn't so exciting this time, though, they must have been loaded.

Here it is only four days from your birthday and where am I, out at sea sooo far away? I'm inclined to believe you at times as if we'll never meet again. The more time I have to my credit overseas, the further I go away from home. What blows my topper is when a guy that has five or six months out here, and the next day he's heading all east. Yes-sir, Honey, it's not what you know, but who you know in this outfit, but definitely. I should be home by June or July at the latest, and that will make a full two years. It seems more like two centuries, and I'm not exaggerating a bit. You'll still be waiting though, won't you, Honey?

Boy, the sea is really choppy today. I suppose you think I'm still drinking beer as I'm writing, but so help me, it's really the sea that is making us bob up and down like a cork. For once, I can't say "I wish you were next to me," because under these conditions, I don't think you would like it. Maybe I'm wrong, though.

Say "money-bags" how many Brinks Express wagons do you hire to carry your wages home on pay day? Take it easy there, Mrs. Rockefeller, now I don't know whether I should marry you for your bank account or just because it is you and only you. If I said the former, you would probably greet me with a shotgun when I got home, so I guess I had better not say.

By the way, The "Spot," that's the joint they opened up on 21st and Marshall Blvd. isn't it? When I get back, we'll take in all the dives from the South side to the North side and throw in the Western suburbs to boot. The latter is the better part anyway.

I'm glad you'll have your bathing suit ready at all times, 'cause after some nights, it'll be an impetuous (whatever that means) mistake not to take a dip in the lake or quarry. Who cares whether the night isn't too warm, I'll have you and vice versa, and that's all that counts, right?

You know, I've written you every other day since the first of March, but I'm afraid that record will have to stop in a few days. Not that I want to, but it's because we're going to be awful busy again and it'll also be longer this time.

I enjoy writing to you, 'cause every time I do, I feel like you're right by my side and that's what I wish for more than anything else in the world.

So before I close, Honey, I want you to know that I love you more than ever and please write as often as possible just to show me that you are thinking of me, "Once in a While."

Love That Will Never Cease, Sal

March 21, 1945

Hiya, Sweets:

Well, we're still at sea and "ain't" it a shame. The ocean is still rough and if you could just see some of these huge swells out here that tosses us around like a feather in a hurricane, it would really make your eyes pop out or your "blinkers" blink, however the case may be.

When this war is over, Honey, you're not going to catch your "worst half" roaming around the seas anymore or any other place as far as that goes. I'm just going to stay "put" as long as it won't be much trouble on your part to put up with me, but it has to be for, "Always," mind you. What, you're going to back out! Say "Simon," if you had another heart in your body it would be an orphan.

If you believe that last sentence, "Irish," I really am going to pound your fannie when I get home.

Did you mention something about Cowb and Scully getting into a little skirmish? (What in the Hell is the matter with those "Marble heads," did they leave all of their "kinicks" roll into the lagoon or what? Make out with a few explicit details on the matter, after all, Honey, I'm quite interested in what goes on amongst my old buddies.

I just got through with a "must" in this outfit, which is mainly a shower. What's this "Navy" turning into when they actually force you to a "bath" once every two weeks? Only kidding, of course. I wish I could take one as often as I wished, then they would have a heck of a time kicking me out.

Turning to an interesting subject for the time being—well what else could it be besides music? Of course, you're a heck of a lot more important to me than some "notes," but when you're both paired together with a little stardust thrown in and I'm around to collect the benefits, what more could one ask for? Any how, did you ever hear a cute little ditty called "Robin Hood?" I have only heard it twice, but it reminds me of you in that it is always running through my mind. So, Honey, next time, take your shoes off, it's a lot easier on my cranium.

I suppose you were quite peeved at me during the latter half of February for not writing at all, but don't blame me, it wasn't my fault. We were "sweeping" at Iwo three days before D day and then we just hung around till March taking in the show. Outside of shelling the beach a couple of times and seeing a few planes shot down, it was pretty monotonous. I wish I were home with you and then there would be some real excitement, you can quote me on that, sis. Now why in the Hell am I calling the girl of my dreams, "sis" for? I guess I really am cracking up.

Ever since we made for Iwo, our mail has really been fouled up. We leave the "pebble" and still no "Straighten Up and Fly Right," in the mail system. I was supposed to be heading home after Iwo, but I'm still out here. I guess I wasn't born right or maybe you have to wait until you're using a cane before they leave you see that dear old "Golden Gate." I wish I knew.

Well you sweet little chick, here it is only forty-eight hours from your birthday and I can't so much as give you a few everlasting kisses for a present. What a life for a mongrel to lead. This must cease, but in a hurry like. What do you suggest, Lor, after all, you're half of this bargain, too. It'll be a great day when we're together again, but "when" is really a question.

I'll drop you a sweet line on your birthday, but we'll probably be too busy by then and for quite some time afterwards. I wish I were there to share it with you (and I do mean share) but what can one do? Keep writing and praying and I'll be home before you know it.

Have to close for now:

Loving You More Than Anything in This World, Sal

P.S. Don't forget to stay sober on your birthday!

March 23, 1945

Hello, Darling:

Happy Birthday to the sweetest and the most interesting young woman I know. You noticed that I said woman! Yes-sir Honey, today "you yam a woman." I hope you didn't celebrate the occasion by stepping out and getting "Pluto." What I wouldn't give to be with you today (and always), Honey. It's a crying shame, so help me that we have to be separated at such a long distance and for such a long time. Things will change though, and in a couple of months "we" will get all of the loving that we want. You can count on that.

We are still at sea, so naturally I can't send you an exquisite gift as I would like to. Instead, Honey, all I can give you is the most prodigious kiss I am capable of producing. You'll find a lot more of them between the lines so don't forget to look for them.

I didn't think I would be able to write to you today, but luck was with us. I hate to mention this, darling, but this will definitely be my last letter for some time. Maybe two weeks, maybe a month and maybe even two months, but when this is over with, I'll be on my way home for thirty days, and most of them will be the time of my life, because they will be spent with you. Yes, you, you Darling.

I'm just dying of curiosity to see who will be affected by "sea sickness" first when we participate on those "Bobs" and other high rides in Riverview Park. You are probably a veteran of the above and at this, I'll have two strikes against me before I even enter the place. I guess you know, you gorgeous young lady, that that is cheating, and in the highest degree. But don't worry, I'm not so dumb, I'll get even with you when we go through all those tunnels that they have. And will I! Yea-man. When we come out of those "tunnels" will I look just dandy wearing "your" lipstick!

When that thirty day leave does arrive, you'll have to help me plan it out to the most precise moment. After all, the good things seem to pass by so fast, and we can't afford to waste even as much as thirty seconds or else you'll have another "trimming" coming to your credit. By the way, you have so many spankings coming that I have neglected to keep an accurate account of them. Now for Heaven's Sake, don't go taking advantage of my sincere honesty and say you have only six coming 'cause I'll swear it's at least ten.

Say, "Irish," have you found any secluded swimming-hole all by your lonesome that we can go swimming in at night and just hang around till the sun comes up? We'll greet that great big ball of fire by harmonizing on "Sunrise Serenade." If you think you can "drown" me once when we're swimming, then you had better start hiring Eleanor Jarret for a tutor.

But don't go worrying your pretty little head off on such trivial matters as "duckings." After all, we're not going to the beach by ourselves at night just to swim, now are we? There is bound to be a gorgeous mellow moon sailing overhead and every now and then between kisses, we'll take a gander at the "Old Man." Then right back to our original plan with me holding you ever so close. I can hardly wait for these glorious days ahead of us to become a reality. How about you?

Then comes the gallivanting around the various night clubs and dives. We'll manipulate around the town even if we have to drag your bike out of the basement. Of course, that will be the last straw, but you have such a lovely "bike" that we're just bound to have fun.

The sea is rather calm today, consequently, I'm not writing you on my head as I usually am. It's not the sea that worries me, but what we're liable to bump into. But don't go worrying 'cause I'll take care of myself to my very best ability. And why shouldn't I? Well I'll tell you. What sane guy wouldn't when he knows, "The Girl of His Dreams—Is Just Around the Corner," waiting for me?

Say, Honey, am I too bold when I ask you if you're going to cook me a meal when I'm home, just to see what your dainty hands can give out with? If you can't make it at your house, we can go somewhere all by our lonesome.

This will be my last night of sleep for some time, so won't you please be there? That is, in my dreams, of course. You

know, "Please give me something to remember you by."
You'll try your best, won't you?

Loving You Forever, Sal

March 25, 1945

*The USS Signet arrives off Kerama Retto, Okinawa
Gunto. She immediately begins sweeping minefields
around a staging area for the battle of Okinawa.*

March 31, 1945

Hiya, Angel:

How is the only girl of my dreams getting along on these
spring days? "Never felt better in my life!" Say, that was an
awful quick answer and a good one at that. I feel pretty good
myself, but I'd feel a Hell of a lot better (at least thirty times)
if I were home with you taking a casual stroll through Douglas
Park on some starry night after previously being "thrown
out" of some dive. Mind you, it wouldn't exactly be a "casual
stroll." After all, what do you think I've been thinking and
dreaming of these last umpteen months? You have just three
guesses, but the first three don't count.

You know, Honey, this is the first chance I've had to
write to you since your birthday! Before you get all hot under
the collar, why don't you take into consideration the number
of letters I have sent your way this month. This makes about
the thirteenth one and that, I think, is pretty good considering
that I never had too much time to myself during the latter
half of this month. This must be a little boresome to you,
especially when some of them haven't ever had a chance to fly
home and are still awaiting censorship.

We're still out at sea (answer me truthfully, can you think
of an uglier word than the last one I just mentioned?) But not
very far from a group of "pebbles," islands to you. These are
the most beautiful ones I've seen yet, with lovely blended
landscape and slopey mountain-sides covered with various

colored rocks. I even saw some wild mountain goats running around one of them. You know, I'll have a lot of "salty yarns" to feed you one of these days. That's of course, if you don't mind cuddling up close beside me and listening. Hey—who gives a damn if you listen, just be sure you cuddle up c-l-o-s-e-! Right-reet.

How is Chicago swinging along these days and is there still any snow on the ground? I suppose it's starting to rain like the dickens about this time of the year, but I wouldn't trade it for any other one in the whole wide world. And that goes for you too, in comparison with girls (scratched out) women (it's a good thing I remembered to scratch that word out or else I'd be suffering a severe case of bumps on the noggin' via mental telepathy of course) on this globe.

Say, what have you been doing with yourself, "Rockefeller," besides getting rich? You're not going out too often now, are you? After all, when I get home, I'd like to see you just as sweet and mellow as can be expected. You're not going to "renege" on me now, I hope. I don't mind you going out and having fun every now and then, just as long as it doesn't become habit-forming. I haven't any "beefs" coming so why should I discuss something that isn't a reality?

I should be speaking of something more interesting, like that dream I had on you the other night. It was really a humdinger, Honey, and if I had more time to explain the details I would most gladly. You'll have to be satisfied in just a few major points, which lead to swimming at McCook quarry on a moonlight night. The whole bunch of us were out there diving off the rocks and gabbing with one another on the small beach. But then it started to rain and everyone went home except us, and that's when the fun really started. We'll re-enact the situation when I get home, that's of course, if you don't think me too bold!

Loving you always, Sal

Chapter 15 April 1945

April 4, 1945

Hiya, Honey:

Well, here I am again, Sweets, writing to my only heart-throb as often and as much as my "brand new" brain can think of.

Say, the mail situation isn't treating you as bad as it treats us way out here, is it? I feel for you, if it is, but I'm afraid I can't reach you. But, oh, how I wish I could, Honey, oh, how I wish I could! It's a good thing one can dream 'cause your sweet face is always around, and that is about the only consolation a guy gets out here.

Right now, I'm further away from you than I've ever been before, but that's relatively in miles, not in thoughts. You're always by my side whenever I have a few minutes to think to myself, and I'm just waiting for that great reality to come when you'll be by my side for always. That day can't come too soon to suit me, and how about you, angel?

The way this damn war has progressed lately, it shouldn't be too long before it's all over with and then I can pack up my sea bag, walk up to the gangway, and drop it in the "drink," just to hear the water splash. Then will I make a bee-line for home and never more no roam. Of course, I may take an occasional trip every now and then, but it won't be very often, and that's a safe bet in almost any country. You no doubt will be with me, so why beef?

You should see these islands we're around now, boy, are they pretty. You can see where the old rough sea has pounded against the massive coral on the beach for centuries and left in its wake various designs of beautifully shaped rocks (it seems that lately all I think of is shapes).

At Iwo Jima, that volcano that's on the southwestern corner was a pretty fantastic sight, but I don't think the Marines liked it too much. Can't say as I blame them either.

You know at Iwo, we only saw one mine and that is only one too many. The less we see of them, the better off we are.

Now how about talking of something more important and exciting—that's us!

Say Irish, when I get home, you'll have to show me around to some new places. After all, "long time no see," and when I hit the lakefront, I'll be just like a hick from Missouri. But don't go worrying your pretty little head off, 'cause it'll only take about three minutes with a steady breeze from the lake acting as a catalyst, to bring me back to my old senses.

Then watch our smoke. We had better bring a fire extinguisher in case the "fire" gets too hot. Have they still got them excursion trips (moonlight of course) on the lake running to Milwaukee, etc? That would really be the berries, don't you think? It would be just like old times again.

I'll probably spend the first three days just admiring you and no one else. After all, Honey, we have to make up for lost time, but in a hurry-like. After all, thirty days flies by awful fast when you're home for the first time in a long time, and we dare not waste any.

Before I close, I want you to know that I love you tremendously and always will, until you say no. So don't ever let me hear you mention that discouraging word while I'm around.

Loving You Forever, Sal

April 7, 1945

Sister ships and combat air patrols take down Japanese planes. In the evening, the USS Signet receives a message from the USS Staunch (AM 307), indicating the approach of an enemy "Betty" (Japanese bomber). Gunners are able to see the bomber's exhaust flames as it approaches. At 2033, the port guns open fire. The plane passes low over the Signet and begins to catch fire as the starboard gunners open fire. Aflame, the plane splashes into the sea about 1,000 yards from the minesweeper. The

207

*wreckage floats and burns while the Signet searches for
survivors. Finding none, she returns to her patrol station.
The pilot's body was later recovered and brought on board.*

April 8, 1945

Hello, Honey:

Boy, these last few days have really been busy for us, but
from now on, I'm going to drop you a line every other day or
at least make a brave attempt at it. I love to write you,
Sweets, but there are a lot of times when it just isn't
permissible. After all, when this pen of mine is making with
the marks, it seems that you're always within kissing distance
and that isn't bad, is it?

Did you ever try writing while standing? Well, that's
what "yours truly" is doing right now. It's pretty rugged with
the ship rolling to and fro. I'm beginning to wonder which will
give first, my legs or elbows. Seeing as how they're both
sharing an equal amount of the weight, it looks like it will take
a little elementary to solve this. I know now that I should
have tried to make fifth grade. So what if I did spend two and
a half years in fourth, a little more study, and it would have
only taken me two.

Whenever we have a few moments to ourselves, we (two
New Yorkers, another Chicagoan and myself) always indulge
in a friendly game of "hearts," but it very seldom ends up that
way. What else could you expect, when these eastern boys
have a better signal system than the Navy has? The
Chicagoan and I are almost always partners, which is rather
logical I think. Anyhow, they seldom win a game. That
shouldn't seem too strange, seeing as how we taught them the
fundamentals of it. They almost always end up with "Dirty
Nora," but I can't blame them. A woman is pretty hard to
find out here in this neck of the woods and every little bit
helps. Whatever you do, don't get me wrong!

We'll leave my leisure time go for the present and get
back to "where I come from" for awhile.

I anticipate that you're quite an artist at the Polish Hop (polka). It's a funny thing, but seeing all of the Polish dance halls I use to go to, I never did get the hang of it. Maybe it was because I was afraid to let go of "steiny" (that's a glass of beer in case you can't make out the spelling) for a few minutes, but then on the other hand, maybe I was too busy picking up the "bodies" off of the deck. After all, there always are quite a number of "casualties" when that "hop" starts blooming. Well, there are always a lot of kicks to it and they fly in almost every unbelievable direction without respect of the fairer sex.

Maybe you're beginning to wonder just why I brought this subject up? Well, it could be that I've been hearing quite a bit of those Polish Hops recently, but I ain't snitching, see! Well, to get to the "purnt," when you and I are all alone either at your house or mine, you'll just have to teach me the fundamentals of it in between loving periods. Don't worry, I'll pay for all of the broken furniture. Okay?

I've been hearing quite a bit of mellow music lately. I heard old B.G. beat out, "Somebody Else Is Taking My Place" (what a gruesome title but such a mellow tune), and also a new one (I believe it's new), "I'm Beginning To See the Light." Gee, Honey, how I wish I could hold you close once again and just rain kisses on you, not just when they play some sweet notes, but always. I guess you know by now that you could be the only girl for me. If perchance you don't know, I think it's about high time you found out. You're always on my mind, Honey, and when I just take a little peek in the near future, when you and I will be together again, I simply start floating on a cloud. My heart starts beating like a Tom-Tom and thrills just run up and down my spine. We'll surely have to have coffee and " " at your house quite a few nights while we're lucky enough to be in each others arms.

Say "Irish," is your lovely brown hair still set up in the same style as when I left you almost two years ago (that is really a long time)? I was just sort of wondering 'cause if you have a new set-up, I might not be able to recognize you at first, but I'll always remember that sweet familiar face.

You know, Lor, we've been out to sea for such a long stretch now that I'm beginning to wonder if I'll ever find my land-legs again when I set foot on terra firma again. I think I remember what port I left them at now. I'll have to be sure we hit that port again. The last time I set my foot on that good old sweet earth was in January and that was quite some time ago.

So, Honey, before I close, don't forget to have a sweet, but luscious dream on me and I'll do likewise. I'll be seeing you soon, so have a lot of love all stacked up for me when I do.

Loving you Forever & then some, Sal

April 10, 1945

Dearest Loretta:

Good morning, Honey. I just got up not so long ago, about eighteen hours ago to be a little more explicit and I sure am feeling great. Maybe it's because I have such a gorgeous creature waiting for me when I get back home. Do you think that might have anything to do with it?

We're suppose to get some mail within a few days and I can hardly wait. Seeing that we haven't had any mail in such a long time, I can safely presume that there ought to be quite a few from you. Here's hoping I'm not disappointed. After all, mail is the closest thing between us and those sweet letters from you send my morale high into the sky. I can hardly wait until that day comes when I no longer will have to put everything I want to say to you down on paper. Instead, I'll just have to hold you ever so close and whisper sweet things in your ear. It isn't very far off when that day will come true.

I've been reading over some of your old letters during the last few weeks and I still "eat them up" just as much as when I first received them.

I'll have to take some of that back, I think I enjoy them a little more now. That's because we haven't had any mail for quite some time and naturally I have more time to study each line. I sure am going to reward you when I get back in more ways than one.

Every time I stop to think of all the time I wasted in not writing to you after that little quarrel, I feel like giving myself a good boot in the pants. I think you should have the honor, but don't forget, don't kick me too hard. My conscience will be relieved quite a bit if you'll only comply.

Did you know that Easter Sunday went by a little over a week ago and I hardly even recognized the fact until a few days later? Something has to be done about it. I think I was not entirely to blame 'cause I was quite busy that day and so were the rest of us.

Say, you remember when you mentioned your being at Rita's house with an apron tied around your waist and about four or five dishes in your hands. Well, I most certainly do, in case just per-chance you forget. And I'll tell you one thing, I didn't have to use much imagination to figure out how cute you must have looked. If you really want to make me happy, you could take a photo of yourself just the way you looked that day and send it to me on the "double." If you do, don't have the "deck" in on it, 'cause there are bound to be a few shattered dishes on it, and that might discourage me a bit. Aw Hell, I'd never let such a natural thing as a few broken dishes disrupt our plans, just as long as they weren't broken over my head.

Last night, after getting off watch, I hit my "rack" but couldn't fall asleep for no how. I just laid there thinking of you and the future. I sure can think of awfully swell things about us when I have the chance. When I get home, then my chance will really burst out into full bloom. I'll tell you everything about the way I think of you. You'll listen, won't you?

How is the water in Lake Michigan these days? I know it's still wet, but is it getting any warmer, that's what is on my mind? After all, I expect to enjoy a few mellow moon-lighted nights on the beach with you. I can just picture us now and, boy, what a picture. I can hardly wait for those days to come true. Take an occasional dip in the rolling waves or else a few dives off of those unforgettable rocks. Then sit down, rest a bit, talk a bit and _____ a Lot (now I've got you worried or have I)?

Lately, as I've been listening to the radio, just about every other number played is "I'm Making Believe" or "I Dream of You," and when I do, I get weak all over. I don't see how they can write such sweet songs, but don't worry I'm not complaining.

Did you actually send those poems and "cedar chest," yet? Or were you just handing me a line? It's pretty hard to come to a conclusion as no mail has been arriving for the last three weeks now.

I had better close for now, Sweetheart, but that's just in writing. My love for you will never cease, always remember that "This Is My Night to Dream, So Please Be Kind," okay?

Always Yours, Sal

April 12, 1945

At Sea

Dearest Sweetheart:

Gee, Honey, we finally got mail for the first time in almost a month. Boy, it sure was good to receive the most important literature that was ever written. Although I received eleven letters, I was slightly (slightly—my eyebrow, I was) disappointed, because only one of them came from you. What's the matter, honey? I told you that there would be periods that I couldn't possibly be able to write. I know I didn't write many letters to you while I was at Iwo Jima, but I couldn't, don't you understand? Almost every time I had a chance to write a letter, it was almost always to you. Maybe that will be sort of a voucher that I'm really in love with you and care for no others in the least!

Anyhow, you're forgiven, as if you really did something wrong, but please, don't forget to send some of your sweet letters out here as often as possible.

It sure is a beautiful day way out here today, but that's only literally speaking. How could any day possibly be beautiful with you and I being away from each other for such a long, long time. We'll have to get a break pretty soon, that's all there is to it, 'cause I can't stand very much of this any longer.

Back to that one, but awfully sweet letter of yours—you know it's a funny thing, but for myself—I could never master the swan dive, but instead, the jack-knife came to me rather easy like. I just can't wait to see you really show that gorgeous swan dive that you now have down "pat." It should really be a humdinger with that lovely shape of yours. When we get on that beach together in the near future, you'll have to teach me the fundamentals of that "bird" dive and I'll try and do likewise as far as the jackknife goes. Since you like swimming so well, and I always was crazy about it, we should have barrels of fun on those moonlight dips. Of course, we're not just going to swim—mind you! (Better take a note of that).

My dear sis sent me a picture of Talman "Terrace" taken during December. It was one of the best pictures I ever received, and I'll have to take her out at least one night to show her that I really appreciate her efforts. It showed the whole street from our house down to the corner, and there must have been at least thirty inches of snow on the ground. I guess I'm slightly exaggerating, but it sure was beautiful. You don't know what it means to a guy to see something like that after missing three winters back home, especially when he's been accustomed all of his life to see about three months of winter out of every year.

As I was listening to the radio the other night, I heard some awful nice numbers. First came T.D.'s, "One O'clock Jump" followed by A.S's (Artie Shaw's), "Begin The Beguine," and then came a very sweet one, "You Are Always In My Heart," and truer words could never be spoken.

I just sat there and made believe you were sitting on my lap and what a glorious feeling it was. Some day soon, we won't have to day-dream or reminisce because everything will be just the way we want it. That remarkable day can't come any too soon to suit me.

213

If you think the solitude is killing you, honey! Then I've been dead for the past two years—ever since I last saw you. It seems that lately my brain will only think of you while my heart is plenty satisfied in just being allowed to "beat" for you.

You sure have me thinking about that snug little parlor of yours and how I wish I was there, especially with the light down low. My, My. There you go, getting me all excited again, but how I love it.

The way you signed that letter of March 8, sort of bewildered me. You know, "curiously in love." I didn't know which way to figure it out because it pointed in about three different directions, especially with the gizmos, "???" behind it. Don't forget to leave me on the secret, and above all, the more you write, the happier you make me.

All My Love & Kisses, Sal

April 14, 1945

Hello, My Darling:

Well, here I am again, writing to the only girl I really care for, and would give anything up in this universe just for the chance to be with "her" again. Gee, Sweets, I miss you something dreadful like, and what can one do? Well, the cards can't be stacked against us forever, and if they try, I'm going to shoot the dealer.

I've only had one letter from you in the last four weeks and that just arrived two days ago. You can readily see the predicament that confronts me in writing, but seeing the way I'm so in love with you, it'll be a snap to get one out. For you "anything goes" and not "almost anything," as you so frequently state.

I'm listening to some mighty mellow music right now, Honey. Even though it's a few years old, it's still mighty "neat." Oh, how I wish I had you close to me and dancing our troubles away. But if I had you beside me, I wouldn't have any troubles. They just finished playing, "Music, Maestro,

Please" and "Melancholy Baby," not to mention, "Somebody Else Is Taking My Place," and gosh, Darling, thrills just go running up and down my spine and I get weak all over as I visualize us together! Oh boy!

I hope you don't mind too much if I forget to put my feet in my pocket and consequently step over your dainty little feet every now and then while we're dancing. I'll gladly pay for all broken arches. After all, Honey, I haven't had a chance to dance in such a long time and a little toe crunching is bound to happen. You won't be too sore at me, will you? If perchance it happens a little too often, we'll walk into the garden and whether a pretty moon is shining or not, I'll make love to you like no one has ever done before!! It won't be too bad after all, now will it?

I just met a buddy from Seattle who I haven't seen in two years. (Say, will you tell that luscious picture of yours that I now have in front of me, to stop making me so nervous, as I'm making too damn many mistakes?) I went to radio school with him in Moscow and he, three other guys from Chicago, and myself, always used to make liberty together. We always had a wild time whenever we went out, and it was more than once that he had to carry me back to the base. As soon as he gets off watch, he's coming over, since he's (his ship is) tied right alongside of us. We sure have a lot of things to talk over, yessiree! Imagine he went and got married since I last saw him.

My Sis said, "I hear that there's a certain young lady that's waiting for you. Every time we meet, I get that funny feeling, you know what I mean. I wish you the best of luck." Now isn't that pretty "neat" of her?

Say, haven't you learned to make Swiss steak, yet? If you haven't, either you or she is going to get a bawling out, savvy? I guess you know I'm still expecting one meal cooked by your own sweet "paws" when I get home. You're not going to try and poison me, now are you? Alright for you, if you do—just see if I go to "our" wedding then.

I just heard "You Tell Me Your Dreams and I'll Tell You Mine," so when I hit my rack tonight, I'll see what I can do in regards to my next letter.

Loving you, Forever, Sal

April 16, 1945

Dearest Darling:

Well to tell you the truth, I have only received one letter from you in a month, and do I worry? No! Do I give a bag beans? No! Do I lose any sleep over you? But definitely no! Just one more thing—what a gosh darned liar I'm turning out to be!

The mail system is rather fouled up out here as you no doubt have already presumed. They bring you a couple of letters one day and then next month they may bring a few more. I'm beginning to think that they're using Christopher Columbus's *Santa Maria* for a mail ship out here. I guess you know it goes rather slow. In fact, if it went any slower, it would be going backwards, so help me! Well, "things like this can't go on forever." I wish I could find where that excerpt came from though!

I suppose you think you have something on me when you stayed in church all day? Well, I guess you know I went to church yesterday, too. If I don't watch myself, and keep this up, I'm afraid I'll have to turn in my heathen papers. Only kidding, of course, and you better believe me.

Here are a few jokes I picked up, and here's hoping you have a few "bus stops" schemed up for me by the time I get back. And if you don't, then I'll do a little scheming of my own, so there!

You know, Honey, I'm beginning to feel (way down deep!) that it won't be very long when I'll have you in my arms and I do mean all of you. "My Dreams Are Getting Better All the Time," and boy are you sweet, mellow and what not. That picture you sent me from way back, keeps my morale up constantly, as I always have it in front of me while

I'm copying in the radio shack. "Sweet and Lovely," that's what I call you, every bit of you, from the tip of your toes to the top of your "noggin." It's going to be a great day when I first set my eyes on you, and just see if I take them off of you, even for a measly minute.

I hope you have a few places of your own that you want to go to when I get there. After all, it's only fair that way. Besides, it'll take me a few days to get my bearings on good old Chicago again. You'll probably be leading me around like a dog at first, but don't let me catch you treating me like one, ha, ha, ha. Now what in the Hell am I laughing at?

We're still out at sea and I can't let you know my whereabouts as yet, but if you have a nice pot of "Jamoke" brewed up for us after I'm taking you home from a lovely and well spent night, then I'll gladly give out with the info. But, only under one condition—you'll have to be sitting on my lap as I'm spinning these yarns and also—strong lights hurt my eyes something awful. Take a note of that.

I made a little bet about a week ago that Berlin would fall by the 1st of May. Old Patton better throw a little more grease in his tanks if I'm to collect. Oh hum, it's just for the principle of the thing anyway—yeah! (*Berlin surrendered on May 1.*)

I wasn't able to listen to any music all day today, but still I'm writing! Savvy? I spent most of the day shooting the bull with that swabby from Seattle. He's a good egg and a barrel of fun to boot.

Well, Honey, I'll close for now, but I'll be back in two days. Don't forget to store up on lipstick, 'cause I have a hint you're going to need a large supply.

Loving you Always, Sal

(Three inserts)

(1) I guess you know nowadays telling some brides what they should know on their wedding night is like giving a fish a bath.

217

(2) Judge: "So you say the defendant stole your money from your stocking"?

Female Plaintiff: "Yes, your honor."

Judge: "Then why didn't you resist?"

Female Plaintiff: "Well, how did I know he was after my money?"

(3) Buss Stop

A boy and girl were walking along a shady road in the moonlight. The boy was carrying a large pail on his back, a chicken in one hand, a cane in the other, and leading a goat. They strolled along silently until they came to a large tree. "I'm afraid to be walking alone here with you," said the girl coyly, "you might try to kiss me."

"But how could I," protested the boy, "with all these things I'm carrying?"

"Well," she answered, "you could stick the cane in the ground, tie the goat to it and put the chicken in the pail."

-Banana Peelings

April 17, 1945

At Sea

Hello, My Dearest:

How is the only young lady that I think constantly of morning, noon, and night, getting along these days? I hope she is in the best of health and spirit, 'cause I don't know what I would do if something ever happened to you. As for me, I'm feeling fine in health, but I can't say the same for my morale. I just found out that I have to wait another two months for my leave and when that time rolls around, it'll probably be another two. By the time my leave actually does happen, I'll probably be using a cane and all set to draw social security. I often wonder how you can wait so long. That is a $64 question, and it's worth it too.

Well, now that I told you "our" troubles, I can get down to writing you a letter.

"At Last," at last (good old Miller), I'm finally beginning to get some "back mail" from you and I do mean "way back." The letter I received yesterday was from the 18th of February. As long as we're way out here, the mail predicament will probably remain that way. Ain't it awful?

So I see you're going to try and drag your five little cousins with us to the beach. Hmmm! Maybe once in the day time, yah, but never on those moonlight dips, 'cause I want you exclusively for myself or am I being too selfish? Even during the day time, those five v 5 IIIII dear cousins of yours might get in my hair and I'm liable to get a sack and drown them one by one! I'm only kidding, of course, but you didn't know my middle name was Frankenstein, did you? Oh well, we'll see when the time comes.

We're still around these picturesque islands, but seeing them day in and day out, more or less, makes them lose their beauty, but in a hurry like. I imagine it would be pretty nice to have a few snapshots of them now to remind you in later years (both good and bad), but that resembles an impossibility in all respects.

I heard "T.D." make with, "I'll Never Smile Again," with Swoonatra and the Pied Pipers exercising their vocal chords, boy it was really mell-ow! You can quote me on the lyrics in expressing the way I feel towards you. We have aboard, the King Sisters recording of, "Heaven by Hideaway," and man— am that luscious. It sure is just right for dancing with those momentarily breaks in it. So when we're dancing together, we'll have to give it a trial, and will I hold you close as I rain kisses all over you, Honey.

You know, Sweets, you shouldn't have told me that, 'cause that leaves me only one alternative—I'm going to run out of words every other second, just so I'll be able to squeeze you so tight. Alreet?

Boy, will I be only too glad to help you overcome any obstacles that may be in your way. You better not be too stubborn, though. After all, honey, we've been separated for ages and I'm going to love you as much as you'll permit, and then some. It's about the only thing that keeps me going out

219

here, just the thought of having you waiting with open arms and willing lips, so there!

Say hello to your sisters and aunt for me, but tell those cousins of yours to start practicing swimming underwater, unless they intend to behave.

I'll close for now my love, but I'll always be with you until my next opportunity to write.

Love that will never cease, Sal

P.S. I liked that, "after all that's what kept me all yours for so long." Please don't change it.

April 18, 1945

The USS Signet supports the stranded crew of an LCVP (Landing Craft, Vehicle, Personnel, which is under fire from entrenched Japanese. They request light from the Signet. Japanese gun fire is silenced each time the Signet uses her searchlight to expose their position. This continues through most of the night. The stranded men are rescued by a tug early on the morning of the 19th.

April 19, 1945

At Sea As Usual

Hello, Sweetheart:

How are you today, gorgeous?

Still saving all your love for me like the sweet young lady that you are? That's marvelous, Honey, 'cause I guess you know that it's getting mighty close to two years that we've been away from each other, although it only seems like two centuries. I figure that in that length of time you should have quite a bit of sweet and tender love put away for me and, Honey-child, "I'se" aiming to collect, but in full! Am I right?

We had a pretty busy night last night, and being up most of the time, they let us sleep all day today. That's of course if we didn't have our regular sea watches. I didn't have to go on until 1600 this afternoon, so I slept all morning and then got up and absorbed some fresh sea breezes until it was time to go on watch.

It rained all afternoon and the breezes were as fresh as a morning glory. I thought of you all afternoon and looked into the future when you and I'll be together again. You know, nice cool rain refreshes you in more ways than one.

After we left Iwo in March, we went down to the Ulithi Island in the Western Carolines. Ulithi is about a hundred miles from Yap Island, which is still a Tojo (a general of the Imperial Japanese army) stronghold. We had six days of rest in those coconut infested islands and managed to hit the beach every other day for an enjoyable beer party.

Those beer parties were really a bit of "alreet." There's where a hunk a coral ran into my "noggin" and that naturally ended my swimming for the day. After that, I had to be contented with solely drinking beer. What a crying shame! Oh well, I didn't mind too much. What am I saying? I know damn right that I could have drank beer there for another month without any strain or pain on my part.

You should have seen the open sea break at the reef and then come rushing towards the beach at an awful fast clip. After the sea broke at the reef, it became crystal clear and so soothing on oneself. The surf was much better than Waikiki will ever be.

That group is the most tropical place I've been to yet. Warm as Hell all day and then cool trade winds all night, usually followed by showers. The winds down there were even better than the soft cool breezes that shoot off the lake on those enjoyable May nights, back home. But don't get me wrong, I wouldn't trade one night back home for a thousand nights in Ulithi.

Even though we were suppose to get as much rest as possible while we were there, old Tojo couldn't see it scoot for no-how. He'd constantly send his kinsfolk over just to keep us from seeing a movie or hitting our "rack" at night.

The sea sure has been rough all night and jogging to and fro as I'm writing this letter. Isn't too easy on a guy, or on the pen either as a matter of fact. But what's an old pen between a couple like us, eh?

You should have heard the sweet, but mellow music old Glen put out for us over the radio, just before coming on watch. It was fifteen minutes of reminiscing and heaven, so help me. What I wouldn't give to hold you close to me and dance to the same numbers that he produced. He started the gong bouncing with "Sunrise Serenade," followed by "Moonlight Cocktails," then "Anvil Chorus," and last but not least, the never dying, "In The Mood." Gee, Honey, I can hardly wait to lay eyes on you again so I can take you out dancing, romancing, swimming, and what not? You follow me, don't you?

I sure had a luscious dream on you last night. Your face was so clear and pretty that it's a crying shame that I can't fly home right now and tell you all the explicit details. Of all the places it happened too, in the old Ogden, can you imagine? I'll have to tell you this one when I get home, so don't forget to remind me, Honey.

It's really a piperoo, so help me.

My dreams keep getting better all the time, but I don't know how when it seems that they reached their peak some time ago. But you won't hear me "beefing," no siree!

I'll have to close for now, Honey, but don't run away, I'll be back soon!

Loving you tremendously, Sal

April 21, 1945

Saturday Nite

Hiya, Sweetstuff:

You know who ever wrote, "Saturday Night—Is the Loneliest Night of the Week," sure hit the nail on the noggin. Of course there are six others that run a close second, but not quite close enough. If I had to count all the Saturday nights that I've missed, I would without a doubt have to take off my shoes, start counting, put them back on again, and then go through the same procedure at least eight more times. That would make it just about right. I'd use my fingers, but I forgot how to count with them. When I get home, I'll have either four or five Saturdays to myself and you can bet a million that they'll all be spent with you. The first Saturday night out with you and they'll have to change the "complexion" of that song to read "Happiest Day of the Week." Right? "Reet"!

Say, what happened to all those sketches you were supposed to send out this way? Remember? Boy, you are getting lazy! Or are you just plain wicked? Well sweetheart, it doesn't make a bit of "dif" to me, which you are, 'cause I honestly love you so much that the only way you could possibly get my goat is to drop a boulder on top of my dome. Even that wouldn't phase me too much, not unless it broke my neck. Then would I take you over my knee and pound the living daylights out of you. Now what do you think of that? But, don't forget you still have about eight coming from previous encounters, and I'm aiming to see that you get them. You can start calling me Simon Legree any day now—I'm tired of monickering you with it.

This whole last week I've been hearing some might sweet numbers, "Saturday Night," "I'm Beginning To See The Light," and some other new "neat" number but I'll be "danged" if I can think of it right off hand. What do you think of the above ditties or don't you? Just as I thought! "I Want to Do What You Do, Go Where You Go, love when you love—and I'll be happy." Right!

We should be getting some more mail within the next two or three days and already I'm praying each night that I'll get a carload from you. I'm not praying in vain, now am I? What? Then you start harping when I call you "wicked."

Say, Honey, how about telling me what you would like to do the first night we're out together, huh? Whatever you want to do, wherever you want to go and whatever you want to see. Your wish will be my command for the entire night. Okay? Good! I just want you to know that I appreciate (not to mention how much I actually love) a fine young lady like you.

We "dogged" the watches this evening, so that means I have that terrible Mid for the next seven days. It won't be too bad though, 'cause I'll have your picture right in front of the "mill" to keep me company until four o'clock in the morning. You won't mind too much, will you? If you start getting— "Sleepy Time Gal," I can always fix you up with a cup of "jamoke." That's the strongest liquor we have aboard, so help me!

I'll have to hit the "rack" for a few hours before I go on the Mid, Honey—so "I'll see you in my dreams."

Loving you forever, Sal

April 24, 1945

My Dearest Sweetheart:

Maybe you don't believe it, but now I'm the one that seems to be lacking letter material. Maybe it's because I have only received two, 2, II, ll, letters from you in the last two, 2, II, ll months. (Say, you are making me form the whackiest habits, I wonder how come?) And then it could be that all the exciting things out here are censored.

The former is by far the most important, especially when the last letter you wrote was dated the 8th of March. Way down deep in my heart, I just know that you've been writing regularly, but still I'm letter-shy. Sooo—my sweet one—there is only one alternative left—and that is you had better hop on your bike and deliver them all in person. Approach me rather slowly, 'cause if I happened to turn around all of a sudden and who should I see, but sweet little you, smiling at me so sweetly, I'm afraid I'd drop dead in my tracks just from sheer happiness.

Are you still going swimming at good old Filmore and how's that jack-knife coming along? Hey—wait a minute— now I know why I'm not getting any mail. You broke you back doing a dive and are now recuperating in some hospital. Why didn't you let me know, which one you are in, so I can send you some flowers or something? Then you wonder why I called you wicked, well I'll be.

You know we always use to go to Filmore, winter, summer, rain or sunshine and after a nice refreshing dip, we'd make a flying run to Fluky's and devour some of their luscious hot dogs. They used to have some nice hot dogs there, but I suppose they closed down due to shortage in labor.

We're still out at sea just bobbing around like corks. I sure hope we get out of this damned area soon as I don't crave for it very well. Besides, Honey, when we leave this Hell-rotten hole, I'll be able to head straight for your arms "At Last," and this time, it's straight dope. I can hardly wait for that blissful moment to arrive and I'm not lying when I say the suspense is killing me. Don't go worrying about this time being different, 'cause it most certainly is. I'm going to squeeze you so tight and I'll never stop kissing you. Gee—you luscious looking creature, you're getting me all excited, but in a hurry like.

Boy, did I hear two mellow songs the other day. "A Million Dreams Ago" and "Indian Summer," and did that take me back to those good old civvy days. Remember the "hard time" you use to give me when we'd go strolling through the park. It'll be quite different this time now, won't it? No more spelling bees, 'cause I have to give the last brain that I possess a rest before it completely passes out on me. I'll just ask you the questions instead. That sounds fair enough or doesn't it?

Say, "curious," how's the coffee company rolling along these days, or aren't you snitching? I suppose you got the forelady's job by now or is it the foreman's? I wouldn't put it pass you, 'cause after all, I don't love you so much just because you're so sweet, but also because you have a few brains up in that "noggin" of yours to give any Einstein some stiff competition.

225

I'll close for now, my loved one, so in the meantime, try and get some of your mail out this way. Okay?

I'll always be loving you, Sal

P.S. What do you think of the "gizmo" inside this letter?

(insert)
Cartoon of sailor and girl in evening dress washing dishes at restaurant.
Sailor says: "Yeah, but wasn't it a swell dinner?"

Sal's note: This could never happen to us now, could it? You better bring your purse along, just in case (ha, ha)

April 28, 1945

Saturday Nite

My Dearest Loretta:

Well, here's your faithful and loving beau, again, trying to get out a few notes to the one he loves more than anyone or anything in this whole wide world.

I have to admit, even though my love for you is growing more ardently each day, that I can't write a letter as fluently as I use to. Maybe it's because none of your mail seems to be coming out this way at the regular pace it use to (I received three letters in the last month and a half from you). Or maybe it's because the last two months, we've been under a strain, more or less, and my nerves have been in that jumpy mood, but regardless of what the cause may be, I'll be loving you until the day I die. Well, anyhow, you should get one consolation out of the fact in that all the letters I do write, you get at least 75% of them. Even Scully is beefing about this, but he doesn't understand, does he, Honey?

Now I'll try and settle down and write you a letter.

We've been rather busy out here with this and that and that and this and a few other things I can't write about at present. Well, it's better this way, anyhow, 'cause when I'm alone with you, in your parlor or some other quiet room with the lights down low (just as picturesque as you describe it), then I'll be able to let go with the tongue. Of course, you have to allow for time out every other minute for a few refreshments and I'm not talking about cake either! Gee, sweets, I just seem to travel out of the world when ever I picture "us" together again when my thirty day leave comes through. I don't want to build our hopes up too high, but I'm inclined to believe that it will take place in the very near future. And if I'm wrong, I'll gladly pay for my error in judgment by helping you out with the largest pile of dishes that you can gather in twenty-four hours. That sounds plenty fair, or am I letting myself in for something? Oh well, here today, gone tomorrow, so we'll have to throw a party on Wednesday.

I haven't heard any mellow music from the States in almost a week now. I suppose, "Saturday Night," is right near the top, but, "Things Ain't What They Use To Be," and I can say that again. Before you used to be able to go to some hipster of a dance, get out about one or two in the morning with your favorite girl, and then hop in a car and roam the city or country with the "radjio" giving out with some might mell-oooh music. Stopping in various dives until about five in the morning. Yes-sir Honey, those were the days—but—"As Long as I Have You, I'll Always Have My Heavenly Hideaway," and that can't be beat for no-how!

For the present though, those back letters of yours (way back) and that luscious snapshot of you and your "bike," will keep my morale up for awhile, but, Honey, don't forget to give out with some new ones.

Loving You Constantly, Sal

Chapter 16, May 1945

May 5, 1945

Dearest Sweets:

Five days have already elapsed of this month, but still this is the first letter I'm writing to you this month. Why? Well I'll tell you, in the last few months I have received only a negligible amount of letters from you, not hardly enough to know that you really still love me. I write as frequently as possible and have given up a lot of sleep and good books because of it. Now surely, you could respond accordingly if not more so. After all, you have a hell of a lot more time to yourself that I can ever think of, so I don't see why you're not writing more regularly. If there's a certain reason, let's be frank with one another and not beat it around the bush as you once said. After all, Honey, I'm still in love with you ardently and hope you feel the same way.

Well, evading the above subject for the time being and getting to this dog's life out here. Right now, the sea is tossing the ship around quite a bit, in fact that's the main reason I'm not using the old pen. It's "weather-beaten" enough and using it on a night like this will surely give it a bad case of rigor-mortis.

There were quite a few letters I wrote you while the sea was choppy and I'm willing to bet that you are still trying to figure them out. There were a few I couldn't even figure out myself after reading it through, but still I let them "ride," knowing that you have a little more intellect that I have.

It sure has been rather disgusting to go into the harbor once each week for mail and not have any from you. For awhile, I thought they just weren't sending any mail all the way out here, but I soon found out different in a hurry when I receive other letters from the neighborhood. Of course they should be coming out here at a better clip, but the last one I received from you was the 8th of March, and that was a long time ago. I don't mean received, but when you wrote it—

maybe it was the 6th. So, when we get mail the next time, I am really praying that there'll be quite a few from you or know the reason why. Now is the time I really could use some of your sweet letters, so don't go letting me down, eh?

Getting back to a more happier moment—a few days ago I picked up Ted Fio Rito's band, coming all the way from some big ballroom in New York City. Boy, he was playing a lot of mellow pieces, including "I Dream of You," and did my heart start beating at an increased rate. What I wouldn't give to be dancing with you as he was putting out that number, and would I hold you close.

Just thinking of it sets me afire—so help me. It isn't coming to be too long from now when that will turn out to be a reality. I expect it to be sometime in the earlier part of summer and the suspense is driving me plumb loco.

Then we can be together again, and go out to dances and the beaches like we planned, or have you forgotten so soon? I bet you have, then you wonder why I call you wicked. Well, now you know.

I'll have to take an exit for a little while, but I'll be back as soon as I get the chance. You better be missing me a little while I'm gone, okay?

I'm back in a flash—if you could call eight hours a flash. I had about five hours of "rack-time" and did that snooze do wonders for your "one and only" (I hope that's the way you think of me), not to mention a rare and refreshing shower I just had. Now, what more could I ask for? I could kick myself right where it would do the most good for asking such a whacky question like that. Sometimes I wonder if I'll ever learn.

Man-a-live, if you could only hear the jive that's coming over right now, it'd make your head spin and your heart would automatically start pounding like rain on a rooftop. The "old licorice-stick man," Artie, promptly gave out with, "Moon Glow," "Summit Ridge Drive," and "Frenesi." Then, what does his competitor, Benny, follow suit with? "Smoke Gets In Your Eyes," "Stardust," and some other might sweet number. I can't catch the title, but I know the record, because

I have it stashed away in the "Chanuke-Box" back home. So when I get back, remind me to play it for you and better yet, we'll dance to it, if you don't mind. You can't help but like the tune and the words will really knock your eyes out. I should have been a little more formal and say "lyrics," but they're both the same difference so why start a riot, eh, Honey?

I'm willing to bet that you didn't lay your dainty little paws on Krupa's "Flamingo." Just as I thought, you're going to leave it up to me to do the hunting. Well, I tell you what, we'll both do the hunting together, besides it'll be a lot more fun that way, but and how.

I suppose the climate back home right now is really beautiful or have those April showers decided to linger around a little longer? Even if that is so, rain can be awfully romantic at times, but and how! It all depends who you are with and where you are at, right?

Now, if I were with you, it could be raining cats and dogs and still it wouldn't phase me in a loathsome manner, but quite on the contrary. You sure would affect me something "awful" with the wind and the rain in your hair. Then, as those soft rain-drops started descending down your equally soft and beautiful cheeks, I would naturally try and kiss each one before they reached the bottom of your unforgettable face.

How could I not help but reach a frantic state in a hurry. Just looking into the crystal ball when you and I will be together again sets me afire in happiness and passion, so darling, always remain true to me.

I really have no reason at all to doubt your integrity (and I don't), but still I like to hear you tell me over and over and over that you love me and nothing will ever change your mind. It is needless to say that my devotion for you is growing more infinite each day.

By the way, how is that cooking of yours coming along? Have you learned to master that exquisite touch of preparing Swiss steak, yet? Aboard ship, they put out a chow that they call Swiss steak, but it is so different from the way my sis used to make it, that makes it as far apart as night and day. So don't forget, Honey, see what you can do to ease my mind a bit.

I'll have to start closing for now my loved one, but I'll be thinking of you constantly in the meantime as I have always been doing.

Loving you Always, Sal

May 12, 1945

My Sweetest One & Only:

Jiminy crickets, sweetheart, they just brought us out Sugar Reports and three of them were from you! Of course, the mail I receive from sweet little you is the only mail I classify as "S.R's,"(Sugar Reports), all the rest being from home sweet home and "me buddies." Every single one of them is so sweet and exciting that I'm going to bring every one of them home with me and I'll let you read each one of them as I'm holding you so close and pouring kiss after kiss on sweet little you. If you get too "warm," I can always run into the kitchen and bring you back a glass of water. Of course, if I know where your Aunt hid some of that more potent liquor, I'd bring you some of that—but I know you, you won't tell me, will you? Please?

Those three sweet, magnificent, gorgeous, luscious, "mellow" (guess what, I ran out of adjectives) letters of yours were all written in February. Being a little more explicit, they were written on the 4th and two on the 13th. Now you know what I mean when I say "back mail." Gee, Honey, the last letter I wrote to you, I believe I blew my top a bit, because I haven't received any mail from you for so long and if you think I was a bit too "wicked," then you can take me over your knee and trim the daylights out of me, alright, sweet? The mail is still fouled up as I have only one letter written by you in March and not one in April. So please, don't stay mad at me if I jumped at conclusions, sweetheart, "What Am I to Say After I Say I'm Sorry?" I'll give you all the loving you can

stand when I get in, honey, if that helps any (I know it helps
me quite a bit, just thinking of it).

Those letters and that "spicy" picture you drew has me
bubbling over with joy, bubbling over with excitement and
bubbling over with passion. Boy, you really have me
bubbling, haven't you? You'll have to excuse this scribbling,
sweetheart, but your letters have me so excited and nervous
(the way this ship is bouncing on this choppy sea doesn't help
matters either) that I can't help it. You got me this way, what
are you going to do about it, eh? Just keep on writing and
waiting, Honey, that's all I ask. Don't think for one moment
that I don't admire your everlasting patience and you'll find
out when I get home. I don't think you'll ever regret that long
awaited moment of bliss when I come "panting" home. I know
I won't.

Speaking of that mellow picture you drew, Honey, it was
really a killer-diller. Just 'perchance, you don't look that sweet
and devouring in the same amount of weaving apparel, do
you? That really has me up on edge just thinking of it. I'll find
out some day, and I sure hope it's soon, don't forget that!
Already, I have the picture slapped up in my locker so I can
take a gaze at it whenever I open it up. I have a hint that I'm
going to be opening up my locker quite a bit in the future, you
don't mind, do you? After all you drew it. Grrrr.

You know, I've been thinking quite a bit lately on just
where we'll meet when I get in. I'm afraid I'd die of excitement
if I stepped off the train (I'll try and take a plane, though, so I
can get home faster) and saw you waiting with such a pretty
smile and open arms. I probably wouldn't be able to control
myself and maybe I'd start drooling and maybe even bawling,
who knows? Of course if I got in about mid-afternoon, I would
take a gallop over to your Aunt's house, knock on the door,
tell who ever answers that I'm the certain one that Loretta has
been waiting for, then "blooyey," I'd flop in a cozy chair and
just wait until my dream girl started approaching the house.
As soon as I saw your sweet little frame coming down the
street, I would rush up to your Aunt and say—"Dear Aunty,
isn't there something you forgot at the store" or "aren't you

suppose to see a man about a dog?" She'd catch on naturally, and would I greet you with the warmest and longest kiss you ever had. What do you think, eh?

I just heard "San Antonio Rose," and did that modernized hick song bring back memories. Wow! After a dance, the whole bunch of us, Scully, Goose, Cowb, Big Horn and a lot more, used to run into good old Al's and start playing that number over and over again, and throw a shot and a beer down the hatch with each number. By five or six in the morning, we were really flying high, but I would always manage to crawl home. I admit my knees would be pretty well bruised by the time I got there, but they served the purpose. After all, what's a couple of knees amongst friends, eh?

I had to get up very abruptly like and leave you for about an hour, but you didn't mind too much, did you? I'll explain to you later, okay?

The weather out here has been rather nice lately, out in these remote parts. Similar to a May back home, with a glorious warm sun in the afternoon and rather cool at night.

Speaking of good old home, it shouldn't be very long before I'll be able to see it. Oh, it'll be so nice to be there again, and seeing you again will make all of my dreams come through. I'll probably be so speechless the first day, seeing Dad and taking you out to show me the sights, you won't mind too much, will you? But I can guarantee you that on the second day, I'll strike it up to my old speed, and then you'll probably get so disgusted, that you'll jab a pillow down my yap,—you sweet old "meanie," you!

Well, my sweet "little woman," it's pretty hard to say how you can tell it's the "real one" or not. Nature always had funny ways in telling you things and she usually tells them to each one differently. Whenever I get something from you (which is exclusively mail out here, but it'll become something else when I get back) you keep me awake for hours with your beautiful self in front of me no matter which way I may look. I'm afraid to close my eyes because you might not be waiting for me in dreamland, but all in all, I've met you quite a few times there and you were always so sweet and kind—don't forget to remind me to tell you of some of those awfully happy moments, won't you?

Then again, how can I help know that it's real—I try eating chow and nothing will go down and I just about gag myself. I start thinking of you and I get goose pimples from stem to stern and most of the time I would walk right past the life lines right into the "drink," if someone didn't grab my arm and break the trance. Last but not least, sweetheart, whenever I hear from you, my heart starts getting St. Vitas' dance and just about jumps right out of my throat, and I'm not exaggerating one minute when I tell you all this, either.

Say, whose kids were you talking about in one of those letters? Didn't I have anything to do with it? (What am I saying?)

You're not just a kidding when you say I have a lot of things to tell you when I get home. All of them are sweet too. You can bet your life on that. You don't mind waiting a while longer so I can hold you in my arms and caress you so tenderly as I tell them to you, do you? After all, a guy gets a little chicken in putting it down on paper, but when I see the real you, oh boy!—Then try and stop me, just try.

I'll have to close for now, honey, mainly because this is the last sheet of stationery I own and could borrow. Don't try and send me any sweets, because I'll probably be on my way home by the time it gets here. I'll probably be using slabs of wood from now on in writing to you.

Loving you, Body & Soul, Sal

P.S.

Say, my sweet artiste, send me all of those marvelous pictures that you possibly can 'cause it reminds me why I am out here and what I can expect when I get in.

May 15, 1945

My Dearest Loved One:

Well, here I am again, sweetheart, scribbling down a few words to remind the receiver that I'm still deeply in love with her and she had better not forget if she knows what's good for her! There are about sixteen "trimmings" that you can expect to collect when I invade Chicago and I don't see how you can possibly stand anymore!

Lately, I've been finding consolation in reading your old mail. It's not that I don't enjoy it, 'cause I do, infinitely. How can I help but not do so when you're always saying such sweet things, those facetious (now there's a two-bit word if I ever did see one) sayings that you put in every now and then, but always in the right place. Yes, how can I not help but have an enormous pride swell inside of me every time I think of that glorious day when I can tell you face to face that I always want you to be mine.

But evading the subject for just a moment, I'd like to know when I'm going to receive a letter written from you in April and maybe another one written in March to make it an even two. I keep blaming it on this critical mail system out here, but I hope I'm not kidding myself. After all, I can't help but worrying maybe something has come between us after all. I can't expect your patience to last forever, especially when it isn't compelled to. If anything accidentally has arisen, Honey, let me know, as I always did admire you for your virtue. Here's hoping that I'm not forming any wrong conclusions.

Recollecting that you've asked if I had changed any, well it's rather hard to say. I know that my thoughts for settling down after this war is over aren't vague anymore, but a reality. I guess it has taken a war to make me arrive to that conclusion so abruptly, but I intend and I will see it through. Outside of that, I can't say whether I have changed much. It's rather difficult for one's self to notice if he has changed any, mostly because it never strikes him to pay too much attention. One is usually more interested in what's going on about him, instead of, in himself.

As for you, my sweet dew drop, you have changed quite moderately. You seem to now have an explanation of just what life is about. You seem much sweeter and more daring in your letters. Here's hoping that they aren't written under false pretenses! You know, I used to have quite a "battle" with you every time I wanted so much as a kiss, but now what are you going to do when I get home and my wantings will be more advanced, eh? All in all, Honey, even though I loved you so-o-o much just the way I left you two years ago, it's my good fortune to see that you have made a turn for the good in almost every respect that is so essential to every woman.

I have a lot of things to tell you, Honey, pertaining to all this, but it's hard to express it on paper. You don't mind waiting just a little while longer so as I can hold you so close in my arms and then tell you all those little things I wanted to tell you.

Say, are you throwing away much of "our" money in that enormous gambling den that you so frequently participate inside of your kitchen? I bet you always have four or five aces hidden inside your sleeves, not to mention how many decks of fixed cards you have ready to use from some intrigue location. I never realized that you played for such high stakes! Imagine sometimes losing as much as a whole quarter in one night! My, my, but you are a spend-thrift! If you ever run out of quarters, just let me know, 'cause I could always advance you a month's stakes, but only on a 50-50 share of the winnings. Say, I didn't like the way you snarled at me just then.

Now to straighten you out on some of this Navy language, mind you, I don't claim to be a "weather beaten salt," but I'll be able to help you out in certain trifles.

First of all, the front of a ship is called the "bow" or "stem" and the very back part, the "stern." Now, comes the "main deck," which strikes one as being the most conspicuous of all the decks. It's the longest deck aboard ship and the very first one that's in the open air coming form the bottom of the ladder. On the "main deck" are located the "fo'castle," "boat deck," or "quarter deck," and then comes the "fantail." The "fo'castle" being up "forward," from the "stem" to the so called superstructure, or the forming of the bridge and its remaining partitions. Then comes the "boat deck," or "quarter deck," as it is most commonly known on the larger ships, covering half of the distance of the main deck. Finally comes the "fantail," which covers the last quarter of the "main deck," beginning where the "boat deck" leaves off, and going to the end of the ship, or "stern," as it is properly called. One thing more, when you speak of going towards the front or up ahead, you say "forward" and towards the back you say "aft."

I just glanced over the above terms and never did realize until now how difficult it was to put the same down on paper. I presume you have a vague idea of the above Navy phraseology or maybe you're more confused than previously. I guess I'll have to wait until I have you underneath some mellow, golden moon and then I'll really give you the sweet and lowdown. That's of course if I can keep this warped mind of mine on my work.

You know, I can't help but gaze at the humdinger of a sketching you drew for "me." Every time I open my locker, there's that gorgeous creature, so "fully clothed" (that's what gets me, yum, yum) just waiting, so serene and contented. I often picture you as being that beautiful chick and you're not far from it, mind you, and then my heart is really set afire.

Just waiting for that day to arrive when I can hold you in my arms and whisper in your little ear all of the things I've always longed to tell you is driving me towards a nervous breakdown, but pronto like. I'll probably be so excited and nervous that first day that I won't be able to utter a word. But give me twenty-four hours to get a hold of myself and then watch the tongue peel off with the sweet lingo!

We're still out at sea and so far away, it isn't even funny. We've been gone from the Hawaiian Islands almost four months now, and all that time has been spent exclusively at sea, except for going into the harbor to get stores every now and then, mostly then!

I'm glad to hear that you're still pal-ing around with Dolly. When you have companionship with a nice girl like her,

I know you won't be doing anything to get me sore. You know what I mean, don't you, Honey?

Well, I stopped this letter for a short while as I deposited myself for a soothing shower. I wasn't gone long, so lay that rolling pin down, Honey.

Here's a little "gizmo" that I thought was pretty "neat." How about saving it as sort of a souvenir and then years hence, we'll pull it out of "our" cedar chest and see if you have changed any as far as cooking goes. Alright?

Well, Honey, I'll have to bring to a close this short means of communication with you, but we won't have to be doing this forever. Some day, when we are in our living room and just taking life easy, we'll look back at these present times and a glow of joy will swell forth inside of us as we think back of those days when the only thing that kept us in close contact were these joyful letters that we are writing now.

Always Yours, Sal

(Inserted cartoon)
Wife in kitchen, lots of smoke, husband with hat in hand,
"Darling! You did all this for me?"
Sal's notes "you" on woman and "me" on man and says
"The first 50 years are the hardest, eh?"

May 27, 1945

Dear Salvatore,

I got your letter the other day and I was glad to hear from you or in good health. So I am, Marie, Uncle Mariano. Once Henry was here today and show the letter you send to him the other day. Hope you be home before the summer is over so you and your brother can help me make the wine. I plant the back yard two weeks ago. Now start to come up because have been rain. Last week was cold. But get warm now. I still work in the same place and the same hours. I hope the war be over soon then I can take a long rest. The best regard from Marie and Uncle Mariano.

I wish the best luck and good future.

Your devoted father, Nick

May 28, 1945

Letter from France
1st Bn5 PJP
333 c/o P.M. N.Y.N.Y.

Dear Little Horn,

I just received your letter and boy was it terrific to hear from you. Dammit guy, I thought maybe you had forgotten all about your buddy, Big Horn.

Yep, Slab, old Heine gave up. The son of a bitch. We should have gassed the bastards.

Stick around, Sal. I'll be in the Pacific before long and we will let it all hang out. Slab, they got some stuff over here called Eau Di Vie (Oh Da Vee) and it is the strongest stuff made. God Oh Mighty, what a bitch, you can pitch on it. I'm going to latch onto a bottle and save it until you and I meet. Also a bottle of Calbados. Which in American means embalming fluid. (Good for rusty joints.)

Yours is the best news I've heard since Adolph took the easy way (off) out. Goose and Boo Boo both out on M.Xes (medical excuse). Wow. I got it twice but not enough to go home with. Godamit!!

I hit a lick for about $2000 bucks. So it looks like we will ride around in style if we ever get back.

Old Mortimer is still working on his quarry. But he sure and hell is getting paid for it, too.

I sure was sorry to hear about Cowboy's and Willie's mother. Boy, that is total war when something like that happens.

Well, chum, so you were in the States in November. Well, you crumb. I was fighting my ass off then and you were drinking good stuff. Boy, but I got you by the balls now. These French girls sleep with you for a bar of candy. Soap sells for $2.00 a bar, Cigs sell for $14.00 bucks a carton and so forth.

Well, Sonny, I've got to run. Hope to Orjses you write soon.

Love and a big kiss, Big Horn

P.S. I've been a good boy

Chapter 17, June 1945

The USS Signet supports landings at Iheya Shima, an island northwest of Okinaw. She then returns to minesweeping and anti-suicide boat patrol.

Friday, June 1, 1945

4606 Hawthorne Ave
Lyons, Ill.

Dear Sal:

Well, you old sea roving pirate, what are you up to now? The way things are moving, it wouldn't surprise me if you are not sneaking into Japan itself.

I got your letter May 15th on Thursday of last week May 24th. Eight days out, which in my figuring puts you about a day beyond Pearl Harbor. And maybe after three or four months aboard, they will pull into the Islands to give you a chance to walk on land again and catch up on your reading while laying on the beach. Boy, what a dream. Especially when you only get my mail about once a month, but don't worry. Some of these days the mail will hit you like the Readers Digest as a testament to their magazine but then I thought it may hurt their feelings to know that it's not delivered every month but at that you can consider yourself lucky in even getting it. Because last Christmas I sent in a subscription for a friend that's stationed in India with the British Forces and he wrote me under March 24th that he has just received a card stating that I had subscribed to the Readers Digest for him and that the first issue would follow immediately.

I got his letter May 29th so just imagine how often he is going to get it, from December to March, he hadn't got a single copy.

Well, Sal, this has been one week for me. I'm dead on my feet and looking forward to next Monday night when I can get to bed by 10 p.m. and get some sleep. It all started Sunday when I went down to see your Dad and hasn't stopped yet. First thing, Aunt went to see her Mother while I went to see your Dad but she didn't get home until 12:30 a.m., Monday. Then Tuesday I wanted to see a certain picture so went to the Lyons show and got home at 11:15 p.m. By the time I had a bite to eat and saw the headlines of the paper, it was midnight. Wednesday being Decorative Day (Memorial Day), I had to work, just my luck and it was worse luck because I had to get up at 5:30 a.m. after getting to bed at midnight. Well, your Aunt wanted to go to Soldier's Field for a Religious Meeting that was held, so after work I met her and Albert and went there. We got out at 10:30 p.m. and by the time we got home it was 1:15 a.m. Your Gods and I had to get up for work the next morning. Well, after raising the whole neighborhood, Aunt finally got me out of bed then. When I got home that night I had to write a letter to Hank (his son) as I usually write him Wednesday nights but was not able to this week on account of going to Soldier's Field. Well I got to bed real early last night, 11:00 p.m., but still wanted to sleep this morning when the little lady called me and now tonight I'm writing you a letter and it's 9:30 p.m. and I haven't seen the paper yet.

Tomorrow night I'll write to Harold (Sal's brother) because Sunday is my day to write to you boys, but I have to go to Great Lakes to see Hank and will probably not be able to write, but Monday. Oh boy, am I ever going to hit that sack. Yes, you can still say, "what do you want to do, sleep your whole life away," but I'll still hit the sack, that is unless the sweet little woman says otherwise and you know I never did like to argue with a woman. I learned that from my mother when I was a kid. I once tried to argue with her once and believe me that was all I did, but it took me close to a week before I could set down with any degree of comfort. She gave me the leather, but it saved me from a lot of trouble since now I know when to keep my mouth shut. Yeah, that's the answer "when the little lady is around." The boys think I can talk like Churchill when the little woman is not around, but I've got Anthony Eden (British Foreign Secretary) backed off the map for diplomacy when she is around. Well ain't that something being a Jekyll and Hyde in my own home?

Well, let's get back to last Sunday. As I said, I was down to see Dad and everything is just fine. The only trouble is that Gends sold their house and the people that bought it says the passageway belongs to their house and blocked it off, but I have a friend of mine who is going to see what that land belongs to. I have to go down to Dad early Sunday morning to get the lot number and sub division number, etc., and then this friend of mine is going to look up the width of the lot in the City Hall, and if the alley belongs to your Dad, well you can bet your last nickel the fence will come down toot sweet. I just want to be sure before I move and then I'll move fast. There hasn't been any trouble yet because your Dad wanted to see me before he did anything and I told him to let them block him off from the passageway and not to say anything that will cause trouble until I find out quick how we stand there. If we own the land, we will wreck the fence and tear it down and move it to the common lot line. But don't you worry about it. There's nothing to worry about. It will all be straightened out. The friend of mine who is handling it is pretty well up in politics and works in the City Hall. So what he says goes. And he will back it up. It won't cost your Dad a penny. He is doing it for me and not Dad.

Dad got a letter from Harold about three weeks ago and considering, he is not too bad off. He sleeps on a cot under a tent and had hot hamburger sandwiches the day he wrote the letter, so if he can do that he is well back of the lines. He said it was possible that you and him were at the same place, but at different times but he says he hardly expects to meet you before he gets home, which means to say he is pretty well inland and not near the sea. He is feeling fine but homesick and hates the Army worse that ever.

He didn't say when he expected to be home, but I think he will be home before the snow flies and maybe you and him will be home about the same time. Say, wouldn't that be a break?

I sent another batch of comics last week and have been sending them every week, but if you get 50% of them, it will be worthwhile to keep lending and by the way, I have a box of tootsie rolls I intend sending to Harold, be he hasn't asked for them. So if you like them, say so, and I'll ship them to you.

I promised you a photo of Hank in this letter, but will have to disappoint you, because they were not ready when I went for them today, so will try and send it in my next letter.

Albert and Jim were up to Great Lakes to see Hank last Sunday and Hank told them that he had got a letter from you. He was tickled pink to get it. I suppose I'll hear more about it Sunday. He was telling me he had to stand in line for an hour at the canteen to get a package of cigarettes this last week and they even ration cigarettes to the Navy. Boy, that's bad, am I glad I smoke Italian cigars. There's plenty of them, but these you have to be a man to smoke them (hope Aunt is not looking over my shoulder). I notice your Dad smokes them now along with Marion (Uncle Mariano). Oh yes, I asked about Eleanor and they have not had a letter from her since February. What do you know about that? She only wrote once to me since she was home on leave and I answered that and will not write her until she writes me, but I'm not worried about her, she is in good hands and is made to toe the mark if she likes it or not, as you and Hank have found out before this.

Well, I guess I'll close. Everybody is in the best of health both here and at Talman Ave. Now I'll see what the paper says for the next ten minutes and then shoot to bed, so good night and God Bless you.

Your Loving Uncle, Henry

June 2, 1945

Lt. Wiggler
COB463 Sig Nuy Conct Bn (aun)
R0246 C/O p.m. San Francisco, Calif.
"Mancianos"

Hello, Henry,

Received your letter last nite of May 29th. Got a letter from Cosmie, too, he said your love life is working at Garden City. Where the hell do you get that shit one can of beer a week. We get all of six. Cosmie said the Duck never comes around the corner. Have you heard from him since he's been home? The last time he wrote me was when he was in the hospital. I got a letter from my bro. What a deal he's got now. They are living in brick buildings in the "Po Valley" (a valley in northern Italy) and getting all the girls they can take for thirty cents and up. He said he may get a leave or come straight out here. Well, Pal, I'm all out of bull. So I'll close for now.

Your buddy, Wiggler

June 6, 1945 (8 p.m.)

WESTERN UNION
USS SIGNET A.M. 302 FPO SFRAN

DEAR SAL; RECEIVED TELEGRAM STATING OUR
BELOVED BROTHER (HAROLD) HAS BEEN KILLED IN
ACTION ON MAY 22, 1945 ON MINDANAO.

Harold was 26.

June12, 1945

Dear Loretta:

Here I am, writing to the only girl I ever really cared for in my whole life and wondering why she hasn't written in return. It's been over a month since I last wrote to you, but I can assure my reasons were just! After all, Honey, not hearing from you in such a long long time has consequently made me come to some definite conclusions and the very first one to pop up is that you no longer care!

If I'm presuming that that is a sufficient answer, well, I guess there isn't anything I can do to change your mind, at least not while I'm way out here on the other side of the Pacific Ocean. But, why in the Hell don't you let me in on the dope or do you get a big kick out of watching a guy fly "blind."

I never thought that you and I would ever separate, but if we did, you would have to be the one to do the breaking first. I knew it could never be me to say, "we better call it quits," because I always was deeply in love with you and thought too much of you to ever possess any sort of idea that would bring us to the above mentioned conclusion.

On my second thought, I began thinking back that maybe I had written something in one of my letters that you didn't exactly crave. Maybe I did get a little bold at times, but after all, Honey, you're not a kid anymore and naturally there wasn't anything in my letters that was too intrepid for a "woman" to conceive. But if so, the least you could have done was to let me know and in return, I could apologize for any rudeness I might have said.

The third reason and the least logical by all means, is maybe you got in some kind of an accident, was hospitalized, and just couldn't write. But how could any harm come to such beautiful and understanding female specie like thou self? I pray that no such thing like the above could ever had happen, but if per chance it did, why didn't someone leave me in on the scoop? Sure your Sis, Dolores, would have let me know, wouldn't she?

Well, I guess I'll change the subject and talk about something else, for instance, your "worst half."

They have finally consented to let us write home that we've indulged in the initial invasions of Keramo Phetta and Okinawa Shima. I guess you've read the papers that it wasn't a Sunday beer party, and I for one, can verify it. Well, that's that! I can't say anymore because the censor would only make with the razor blade with any other additions. The Gyrenes (Marines) and Doggies (Army) usually are allowed to spurt out with all the info they have at hand, but the Navy isn't quite so lenient. You usually have to wait till the war is over before you say anything.

Well, Honey, I'll have to close for now, but I find it rather difficult to write when I don't know if I was "thrown out at home" or "crossed the goal line!"

Thinking of You Always, Sal

P.S.

Please write soon, eh?

News received Radio, San Francisco and transcribed by Sal in the radio shack

Guam:
Nearly 200 superforts loosed high explosive
bombs Sunday on 5 factory and military targets
in Tokyo and Yokahama area subjecting Japan
Mustangs. It was the worst week-end of the war
for Japan and Tokyo admits one of every 15
residents have been burned out of or blown from
home by raid.

Berlin:
Marshal Gregory Zhukov said Sunday that Russia
was now studying the question of demobilization
of her mighty army. It was the first such
disclosure he did not deliberate.
Washington:
Germany lost average one submarine by sinking
every 3 days between Sep. 3, 1939 and May 8,
1945 official records disclosed Sunday.

San Francisco:
Melbourne radio said Sunday Australian forces
in northern Bouganville had landed on the west
coast of Machin Bay posing threat heavy troop
concentration on the Bonen Peninsula.

Calcutta:
British and Indian troops cleaning out
resisting Japanese remaining nests in South
Burma have captured 3 enemy held villages in
Pagru Hill area between the Irratd and Rangoon
Mandalay Railway Admiral Mountbattens
Headquarters announced last Sunday night after
Chinese capture the important junction center
in South China, rare hub outlying bastion of
Shanan Province. Monday Chinese Headquarters
reported its troops had captured the port of
Futing on China's East Coast 450 miles west of
Okinawa in second of 4 important victories
paving the way for profitable American invasion

Asiatic mainland. In two other successes
Chinese forces seized highway strong hold of
Lungchow 12 miles from Indo-China from Japanese
retiring from South China and smashed within 25
miles of former U.S. Air Base at Kweslin 350
miles southeast of Chunking.

Guam:
June 10, 1945 attacking vital war industries on
Honsu Island for second time within 23 hours,
150 to 200 superforts today bombed 5 industrial
plants and repair base on Jap homeland. The
superforts carried both high explosive and
incendiaries and primary targets where aircraft
and superforts were over their targets. The
21st bomber command reported that
reconnaissance photos showed clearly that 2
primary targets were virtually destroyed in
yesterday's attack and third target slightly
damaged in 3 prong assault on Nagoya, Naruo and
bomber flights which hit the three targets in
Tokyo area today.

June 20, 1945

S.H. O. R.M. 2/c
USS Signet (AM 3 02)
o/o NPO
San Francisco, Calif.

*(Above address scratched out and below it is written: 1319
Talman Ave., Chicago, Ill.)*

My dearest Sal,

I just received your letters dated the twelfth and I really
sorry I didn't write any sooner. But then I did try to sooo
many times, and that's what happened, I just couldn't finish
off a letter to you. I'd start, and get about one page written
and then I'd sit and wrack this lonesome brain of mine for
about a half hour trying to find something suitable to tell you.
But no soap. And before, I could finish off a letter 1-2-3. No
strain, nothing, why?

Then I was beginning to think, "Well maybe, I don't love him anymore." Well, do I? Do I? I kept thinking about it. Honey, I don't even think I know my own mind.

Although it is in quite of a rut now. Maybe you'll be able to enlighten me, huh? You're coming home soon aren't you, for sure now?

And you want me to tell you another silly thing too? Are you sure you won't mind if I'm as tall you? Whew! I finally said it, but believe it or not, I was quite conscious of it. Oh, in case you had any doubts, may I confirm the three "definite conclusions" you gave for me not writing.

I still do care a lot for you (although I have a very funny way of showing it) and I told you I'd wait 'til you got "home" before I'll ever change my heart. (Slight chance, tho.) It's just that I get in those "moods." And don't think I'm lying to use that for an excuse either—it's just that I write like I feel—I know you wouldn't want me to write under "false pretenses," would you?

Secondly... although you were a little "bold" at times, but I'm glad you write to me as a grown up. (It's so hard to make people around here realize I'm a "woman" now.) I guess I got broadminded with my age, eh? And thirdly, don't you know you can't harm a good Pole?

Say, when is my "better half" gonna make (draws sergeant strips)?

Well, I'll have to be closing now—and don't forget to answer soon.

Oh, before I forget, did you even hear one of the latest hits? Vaughn Monroe's arrangement of, "There I Said It Again." Anyway. I've decided to learn all the words to. it.

Well, goodnight, Honey.

Have a dream on me, Love Loretta

Chapter 18, July - September 1945

July 8, 1945

The USS Signet departs Okinawa heading for the Phillipines.

July 13, 1945

The USS Signet arrives at Leyte Gulf in the Philippine Sea on the 13th and remains until the end of the successful campaign on August 15.

August 18, 1945

The USS Signet departs Leyte.

August 24-30, 1945

Returning to Okinawa on the 24t, the Signet remains there until the 30th. She gets underway with a large group of minesweepers to help sweep the Yellow Sea in support of Korea occupation forces.

September 1-7, 1945

The USS Signet makes daily sweeps in the Yellow Sea and clears the area at night.

September 8-October 10, 1945

Heading for Japan the next morning, the Signet begins sweeping the approaches to Sasebo. For two months, she sweeps the area around Sasebo during the day and anchors at Matsu Shima, Kyushu at night.

From late September until early October, the crew enjoys liberty in Sasebo.

Chapter 19, October-December 1945

October 11-21, 1945

The USS Signet sweeps the area around Iki and Tsushima Islands off the northwestern coast of Kyūshu, Japan.

October 26-November 10, 1945

The USS Signet conducts operations in the East China Sea southwest of Kyushu.

November 30, 1945

1 p.m.
WESTERN UNION
MISS LORETTA
2ND FL FRONT 1934 STATE ST
CHICAGO

WILL ARRIVE ON THE 5 OR 6 TONIGHT BUT NO
TOOTH LOVE SAL

November 17-December 5

The USS Signet makes her final sweep and returns to the vicinity of Tsushima, an island of the Japanese archipelago.

December 11, 1945

Departing Sasebo with her homeward-bound pennant flying, the Signet with *the other ships of Mine Squadron 12, steams out of the harbor, passing in review before the Rear Admiral Commander, Pacific Fleet, and receives the salutes of the assembled ships of the U.S. Pacific Fleet.*
She earns four battle stars for meritorious participation in battle.

About the Author

Laura Lynn Ashworth is an award-winning copywriter and political cartoonist. While helping an elderly family member with veterans administration paperwork, she ran across "the letters" and instantly knew of their rarity, freshness and historical significance. Although she received three publishing contracts within two months of sending the letters to major publishers, Ashworth decided to publish them herself on the advice of best-selling authors. She currently lives and works in a northwest suburb of Chicago.